ENHANCING ASEAN'S CONNECTIVITY

ENHANCING ASEAN'S CONNECTIVITY

EDITED BY
SANCHITA BASU DAS

ISEAS

INSTITUTE OF SOUTHEAST ASIAN STUDIES
Singapore

First published in Singapore in 2013 by ISEAS Publishing
Institute of Southeast Asian Studies
30 Heng Mui Keng Terrace
Pasir Panjang
Singapore 119614

E-mail: publish@iseas.edu.sg
Website: <http://bookshop.iseas.edu.sg>

The responsibility for facts and opinions in this publication rests exclusively with the authors and their interpretations do not necessarily reflect the views or the policy of the publisher or its supporters.

ISEAS Library Cataloguing-in-Publication Data

Enhancing ASEAN's connectivity / edited by Sanchita Basu Das.
1. Transportation and state—Southeast Asia—International cooperation.
2. Information technology—Southeast Asia—International cooperation.
3. Energy policy—Southeast Asia—International cooperation.
4. Power resources—Southeast Asia—International cooperation.
5. ASEAN.
I. Basu Das, Sanchita.
HC441 E58   2013

ISBN 978-981-4414-11-1 (soft cover)
ISBN 978-981-4414-12-8 (E-book PDF)

Cover photos: The photos of the cable lines and that of the roads were taken by Mr Subhramit Das (reproduced with kind permission) while the photo of the water pipes is from Shutterstock.

Typeset by International Typesetters Pte Ltd
Printed in Singapore by Mainland Press Pte Ltd

CONTENTS

Foreword by High Commissioner Ong Keng Yong   vii

Message by Mr Rodolfo C. Severino   xiii

Preface   xv

The Contributors   xix

List of Abbreviations   xxi

I. OVERVIEW

1. Understanding the MPAC   3
   Sanchita Basu Das

2. Current State of ASEAN Infrastructure   9
   Nguyen The Phuong

3. Building Greater Connectivity Across ASEAN   28
   Michael Yeoh, Ng Yeen Seen, Tilottama Roy

II. TRANSPORTATION, TELECOM, ICT AND ENERGY INFRASTRUCTURE

4. The Development of Logistics Infrastructure in ASEAN: 37
   The Comprehensive Asia Development Plan and the
   Post-AEC Initiative
   Fukunari Kimura

5. Challenges for Building Better Transportation Infrastructure   59
   Linkages Across ASEAN: Indonesia's Perspectives Towards
   an Integrated Asian Economic Community
   Bambang Susantono

6. Connecting Southeast Asia through Broadband   72
   Arne Jeroschewski, Andre Levisse, Lorraine Salazar,
   Robert Tesoriero, and Shaowei Ying

7. The Current State of ICT Systems across ASEAN   91
   Lee Yu Kit

8. ASEAN and ICT: A Tale of Two Cities?   108
   Emmanuel C. Lallana

9. Integration of Energy Infrastructure towards ASEAN's   121
   Connectivity
   Nguyen Manh Hung and Beni Suryadi

10. ASEAN Energy Integration: Interconnected Power and Gas   142
    Pipeline Grids
    Tilak K. Doshi

III. IMPLEMENTATION AND POLICY RECOMMENDATIONS

11. Master Plan on ASEAN Connectivity "From Plan to   165
    Implementation"
    Somsak Pipoppinyo

12. Conclusion and Policy Recommendations   175
    Sanchita Basu Das

Index   186

FOREWORD

ASEAN is the only organization of its kind in the vast region that stretches from the Indian Subcontinent to the Kamchatka Peninsula. Geographically, it covers Southeast Asia, where there are more seas and islands than continuous land mass. In the past four decades, economic development and trade have flourished impressively amongst the ten ASEAN member states, culminating in a combined Gross Domestic Product (GDP) of nearly US$2 trillion in 2011. Going forward, future economic growth and prosperity will depend on greater and improved connectivity not only within ASEAN, but between ASEAN and its trading partners as well. A well-connected ASEAN with good connections to the wider region will create a much larger and integrated market with more production and distribution networks. This will help to realize the full potential of the ASEAN Free Trade Area (AFTA), as well as the various ASEAN Plus One Free Trade Agreements (FTAs), and the envisioned Regional Comprehensive Economic Partnership.

However, the imperative for enhancing connectivity in ASEAN is not merely economic. More importantly, ASEAN is building a community from among the diverse nations of Southeast Asia. To do so, they must have mutual trust and understanding, and in turn develop greater cohesion and solidarity. If ASEAN remains separated by the mountains and seas, and if its people cannot interact easily with each other, the feeling of togetherness and the sharing of a common future cannot be forged and developed. More time and attention must therefore be given to one another, and it is through greater connectivity that this can be achieved.

History is full of remarkable success stories about how diverse nations were connected to develop trade and other relations across vast distances.

For example, the Roman Empire had more than 400,000 kilometres of roads, covering more than one hundred provinces around the whole of the Mediterranean Sea. Of these, 80,500 kilometres were paved roads, allowing the Roman authorities to reach a considerably extended territory. The different multiracial communities within the Roman Empire were able to leverage on each other's strengths to expand economic activities, especially in trade. Another example would be the Persian Empire, which built roads and canals to link the land mass from the Persian Gulf to the Black and Mediterranean Seas. The most famous of these Persian construction projects was the "Royal Road" that stretched 2,700 kilometres, from the south-western part of present-day Iran to the north-western coast of Turkey. We also have the Mongols who effectively organized their transcontinental communications and connectivity through their unique "Yam" postal system, which stretched on land from the Pacific Ocean to Eastern Europe. In modern times, we have the Asian Highway Network developed by UNESCAP, which covers more than thirty-two countries across the Asian continent to Europe, and includes more than 140,000 kilometres of vehicular roads. Big countries like the United States of America and China have also built extensive road networks to connect their citizens over vast territories. In India, there are as many as 4.32 million kilometres of roads and highways, connecting the huge subcontinent as a unified state.

ASEAN is of course not building any empire. What the ASEAN Leaders do wish to sustain is the economic competitiveness of their region, and to provide a strong foundation for continued peace and prosperity in Asia. History has taught us that connectivity is essential in this endeavour, and this can explain why the ASEAN leaders have embarked on the purposeful development of the necessary physical, institutional and people-to-people links to support ASEAN's integration. The key to this concerted effort was the ASEAN Connectivity initiative, which was first endorsed by the ASEAN leaders in October 2009. This was followed by the landmark Master Plan on ASEAN Connectivity that was formulated and adopted a year later. Today, the challenge for ASEAN is to implement the ambitious elements in this Master Plan. If we can accomplish a 50 per cent implementation of the Master Plan by 2015, ASEAN will already be well positioned for an unprecedented era of regional economic expansion and progress.

In fact, individual pieces of physical infrastructure and frameworks are already in place, and what is urgently needed is to connect the respective existing facilities and projects. There is also the other challenge of reconciling the different mindsets and priorities of the different ASEAN member states, which thus far have complicated the implementation of the Connectivity initiative. Nevertheless, the will of the political leadership remains evident, and a constant monitoring effort to supervise and review the well-thought through plans should produce a level of connectivity that will be the basis for a strong ASEAN Community.

Another big challenge for ASEAN is the ability to mobilize the necessary resources to sustain the implementation of the Master Plan on ASEAN Connectivity. In the wake of global economic difficulties and financial woes, ASEAN's major trading partners are encountering their own fiscal and public policy problems. Inevitably, there are not much extra resources to go around, let alone provide completely for ASEAN's connectivity projects. Accordingly, ASEAN must develop creative and innovative ways to mobilize resources from all potential donors and collaborators to execute its Connectivity plan. This also means that it will be necessary for ASEAN to go beyond the concept of "other people's money" to develop its own agenda. In the early days of ASEAN's development, the organization was an aid recipient, and the traditional donors from the West were happy to help in the development of the member states. Today, the more developed economies of ASEAN must be prepared to make increased contributions to the Connectivity initiative to incentivize other donors and collaborators to provide sufficient funding for the relevant projects. The private sector and other capable non-governmental organizations should also be roped in, through mutually beneficial policy measures and frameworks. The institutional capacity of the ASEAN Secretariat and other ASEAN-centric bodies also need to be strengthened to enable them to play useful roles in resource mobilization.

ASEAN is fortunate in having its Connectivity initiative supported by its major trading partners, who see a more connected ASEAN as bearing positive results for their respective national interest *vis-à-vis* the region. The immediate neighbours surrounding ASEAN will reap significant economic benefits, particularly increased trade, with ASEAN's member states. Such benefits will not just help the growth of ASEAN but also its immediate neighbours, and will contribute to broader initiatives for global economic development. At the same time, it is also important to manage the expectations of ASEAN's partners, particularly when the specific priorities for ASEAN and its friends may not be completely aligned. In this respect, the various ASEAN-centric mechanisms, such as the ASEAN Plus Three, the East Asia Summit, and the ASEAN Regional Forum, should help and facilitate the efforts on both sides to map out mutually beneficial time schedules and cooperative projects.

Connectivity is the basis for realizing a community from among the different existing cultural, social, economic and political systems in Southeast Asia. To this end, the implementation of the Master Plan on ASEAN Connectivity must require a significant expansion of capacity-building programmes in the region. The human capital of ASEAN must be equipped with the necessary knowledge and wherewithal to undertake the Connectivity initiative in a concerted and sustained manner. Leadership and stewardship continue to be important, but specific frameworks and institutions have equally important roles to play as well, given the current paucity of ASEAN-wide organizations that could help generate enthusiasm and practical projects to push the Connectivity agenda forward. As the momentum to strengthen connectivity increase, basic issues of ASEAN's organizational structure and mandate must also be addressed. The best champion for ASEAN Community building and the implementation of ASEAN Connectivity is in fact the ASEAN Secretariat based in Jakarta. The Secretary-General of ASEAN must be empowered to take the lead and harness all available technology and resources to deliver the ASEAN Connectivity initiative. He should also work closely with the ASEAN Connectivity Coordinating Committee to streamline efforts and clear identified roadblocks as early as possible.

For now, it is imperative that ASEAN steps up the pace of implementation, and spur the momentum needed to accomplish the identified prioritized projects in the Connectivity initiative. ASEAN has to stay focused and keep to its consistent and systematic building block approach, harvesting low-lying fruits where it can — such as completing the various "missing links" in the physical sectors like road networks, rail infrastructure and a regional power grid — before steadily progressing to new targets. More efforts should be undertaken to lower, if not remove, the existing barriers to trade, as well as to align national procedures, rules and regulations to rigorous, world-class standards. The private sector also needs to be better informed and more involved through tangible and bankable public-private partnerships.

The people-to-people factor of ASEAN Connectivity needs to be particularly emphasized. More effort and resources should be placed in youth exchanges, cultural programmes and tertiary institutional collaborations, which thus far have proven to be useful strategies to help promote the growth of cultural and educational networks and linkages among our people. The easing of visa requirements for ASEAN nationals travelling amongst ASEAN member states meanwhile would not only be a boon for the regional tourism industry, but would also help to facilitate greater intra-ASEAN people mobility and interaction. Looking ahead, it will be useful for ASEAN to consider moving the Connectivity initiative from a people-oriented to a people-centred one, with the necessary reviews and stocktake conducted to see if the people have benefitted from the various measures undertaken, and if more can be done. Here, the ASEAN Secretariat and National Coordinators are especially well-placed to carry out public outreach and feedback surveys to better involve the people of ASEAN and give them a sense of ownership to ASEAN Connectivity.

This book, *Enhancing ASEAN Connectivity*, is an excellent example of "people-to-people" sharing as it brings together the experts and thinkers from various ASEAN member states (as well as the partners of ASEAN) to discuss and review the cooperation and collaboration needed to achieve the goals laid down in the Master Plan. This book is also a useful reference to policy-makers across ASEAN, who could use the studies compiled in it to fine-tune their programmes and policies where necessary. The publication of this book is timely. It will stimulate an assessment of the current state of the Connectivity initiative and identify the implementation gaps that can be addressed by the stakeholders. Indeed, a number of chapters in *Enhancing ASEAN Connectivity* have made considerable effort in this regard, having looked at issues like capacity, bandwidth, infrastructure disparities and private sector financing.

An important dimension that *Enhancing ASEAN Connectivity* addresses is Information and Communication Technology (ICT) connectivity. The significance of ICT is two-fold as it is not only a key driver in the modern economy surrounding us, but it is also the medium of personal communication and messaging today, particularly for the younger generation. How ICT connectivity is developed within each ASEAN member state and the grouping as a whole will determine the future connectedness of this region and its people with the rest of the world. The impact and reach of ICT is also considerably greater and more immediate compared to physical roads and highways, as people can save costs and travelling time to communicate with one another across borders. One chapter of this book also noted that the youth of ASEAN are at the forefront of the "global social network revolution". Looking ahead, it will be useful to consider how the creativity and passion of the young people can further energize the Connectivity agenda in ASEAN.

In conclusion, ASEAN Connectivity has been widely billed as the twenty-first century "passport" to regional economic growth, but what will clearly, and must, remain core is its contribution to the viability and cohesion of ASEAN. As a comprehensive, ambitious and far-reaching endeavour, just the implementation of the Connectivity initiative alone will bring the ten ASEAN member states and its people closer than ever before, as they unite towards a common purpose and prepare collectively for a positive future. Mutual trust and understanding will grow and strengthen, and a deeper sense of belonging to a regional "community" will be forged. This, I believe, is the true essence and vision of ASEAN Connectivity, and is something that every one of us must aspire towards.

Ong Keng Yong
Singapore High Commissioner to Malaysia
Secretary-General of ASEAN (2003–07)

MESSAGE

I have a couple of thoughts on connectivity in the Association of Southeast Nations, or ASEAN.

The first is that an ASEAN Community, including an ASEAN Economic Community, which ASEAN has proclaimed as a goal, cannot be realized without connectivity, without the connectivity as comprehensively conceived in the Master Plan on ASEAN Connectivity. Connectivity is essential for achieving ASEAN's objectives of closer political cohesion, deeper economic integration, and more effective regional cooperation. Connectivity has to be attained comprehensively, in all its three inter-dependent dimensions.

The leaders of the ASEAN member states, gathered at their annual summit meeting in Hanoi, adopted the Master Plan on 28 October 2010. In it, connectivity has three interconnected components — physical, institutional and people-to-people. Physical connectivity is the infrastructure required to link the ASEAN countries together, mainly in terms of transport, information and communications technology, and energy. Institutional connectivity consists of the measures agreed upon and implemented by governments to facilitate trade and invest-ments within the region. People-to-people connectivity means personal exchanges through education, culture and tourism.

This is the second idea: that these three elements of the Master Plan are interrelated, interdependent and interconnected. Infrastructure is of little use if institutional, legal, practical and other barriers prevent trade, investment, information and people from flowing more freely over it. Trade, investment, information and people cannot flow more freely or flow at all if the requisite infrastructure is not improved or built. Infrastructure will not be built or improved and facilitating measures will not be agreed upon and carried out if people do not have contact with and know one another across national boundaries.

It is with these in mind that one should regard the chapters in this volume and the ASEAN Roundtable 2011 at which they were presented.

Rodolfo C. Severino
Head, ASEAN Studies Centre
Institute of Southeast Asian Studies
Secretary-General of ASEAN (1998–2002)

PREFACE

This book is a result of the ASEAN Roundtable 2011 on "Enhancing ASEAN's Connectivity" organized by the ASEAN Studies Centre (ASC) at the Institute of Southeast Asian Studies (ISEAS), along with the Konrad Adenauer Stiftung (KAS) on 5 May 2011 at Shangri-La Hotel, Singapore. The primary objective is to examine the current state of infrastructure development across ASEAN and to discuss how greater connectivity can contribute to the process of ASEAN economic integration. The ASC hopes that the roundtable would produce a set of policy recommendations that would help ASEAN to address the national- and regional-level challenges to build a robust infrastructure and to suggest approaches to resource mobilization for this purpose.

The roundtable focused on four areas: *transportation* for the movement of goods and people, *telecommunications* for business and people, *information and communication technology (ICT)* for businesses, education and other developments in the region, and *energy infrastructure* for better use and distribution of resources.

Road, rail, water and aviation corridors assume importance for the movement of goods and people. The development of transnational transport projects, such as the ASEAN Highway Network and the Singapore–Kunming Rail Link, is also key to realizing a seamless ASEAN. In the dynamic global telecommunications environment, ASEAN needs to promote telecommunications as a fundamental infrastructure in accomplishing its vision of an AEC. Given the importance of the Internet in business and other economic and social development, it is crucial to promote the utilization of ICT. The absence of such linkages will threaten to accentuate the already existing gaps between different countries both within ASEAN and around the world. Finally, integrated power grids and gas pipelines for ASEAN countries aim to improve energy efficiency and develop indigenous energy resources. It is expected to bring huge economic efficiency, creating opportunities to expand the power market, stimulate investment, and contribute to member countries' energy security.

At the end of the one-day roundtable discussion, it was concluded that:

1. For ASEAN, to build an economic community, even though the tariff cutting component is on track on paper, there exist many non-tariff barriers which would lower the potential benefits under the economic integration. One such barrier is the lack of physical and personal connectivity across the ASEAN region. Hence, it is a crucial time for ASEAN to enhance regional connectivity.

2. Greater connectivity results in better cooperation not only among the member countries, but also between the ASEAN region and the rest of the world. It would also help in the multifaceted growth of the region and would significantly narrow the development gap within ASEAN.

3. In ASEAN, the physical infrastructure, particularly in the less developed members, is characterized by structural weaknesses — low responsiveness to users, organizational inefficiencies, insufficient funding, heavy dependence on official development assistance, low foreign direct investments, and lack of environmental awareness. Most ASEAN countries are also short of the "soft" infrastructure (ICT), which are important prerequisites for the next stage of development. This calls for the upgrading of existing infrastructure, the construction of new infrastructure and the harmonization of regulatory framework.

4. The MPAC can potentially transform the ASEAN region, providing the conditions for a single market and production base. It is an expensive initiative, and funding remains a major challenge. The private sector should be actively involved as a number of infrastructure projects identified in the MPAC are still waiting for substantial investment. Hence, what is needed is to develop economically viable and bankable projects.

This book is divided into three parts. The first part contains three chapters which present an overview of ASEAN's state of physical connectivity and challenges in building better infrastructure. The second part hosts a collection of chapters that discuss specific issues pertaining to each kind of physical connectivity — a) transportation infrastructure; b) telecom connectivity; c) ICT, and d) energy infrastructure. The third part covers the issues in implementing the MPAC and gives concrete policy recommendations.

The book has several distinguished writers from academia, private sector and government bodies: Dato' Michael Yeoh (Asian Strategy and Leadership Institute), Nguyen The Phuong (Ministry of Planning and Investment, Vietnam), Fukunari Kimura (ERIA), Bambang Susantono (Transportation Department, Republic of Indonesia), Andre Levisse (McKinsey & Company), Lee Yu Kit (IBM), Emmanuel C. Lallana (Ideacorp), Nguyen Manh Hung (ASEAN Centre for Energy), Tilak K. Doshi (Energy Studies Institute) and Somsak Pipoppinyo (ASEAN Secretariat). The ASC would like to thank all of them for making the roundtable a success and this publication possible.

The ASC would also like to thank Ambassador Pradap Pibulsonggram (Thailand's Representative to the ASEAN Connectivity Coordinating Committee, Ministry of Foreign Affairs of Thailand), Dr Denis Hew (Director, Policy Support Unit, APEC, Singapore) and Dr K. Venkat Ramani (Senior Advisor for ASEAN-UN Partnership, ESCAP, Thailand), who shared their thoughts and research during the roundtable.

On behalf of Mr Rodolofo C. Severino, head of the ASC, we would like to sincerely thank Ambassador K. Kesavapany for his encouragement and support. We also thank Dr Wilhelm Hofmeister, Director, Regional Program "Political Dialogue with Asia", Konrad Adenauer Stiftung, Singapore, for his interest in the ASEAN Roundtable 2011. We are grateful that both Ambassador K. Kesavapany and Dr Hosfmeister delivered the opening remarks at the roundtable, highlighting the need for better infrastructure in ASEAN to realize its ultimate goal of "single market and production base".

Personally, I would like to thank H.E. Ong Keng Yong for writing the foreword for this volume. I would like to thank Mr Rodolfo Severino who oversaw the whole project and shared his insights for enrichful discussion. I was assisted by Lily Koh and Hnin Wint Nyunt Hman at critical junctures of the roundtable and production of this book and I thank them for that. Last, but not least, I thank the staff of the ISEAS Publications Unit, especially its head, Mrs Triena Ong, for their professionalism in getting this book published. Finally, I wish to thank the contributors of the volume who made the conference a success and the publication of its material possible.

I hope this book will help the ASEAN stakeholders and other interested public in understanding ways to strengthen ASEAN's connectivity both internally and externally. I hope that the policy-makers are benefited by the recommendations.

Sanchita Basu Das
Editor

THE CONTRIBUTORS

Sanchita Basu Das is Lead Researcher for Economic Affairs at the ASEAN Studies Centre, Institute of Southeast Asian Studies, Singapore.

Tilak K. Doshi is Principal Fellow and Head of Energy Economics Division, Energy Studies Institute, NUS, Singapore.

Arne Jeroschewski is an Engagement Manager at McKinsey & Company, Singapore.

Fukunari Kimura is Chief Economist at the Economic Research Institute for ASEAN and East Asia (ERIA) and Professor at the Faculty of Economics, Keio University.

Emmanuel C. Lallana is Chief Executive at Ideacorp, Manila, the Philippines.

Lee Yu Kit is Chief Technologist and Executive IT Architect at IBM Public Sector, Growth Markets Unit, IBM, Malaysia.

Andre Levisse is Senior Partner, Telecom, Media and High Tech at McKinsey & Company Asia.

Nguyen Manh Hung was the Executive Director of the ASEAN Centre for Energy.

Nguyen The Phuong is the Vice-Minister of the Ministry of Planning and Investment, Vietnam.

Somsak Pipoppinyo is Director of Finance, Industry and Infrastructure at the ASEAN Secretariat, Jakarta.

Tilottama Roy is a Research Associate at the Centre for Public Policy Studies (CPPS), Asian Strategy and Leadership Institute (ASLI).

Lorraine Salazar is Knowledge Specialist, Telecom, Media and High Tech at McKinsey & Company, Singapore.

Ng Yeen Seen is Director of the Centre for Public Policy Studies (CPPS), Asian Strategy and Leadership Institute (ASLI).

Robert Tesoriero was Research Manager, Telecom, Media and High Tech at McKinsey & Company, Asia.

Michael Yeoh is CEO of the Asian Strategy and Leadership Institute (ASLI) and a Member of the ASEAN High Level Task Force on Connectivity.

Shaowei Ying is Associate Principal at McKinsey & Company, Singapore.

Beni Suryadi is Regional Energy Policy Analyst at the ASEAN Centre for Energy.

Bambang Susantono is the Vice-Minister of the Transportation Department, Republic of Indonesia.

LIST OF ABBREVIATIONS

ABC	ASEAN Broadband Corridor
ADB	Asian Development Bank
AEC	ASEAN Economic Community
AFTA	ASEAN Free Trade Area
AGC	ASCOPE Gas Centre
AHN	ASEAN Highway Network
AIF	ASEAN Infrastructure Fund
APAEC	ASEAN Plans of Action on Energy Cooperation
APG	ASEAN Power Grid
APSC	ASEAN Political Security Community
ASAM	ASEAN Single Aviation Market
ASCC	ASEAN Socio Cultural Community
ASCOPE	ASEAN Council on Petroleum
ASEAN	Association of Southeast Asian Nations
ASEAN+3	ASEAN, China, Japan and South Korea
ASEAN+6	ASEAN+3, India, Australia and New Zealand
ASTP	ASEAN Strategic Transport Plan
ATAP	ASEAN Transport Action Plan
ATM	ASEAN Transport Ministers
AVLRC	ASEAN Virtual Learning Resource Centres
BIMP-EAGA	Brunei–Indonesia–Malaysia–Philippines East ASEAN Growth Area
BOO	Build-Own-Operate
BOT	Build-Operate-Transfer
CADP	Comprehensive Asia Development Plan
CCC	Connectivity Coordinating Committee
CGIF	Credit Guarantee Investment Facility

CLMV	Cambodia, Laos, Myanmar and Vietnam
EE&C	Energy Efficiency and Conservation
ERIA	Economic Research Institute for ASEAN and East Asia
FDI	Foreign Direct Investment
GDP	Gross Domestic Product
GMS	Greater Mekong Subregion
GNI	Gross National Income
GSM	Geographical Simulation Model
HAPUA	Heads of ASEAN Power Utilities/Authorities
ICT	Information and Communication Technology
IMT-GT	Indonesia-Malaysia-Thailand Growth Triangle
LCCs	Low Cost Carriers
LPI	Logistics Performance Index
MNEs	Multi-National Enterprises
MPAC	Master Plan on ASEAN Connectivity
MRAs	Mutual Recognition Arrangements
MRC	Mekong River Commission
NTB	Non-tariff barriers
ODA	Official Development Assistance
PPP	Public-Private Partnership
Ro-Ro	Roll-on/Roll-off
SEZs	Special Economic Zones
SKRL	Singapore-Kunming Rail Link
TAGP	Trans-ASEAN Gas Pipeline
TELMIN	Telecommunications and Information Technology Ministers
TELSOM	Telecommunications and Information Technology Senior Officers Meeting
TTRs	Transit Transport Routes
USD	US Dollar
UNCTAD	United Nations Conference on Trade and Development

I
OVERVIEW

1

UNDERSTANDING THE MPAC

Sanchita Basu Das

ASEAN leaders proclaimed to create an ASEAN Economic Community (AEC) by 2015. While the fundamentals for creating a single market and production base are a work in progress, it is also crucial for ASEAN to facilitate the realization of the ASEAN community through "connectivity" (see Figure 1.1). This is because community building through physical, institutional and personal connectivity is not only expected to reduce business transaction cost, time and travel cost, but also to connect the "core" and the "periphery" in ASEAN, thus distributing the benefits of multifaceted growth wider in the region and reducing the development divide in ASEAN. Moreover, better connectivity within ASEAN is essential for further connectivity with other regions, such as East and South Asia, which will help ASEAN to maintain its centrality in the evolving regional architecture.

In 2010, during the 17th ASEAN Summit in Vietnam, the Leaders adopted the Master Plan on ASEAN Connectivity (MPAC). The plan strives to integrate a region of over 600 million people with a combined GDP of about US$1.5 trillion. The Master Plan identified several

FIGURE 1.1

Interaction between ASEAN Connectivity and ASEAN Community

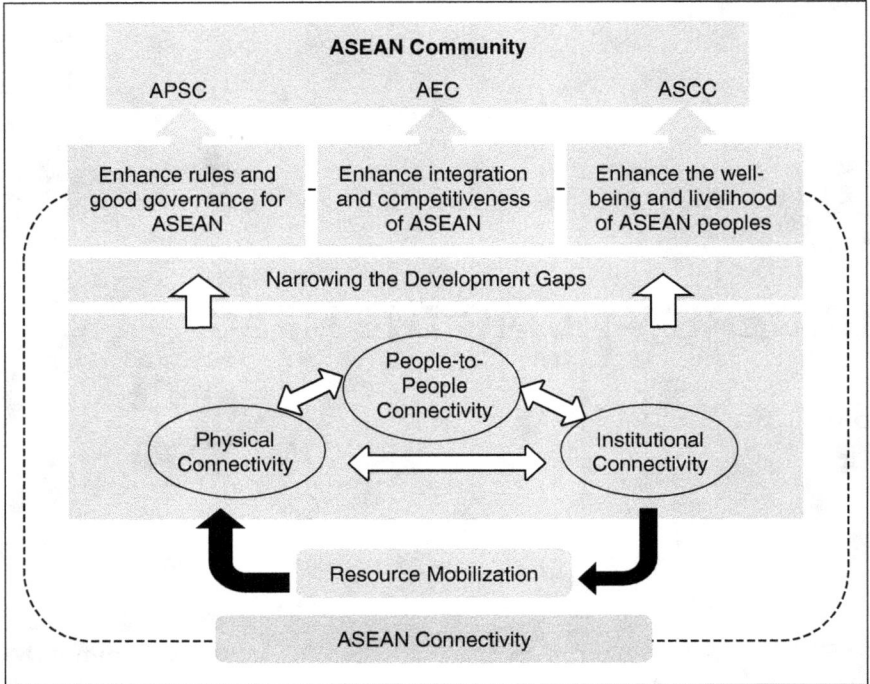

Source: MPAC, ASEAN Secretariat, June 2011.

priority projects, including the ASEAN Highway Network, a roll-on roll-off network and the ASEAN Broadband Corridor. It reviewed the achievements made and the challenges encountered to build up the linkages in ASEAN. It also provided key strategies and essential actions with clear targets and timelines to address the challenges.

Three linkages and strategies

The MPAC has three components:
- physical connectivity;
- institutional connectivity and;
- people-to-people connectivity

(a) Physical Connectivity

Currently, in ASEAN, the physical infrastructure, particularly in the less developed members, is characterized by structural weaknesses — low responsiveness to users, organizational inefficiencies, insufficient funding, heavy dependence on official development assistance, low foreign direct investments, and lack of environmental awareness. Most ASEAN countries are also short of the "soft" infrastructure (ICT), which are important prerequisites for the next stage of development. This calls for the upgrading of existing infrastructure, the construction of new infrastructure and the harmonization of regulatory framework. They are all vital for the seamless movement of goods and tradable services within the region and to the rest of the world.

The key strategies for enhanced physical connectivity include the completion of the ASEAN Highway Network (AHN); fully implementing Singapore-Kunming Rail Link (SKRL); establishing an efficient and integrated inland waterways network; forming an integrated, efficient, and competitive maritime transport system; building integrated and seamless multimodal transport systems; accelerating ICT infrastructure and services development in member states; and prioritizing the processes to resolve institutional issues in energy infrastructure projects.

(b) Institutional Connectivity

While ASEAN has been successful in eliminating tariffs, it is still struggling with the issue of non-tariff barriers (NTBs) to trade and investment. While some such barriers are necessary — for example, to protect the environment or the health of humans, animals and plants — others unnecessarily distort trade flows and restrict competition. To address this, ASEAN must harmonize standards and conformity assessment procedures, and operationalize key transport facilitation agreements to reduce the costs of moving goods across borders. In addition, ASEAN member states must fully implement their respective National Single Windows towards realizing the ASEAN Single Window by 2015.

Key strategies to enhance institutional connectivity include fully operationalizing the three Framework Agreements on transport facilitation; implementing initiatives to facilitate interstate passenger land transportation; developing the ASEAN Single Aviation Market (ASAM); developing an ASEAN Single Shipping Market; eliminating barriers to merchandise trade to accelerate the free flow of goods within the region; accelerating the development of an efficient and competitive logistics sector, in particular transport, telecommunications, and other connectivity-related services in the region; substantially improving trade facilitation; enhancing border management capacities; increasing Member States' openness to both intra-regional and extra-regional investment under fair investment rules and strengthening institutional capacity where necessary to improve coordination of policies, programmes, and projects between the regional and subregional levels.

(c) People-to-People Connectivity

This entails deeper intra-ASEAN cultural interaction, greater intra-ASEAN people mobility through progressive relaxation of visa requirements and development of mutual recognition arrangements (MRAs) to facilitate the ongoing efforts to increase greater interactions between the peoples of ASEAN.

Key strategies for people-to-people connectivity include promoting deeper intra-ASEAN social and cultural understanding and encouraging greater intra-ASEAN people mobility.

Prioritized Projects for ASEAN Connectivity

MPAC has identified fifteen prioritized projects for ASEAN Connectivity (see Table 1.1). Physical connectivity includes six projects related to land and maritime transport, ICT, and energy. Institutional connectivity includes five related to the free flow of goods and investment and transport facilitation. People-to-people connectivity consists of four projects related to the movement of people (tourism in particular), culture, and education.

Prioritized projects were chosen on the basis of high likelihood of success and impact and of balanced synergies between the three pillars of connectivity and between mainland and archipelagic member states. These projects included the completion of the AHN and upgrading of transit transport routes; building missing links in the SKRL; interconnection between the sub-regions of IMT-GT and BIMP-EAGA; and the continued development of the Ro-Ro Network.

An ASEAN Broadband Corridor (ABC) will also be established to utilize ICT as an engine for growth and integration with the aim to turn ASEAN into a global ICT hub. ABC involves ICT infrastructure

TABLE 1.1

List of Fifteen Priority Projects which will have Substantial Impact upon Implementation

6   Projects under Physical Connectivity

- Completion of the ASEAN Highway Network (AHN) missing links and upgrade of Transit Transport Routes (TTRs);
- Completion of the Singapore Kunming Rail Link (SKRL) missing links;
- Establish an ASEAN Broadband Corridor (ABC);
- Melaka-Pekan Baru Interconnection (IMT-GT: Indonesia);
- West Kalimantan-Sarawak Interconnection (BIMP-EAGA: Indonesia);
- Study on the Roll-on/Roll-off (RoRo) network and short-sea shipping

5   Projects under Institutional Connectivity

- Developing and operationalizing mutual recognition arrangements (MRAs) for prioritized and selected industries;
- Establishing common rules for standards and conformity assessment procedures;
- Operationalize all National Single Windows (NSWs) by 2012;
- Options for a framework/modality towards the phased reduction and elimination of scheduled investment restrictions/impediments;
- Operationalization of the ASEAN Agreements on transport facilitation

4   Projects under People-to-People Connectivity

- Easing visa requirements for ASEAN nationals;
- Development of ASEAN Virtual Learning Resources Centres (AVLRC);
- Develop ICT skill standards;
- ASEAN Community Building Programme

Source: MPAC, ASEAN Secretariat, June 2011.

development, human capital development in terms of a skilful and knowledgeable ICT workforce, and undertaking actions to bridge the digital divide within ASEAN.

Strengthening institutional connectivity includes developing and operationalizing mutual recognition agreements (MRAs) for prioritized industries; establishing common rules for standards and conformity assessment procedures; operationalizing all National Single Windows by 2012; phased reduction and elimination of investment restrictions; and activating ASEAN agreements on transport facilitation.

People-to-people connectivity includes a more free and improved visa regime with the full implementation of exemption for intra-ASEAN travel by ASEAN nationals by 2012; development of ASEAN Virtual Learning Resource Centres (AVLRC); development of ICT skill standards; and development of a comprehensive ASEAN Community Building Programme.

According to the Asian Development Bank (ADB), the complete realization of ASEAN Connectivity requires around US$596 billion, underscoring the need for cooperation with the ten Dialogue Partners and public-private partnerships. Meeting this financing requirement will pose tremendous challenge in realizing full ASEAN connectivity by 2015.

There are several funding sources and most of the time it is likely to be mixed for a particular project. While international financial institutions (like the World Bank or ADB) are expected to contribute substantially, bilateral agencies (like the Japanese, Chinese or US ODA) and commercial banks are equally important. ASEAN is also trying to increase the role of private sector participation through approaches like Public-Private Partnership (PPP). It is looking at new sources of funding like developing the domestic and regional capital markets and establishing an ASEAN Infrastructure Fund (AIF).

Thus, although MPAC is one of the important solutions to the problems obstructing the process of ASEAN Community Building, in the next few years, what is needed is for the multiple ASEAN stake-holders to work together with various sources of funding. It should be noted that besides the investment and technology, what is also crucial is good governance as all this together will finally lead to rise in flows and volumes of goods, services, people and information across the ASEAN region.

2

CURRENT STATE OF ASEAN INFRASTRUCTURE

Nguyen The Phuong

Introduction

With a population of nearly 600 million and a combined Gross Domestic Product (GDP) of US$1.5 trillion, ASEAN is one of the world's most diverse and dynamic regional organizations. Currently, ASEAN's priority is to build a people-centric ASEAN Community by 2015.

If ASEAN can achieve its objective, its centrality could be more effectively promoted in the evolving regional architecture. One of the critical factors for an effective ASEAN community is the enhancement of connectivity within ASEAN. Connectivity does not only mean eliminating tariffs, but also removing non-tariff barriers, reducing obstacles to investment, and easing restrictions on trade in services. It also means binding ASEAN members through necessary physical infrastructure. This will bring people, goods, services, and capital closer together in accordance with the ASEAN Charter.

Infrastructure can be categorized into hard and soft infrastructure. The former refers to main physical structures or facilities that support the society and economy, such as transport (e.g., ports, roads, railways); energy (e.g., electricity generation, electrical grids, gas and oil pipelines); telecommunications (e.g., telephone and Internet). The latter refers to non-tangibles supporting the development and operation of hard infrastructure, such as policy, regulatory, and institutional frameworks; governance mechanisms; systems, procedures and so on.

This chapter is an overview of the current state of ASEAN infrastructure. The sectors covered in this chapter include: (1) transport, (2) ICT, and (3) energy. The chapter also provides a compilation of existing infrastructure development programmes for reference.

Current State of ASEAN Infrastructures

1. Transport Infrastructure Development

(a) Strategies

Having an integrated transport system in ASEAN is always an important goal of the ASEAN cooperation in the transportation sector. This is crucial for realization of the ASEAN Free Trade Area (AFTA) and for ASEAN to integrate with the global arena. To achieve this objective, a series of action plans have been adopted. These are: the Successor Plan of Action in Transport 1999–2004, the ASEAN Transport Action Plan (ATAP) 2005–2010 and the ASEAN Strategic Transport Plan (ASTP) 2011–2015.

The ASTP identifies strategic actions that have to be implemented during 2011–12 in order to support the realization of the ASEAN Economic Community (AEC) by 2015. It also supports the new priorities identified under the Master Plan on ASEAN Connectivity. The ASTP is developed on the ATAP and on a comprehensive assessment of the current transport situation in ASEAN. The ASTP is also formulated to reflect other ongoing developments in the world such as a changing economic landscape, mainly due to the emergence of new economic powers such as China and India, and growing global concerns over the environment, climate change, and safety and security. It also seeks to identify the long-term vision of ASEAN transport cooperation beyond 2015.

Till 2010, under the ATAP, forty-eight actions covering the four sub-sectors of air transport (ten actions), land transport (thirteen actions), maritime transport (fourteen actions), and transport facilitation (eleven actions) have been implemented. Out of this, three have been completed, forty-two are at various stages of implementation, and three are in the preparation stage. The ongoing actions will be carried over to the ASTP 2011–2015, as they are still highly relevant for the next five years and beyond.

(b) Progress and Challenges

Land Transport

ASEAN cooperation in roads and rail aims to establish efficient, integrated, safe, and environmentally sustainable regional land transport corridors linking all ASEAN member states and countries beyond. There are two flagship land transport infrastructure projects within ASEAN, namely the ASEAN Highway Network (AHN) and the Singapore–Kunming Rail Link (SKRL).

Road Infrastructure

The ASEAN Transport Ministers (ATM) adopted a plan to develop the AHN with the following time-frame at its fifth meeting in Hanoi, Vietnam in September 1999:

- *Stage 1:* Network configuration and designation of national routes to be completed by 2000.
- *Stage 2:* Installation of road signs at all designated routes, upgrading of all designated routes to at least Class III standards, construction of all missing links, and commencing operation of all cross-border points by 2004.
- *Stage 3:* All designated routes to be upgraded to at least Class I standards and the upgrading of low traffic volume non-arterial routes to Class II standards by the year 2020.

The AHN is an expansion of the "Trans-Asian Highway" network within ASEAN. To date, while there have been significant progress made by ASEAN member states in terms of increasing the length and upgrading the road quality of highways, there are still missing links and below standard roads in some Member States. As far as the missing links of the AHN are concerned, it is located mostly in Myanmar with a total length of 227 kilometres. Whereas for the roads which are below Class III standards under the AHN, it stretches over 5,300 kilometres encompassing six Member States — Indonesia, Lao PDR, Malaysia, Myanmar, the Philippines, and Vietnam.

The AHN also identifies transit transport routes (TTRs), which are considered critical for facilitating goods in transit and have been prioritized for upgrading and construction. Below Class III roads of these TTRs includes approximately 2,069 kilometres of transit transport routes in Lao PDR, Myanmar, and the Philippines. Access to financing is the key challenge to the timely completion of the upgrading of the below Class III standards by 2004, as planned by the ATM (see Table 2.1).

TABLE 2.1
Designated TTRs in ASEAN

Country	Total Length of TTRs (km)	Total Length of Below Class III TTRs (km)
Brunei Darussalam	168	0
Cambodia	1,338	0
Indonesia	4,143	0
Lao PDR	2,170	391
Malaysia	2,242	0
Myanmar	3,018	1,467
Philippines	3,073	211.5
Singapore	$-^1$	–
Thailand	4,477	0
Vietnam	577	0
Total	21,206	2,069.5

Note: [1] Designated TTRs for Singapore to be submitted at the time of deposit of Instrument of Ratification for Protocol 1 of the ASEAN Framework Agreement on the Facilitation of Goods in Transit.

Sources: Thailand Report, "The Updated Status of the AHN Project", presented at the 29th Senior Transport Official Meeting in Brunei Darussalam, 1–3 June 2010; ASEAN Secretariat.

Rail Infrastructure

The SKRL flagship project was proposed at the Fifth ASEAN Summit in December 1995, targeted for completion by 2015. It covers several routes through Singapore–Malaysia–Thailand–Cambodia–Vietnam–China (Kunming) and spurs lines in Thailand–Myanmar and Thailand–Lao PDR.

Currently there are 4,069 kilometres of missing links (see Table 2.2), or links that need to be rehabilitated in six Member States including Cambodia, Lao PDR, Malaysia, Myanmar, Thailand, and Vietnam. Due consideration should be given to CLMV (Cambodia, Laos, Myanmar, and Vietnam) Member States with regard to securing both financial and technical assistance from ASEAN, its dialogue partners, and other international organizations to help them in the undertaking of the SKRL project.

Inland Waterways Transport

Although inland waterways transport has large potential in reducing freight transport costs, the current utilization rate within ASEAN is still very low. The ASEAN region is generously endowed with around 51,000 kilometres of navigable inland waterways, which can play an active role in transport development, especially in the CLMV states and Thailand. The reasons for low utilization are the underdeveloped

TABLE 2.2
Missing Links in the SKRL Project

Missing Links	Kilometres
Vientiane – Thakek – Mu Gia	466
Mu Gia – Tan Ap – Vung Ang	119
Poipet – Sisophon	48
Phnom Penh – Loc Ninh	254
Loc Ninh – Ho Chi Minh	129
Thanbyuzayat – Three Pagoda Pass	110

waterways network, poor river ports and facilities, and poor interposal connectivity. Considering the advantage in economic activities, these infrastructure issues need to be addressed, together with improved rules and governance for managing the inland waterway transport system.

Maritime Transport

ASEAN has designated forty-seven ports as the main ports in the trans-ASEAN transport network. Given the varying levels of port infrastructure development, there are a number of issues faced by the designated ports in ASEAN. For example, the handling of cargo depends on the capacity of ship calling at the ports, cargo handling capacity, land transport and logistics capacity, and customs and administrative clearance procedures.

Maritime transport is the most important mode of transportation in international trade. However, many ASEAN countries, with the exception of Singapore and Malaysia, rank poorly compared to China and Hong Kong in the United Nations Conference on Trade and Development (UNCTAD) Liner Shipping Connectivity Index. At the same time, most of the gateway ports of the ASEAN member states are "fairly full", which means that investments in capacity expansion would have to be made in order to meet the growth in trade expected from the deeper economic integration of the ASEAN member states among themselves and with the rest of the world.

In order to enhance intra-ASEAN connectivity, the archipelagic regions of ASEAN must be connected through efficient and reliable shipping routes. The results of the initial impact assessment of the Philippines Nautical Highway System (also referred to as Roll-on/Roll-off [RoRo]) demonstrate significant benefits in terms of reduction in transport costs, the creation of new regional links and expansion of regional markets, more efficient shipment of goods and people that have particularly benefited the poorer provinces in the maritime routes, acceleration of local area development, realignment of logistical practices with more frequent deliveries, and greater competitive pressure on the domestic shipping industry (ADB 2010).[1]

Air Transport

In the area of air transport infrastructure, capital airports of ASEAN member states are sufficient in terms of runway lengths to accommodate the existing operation of aircrafts. However, some of these airports still face problems in providing airport facilities, particularly runways and warehouses. Aside from the development of airports, attention to harmonizing ASEAN air navigation system and procedures, including air routes, should be given. Failure to improve these facilities could result in limited growth potential. Some ASEAN member states have recently implemented projects to improve airport facilities and services, including the construction of terminals for private low cost carriers (LCCs). However, a lack of storage facilities at the airports of some ASEAN member states still remains (see Annex 1).

2. Information and Communications Technology (ICT) Infrastructure Development

(a) Strategies

ASEAN cooperation and integration in the ICT sector is currently governed by the e-ASEAN Framework Agreement, signed by ASEAN leaders on 24 November 2000 in Singapore, and the ICT components of the AEC Blueprint. The e-ASEAN Framework Agreement sets the objectives of ASEAN ICT cooperation to:

   a.   Develop, strengthen, and enhance the competitiveness of the ICT sector in ASEAN;
   b.   Reduce the digital divide within individual ASEAN member states and amongst ASEAN member states;
   c.   Promote cooperation between the public and private sectors in realizing e-ASEAN;
   d.   Promote the liberalization of trade in ICT products and services, and investments to support the e-ASEAN initiative.

Under the Agreement, ASEAN would implement various measures aimed at: (a) facilitating the establishment of the ASEAN Information Infrastructure; (b) facilitating the growth of electronic commerce in ASEAN; (c) promoting and facilitating the liberalization of trade in ICT products and services, and of investments in support of the e-ASEAN initiative; (d) promoting and facilitating investments in the production of ICT products and the provision of ICT services; (e) developing an e-Society in ASEAN and capacity building to reduce the digital divide within individual ASEAN member states and amongst ASEAN member states; and (f) promoting the use of ICT applications in the delivery of government services (e-government).

The ASEAN Telecommunications and Information Technology Ministers (TELMIN) have also made a number of important decisions to enhance ASEAN ICT cooperation to help build a connected, vibrant, and secure ASEAN Community through, among others: (a) building a next generation infrastructure backbone; (b) creating a skilful ICT workforce and knowledgeable community; (c) promoting digital inclusion/e-government; (d) promoting e-society and ICT engine for sectoral transformation (including creative, innovative and green ICT) and; (e) facilitating the development of e-commerce and investment in the ICT sector. The decisions also include, among others, the "Bali Declaration on High Speed Connection to Bridge ASEAN Digital Divide" and the "Vientiane Declaration on Promoting the Realization of Broadband across ASEAN" in 2008 and 2009, respectively, to provide principles and specific actions that need to be implemented for the development of the high speed national information infrastructure and regional secure broadband networks in ASEAN.

The 8th TELMIN Meeting in August 2008 tasked the ASEAN Telecommunications and Information Technology Senior Officers Meeting (TELSOM) to discuss and come up with recommendations on the new ICT thrusts and strategies that ASEAN should focus on until 2015.

Following up on the TELMIN mandate, TELSOM agreed to develop an ASEAN ICT Master Plan as a strategic document to reinforce ICT's enabling role in the implementation of the Roadmap for the ASEAN Community (2009–2015). The Master Plan would need to identify and incorporate meaningful and effective outcomes to bring the ASEAN ICT sector to a higher level. The Master Plan would also include new and emerging areas of cooperation, such as international roaming charges, information security, universal service (including universal access to broadband), new media (e.g. Internet-based social networking) and digital contents, e-government, industry structure, empowerment of consumers, broadcasting, and green ICT.

The 9th TELMIN Meeting in October 2009 endorsed the vision of the ASEAN ICT Master Plan 2015 in "Towards an Empowering and Transformational ICT: Creating an Inclusive, Vibrant and Integrated ASEAN". TELMIN also endorsed the outline, including the strategic thrusts and key initiatives, of the Master Plan.

(b) Progress and Challenges

ICT infrastructure is fundamental to supporting trade, facilitating investments, and enlarging markets through its ability to facilitate information exchange, to connect people, to support delivery of services, and to reduce the cost of business and trade-related transactions. ICT infrastructure is broadly defined to include fixed, mobile, and satellite communication networks and the Internet, as well as the software supporting the development and operation of these communication networks.

Developing ASEAN ICT infrastructure faces a number of challenges. The most important challenge would be to find solutions to the extensive digital divide in ASEAN. Bridging the digital divide requires commitment from Member States to improve the competitiveness of their national ICT sectors.

Other challenges include insufficient coordination to ensure connectivity amongst national information infrastructure, the need to nurture technological innovation, as well as the lack of financing schemes for infrastructure projects that involve significant participation of private capital. Significant challenges also lie in the ability of ASEAN member states to develop and harmonize ICT regulations necessary for connectivity projects (i.e., cross-border transactions) and to encourage national and private investments in ICT infrastructure and services.

3. Energy Infrastructure Development

(a) Strategies

ASEAN cooperation on energy is guided by the Agreement on ASEAN Energy Cooperation 1986 and the consecutive series of five-year ASEAN Plans of Action on Energy Cooperation (APAEC) starting from APAEC 1999–2004. The current plan of action is the APAEC 2010–2015, which was adopted by the ASEAN Ministers on Energy at their 27th AMEM Meeting in July 2009 in Myanmar, with the theme of "Bringing Policies to Actions: Towards a Cleaner, More Efficient and Sustainable ASEAN Energy Community". The main strategy and thrusts of ASEAN energy cooperation are also reflected in the AEC Blueprint 2015.

In general, the overall objective of ASEAN energy cooperation is to enhance energy security and sustainability for the ASEAN region, while at the same time giving due attention on the issues of health, safety, and environment. ASEAN energy cooperation is carried out in seven main Programme Areas: a) ASEAN Power Grid (APG), b) Trans-ASEAN Gas Pipeline (TAGP), c) Coal and Clean Coal Technology, d) Renewable Energy, e) Energy Efficiency and Conservation, f) Regional Energy Policy and Planning, and g) Civilian Nuclear Energy.

Directly relevant to the ASEAN Connectivity initiative, is the development of the two major ASEAN energy infrastructure interconnectivity projects, namely the TAGP and the APG.

(b) Progress and Challenges

Energy plays a crucial role in economic development and will remain critical to the continued economic growth of the ASEAN region. Under the first Plan of Action (1999–2004), the conclusion of the TAGP Master Plan by ASEAN Council on Petroleum (ASCOPE) and the ASEAN Interconnection Master Plan Study by Heads of ASEAN Power Utilities/Authorities (HAPUA) paved the way for an enhanced regional energy security framework, while promoting efficient utilization and sharing of resources.

In the second Plan of Action (2005–2009), significant achievements were: the signing of a MOU for the APG, the establishment of the APG Consultative Council, and the establishment of the ASCOPE Gas Centre (AGC).

The current Plan of Action (2010–2015) placed greater emphasis on accelerating the implementation of action plans to further enhance energy security, accessibility, and sustainability for the region with due consideration to health, safety, and environment; especially in relation to APG, TAGP, clean coal technology, and renewable energy amongst others.

APG is a flagship programme mandated in 1997 by ASEAN leaders, which aims to help ASEAN member states meet the increasing demand for electricity and improve access to energy services by enhancing trade in electricity across borders, optimizing energy generation and development, and encouraging possible reserve sharing schemes.

Challenges for the APG remain, since a significant number of the future interconnected projects will either require marine/undersea cable connections or inland connections involving the grids of the CLMV countries. The economic viability of the planned grid interconnected projects has yet to be established and accepted by participating economies, even though the projects have already been assessed by HAPUA to be technically feasible. Economic viability will affect prospects for financial viability in particular. Issues regarding the need to introduce an effective regulatory framework and a mechanism for raising capital also need to be addressed.

TAGP aims to develop a regional gas grid by 2020, by interconnecting existing and planned gas pipelines of Member States and enabling gas to be transported across borders. By 2013, there is likely to be a total of 3,020 kilometres of pipelines in place, with the completion of the M9 pipeline linking Myanmar to Thailand. The region is also looking into establishing infrastructure for the transportation of liquefied natural gas (LNG), as countries such as Malaysia, Singapore, and Thailand undertake construction of LNG terminals. The challenges are in obtaining an adequate supply of piped natural gas, increase in investment costs, synchronizing national technical and security regulation requirements, and differences in the processes of supply, distribution, and management for natural gas across the countries.

The realization of TAGP is expected to encounter substantial financial and legal complexities. The challenges include increasing investment costs, synchronizing national technical and security regulation require-ments, and differences in the supply, distribution, and management procedure of natural gas across the countries. Rivalry between the pipeline-delivered natural gas and other energy sources, such as coal and LNG, also needs to be addressed. In addition, there is also a need to overcome the issue of political trust common in energy markets cooperation, which can be a huge barrier to the trade in pipelined gas and electricity.

To date, eight bilateral gas pipeline interconnection projects are operating, with a total length of some 2,300 kilometres. This is more than half of the total planned length for development (4,500 kilometres). The developed projects link pipelines between Thailand and Myanmar, West Natuna and Duyong, West Natuna and Singapore, South Sumatera and Singapore, Malaysia and Thailand, and Singapore and Malaysia.

Other Energy Connectivity Policies and Concerns

ASEAN energy cooperation also concerns the promotion of effective competition in the energy market, ensuring reliable and secure energy supply, and the development of a dynamic energy sector in the region.

A significant increase in activities have been seen in the ASEAN Energy Efficiency and Conservation (EE&C) cooperation sector as well as in renewable energy, covering numerous institutional capacity building programmes, increasing private sector involvement in ASEAN EE&C and renewable energy programmes, and in expanding markets for energy efficiency and renewable energy products. The APAEC (2010–2015) sets a goal for ASEAN to pursue the ideal target of reducing regional energy intensity of at least 8 per cent by 2015 based on the 2005 level, and to achieve a 15 per cent collective target for regional renewable energy in the total power installed capacity by 2015.

In the coal industry, notable efforts and activities have been under-taken to promote sustainable development and the utilization of coal and clean coal technology. The ASEAN member states' energy plans indicate the rapid growth of coal utilization for power generation, which presents itself an opportunity to promote and increase cleaner coal use and trade that could bring in mutual economic benefits towards regional energy integration.

To enhance ASEAN's position as a regional energy player, ASEAN's energy cooperation with Dialogue Partners is in progress with imple-mentation of various programmes, and projects under the frameworks of ASEAN Senior Officials on Energy Meeting+3 (SOME+3)/ ASEAN Ministers on Energy Meeting+3 (AMEM+3), East Asia Summit Energy Cooperation Task Force (EAS ECTF)/ EAS Environment Ministers Meeting (EMM), SOME-Ministry of Economy, Trade, and Industry Japan (SOME-METI), and SOME-European Union (SOME-EU). The major activities being undertaken include: implementation of the 2010 ASEAN-EU Energy Cooperation Work Plan, development of the Oil Stockpiling Roadmap for ASEAN+3 countries, and implementation of the Clean Development Mechanism project as well as a civilian nuclear energy capacity building project.

Regional and Subregional Infrastructure Development Programmes[2]

ASEAN Initiatives

- ASEAN Highway Network Project: The AHN Project consists of twenty-three designated routes totalling about 38,000 kilometres.

- The SKRL Project is expected to link major cities in eight countries, namely Singapore, Malaysia, Thailand, Cambodia, Vietnam, Lao PDR, Myanmar, and China.
- ASEAN's initiatives to integrate member countries' transport systems include the Framework Agreement on the Facilitation of Goods in Transit, the ASEAN Framework Agreement on Multimodal Transport, and the ASEAN Framework Agreement on the Facilitation of Inter-State Transport. Member countries have also designated fifty-one airports and forty-six ports to form integral parts of the trans-ASEAN transportation network.
- ASEAN initiatives in telecommunications and information technology include the development of ASEAN information infrastructure, bridging the digital divide within ASEAN by encouraging capacity building and human resource development, enhancing access to and the use of telecommunications and information technology, and coordinating and harmonizing policies and programmes.

Greater Mekong Subregion (GMS)

The GMS's prioritized area is the development of three economic corridors — East–West, North–South and Southern — in accordance with a ten-year strategic framework adopted in 2001. In 2008, the GMS cross-border transport agreement (CBTA) was signed and ratified, covering all the relevant aspects of cross-border facilitation such as single window, single-stop, custom inspections, cross-border movement of people, exchange of commercial traffic rights, and issues related to road and bridge design standards, including road signs and signals.

Mekong River Commission (MRC)

The Mekong River Commission (MRC) was established in 1995 by an agreement between the governments of Cambodia, Lao PDR, Thailand, and Vietnam. The Agreement on the Cooperation for the Sustainable Development of the Mekong River Basin came about as the four countries saw a common interest in jointly managing their shared water resources and developing the economic potential of the river.

Since the 1995 Agreement, the MRC has launched a process to ensure "reasonable and equitable use" of the Mekong River System, through a participatory process with National Mekong Committees in each country to develop procedures for water utilization. The MRC is supporting a joint basin-wide planning process with the four countries involved, called the Basin Development Plan, which is the basis of its Integrated Water Resources Development Programme. The MRC is also involved in fisheries management, promotion of safe navigation, irrigated agriculture, watershed management, environment monitoring, flood management, and exploring hydropower options.

The two upper states of the Mekong River Basin, the People's Republic of China and the Union of Myanmar, are dialogue partners to the MRC.

Brunei–Indonesia–Malaysia–Philippines East ASEAN Growth Area (BIMP-EGA)

BIMP-EAGA's regional projects have focused on air and maritime services, as well as on software aspects. A memorandum of agreement on promoting cross-border movement of commercial buses and vehicles, and establishing efficient and integrated sea links in the subregion, was signed by the members in 2007.

Indonesia–Malaysia–Thailand Growth Triangle (IMT-GT)

IMT-GT aims to expand opportunities for trade and investment through improved infrastructure and connectivity. The private sector plays an important role through the joint business councils. There are six working groups, including one focused on infrastructure and transport. To date, five economic connectivity corridors have been identified. In partnership with the Asian Development Bank (ADB), it provides capacity-building support, helps to mobilize technical and financial resources, and to promote an enabling environment for private sector development.

The Asian Highway and Trans-Asian Railway Network (AH-TAR)

The AH and TAR networks are part of the United Nations Economic and Social Commission for the Asia Pacific's (UNESCAP) initiative to improve economic links among Asian countries through better and increased connectivity. Its other pillar is the facilitation of land transport projects through intermodal transport terminals (dry and inland ports).

ASEAN Infrastructure Hindrance for Economic Integration

According to the Master Plan on ASEAN Connectivity, the main focus in terms of physical connectivity is to integrate transport, ICT, and energy infrastructure. However, the hindrances to accelerate infrastructure development in ASEAN are many. Some of them are mentioned as below:

1. Geographical diversity;
2. Different levels of economic and infrastructure development;
3. Country capacity (e.g., the infrastructure of some ASEAN members is relatively underdeveloped; on the other hand, the more mature ASEAN countries may have more developed infrastructures, but the cost of linking them can be prohibitive due to geographical barriers);
4. Asymmetric distribution of regional infrastructure costs and benefits across participating countries;
5. Synchronization of national and subregional infrastructure planning and financing;
6. Massive financing requirements: The ADB estimates that ASEAN countries will require infrastructure investment amounting to US$596 billion during 2006–15, with an average investment of US$60 billion per year (see Table 2.3). Meeting this financing

TABLE 2.3
Projected Infrastructure Requirements in ASEAN 2006–15
(US$ billion)

Sector	New Capacity	Maintenance	Total
Power	170.3	46.0	216.3
Transport	95.6	61.2	156.8
Water and Sanitation	98.8	60.6	159.4
Telecom	30.9	32.7	63.6
Total	395.6	200.5	596.1

Source: ADB.

requirement will pose a tremendous challenge in realizing full
ASEAN connectivity by 2015; and

7. In addition, another challenge is to minimize the overlap or
    duplication of work plans and activities, and overstretching of
    resources. The task forward is to ensure that implementation
    mechanisms work effectively.

Addressing these difficulties will require the following measures:

1. Creation of an enabling environment for cross-border infrastruc-
    ture (CBI) investment;
2. Effective coordination among multiple stakeholders (central
    government, local government, the private sector, and civil
    society) for CBI development;
3. Identification, development, prioritization, and preparation of
    "bankable" or commercially-viable projects;
4. Mobilization of ASEAN member countries' private savings to
    finance "bankable" projects;
5. Evaluation of capital intensive projects in terms of symmetric
    distribution of cost and benefits; and
6. Identification of the limitations of traditional infrastructure
    financing.

Concluding Remarks

In order to achieve ASEAN's vision of a stable, prosperous, and highly
competitive region, regional infrastructure cooperation for connectivity
must complement efforts in infrastructure development at the country
level. By working together, ASEAN countries can sustain economic
growth as well as move closer to their goal of integration.

To build up infrastructure, ASEAN members should utilize their
own national resources, as well as tap those of other Asian countries.
They should mobilize resources from Dialogue Partners, International
Financial Institutions, bilateral donors, and the private sector. The role
of ASEAN is to ensure cooperation and coordination of its members'
infrastructure projects: harness shared resources such as capital,
energy, services, and technology; harmonize cross-border rules and
regulations; and facilitate exchange of good practices on institutions
and policies.

Key Air and Sea Ports in ASEAN   ANNEX 1

1. Brunei Darussalam

   Port

   1. Muara Port
   2. Kuala Belait Port
   3. Bangar wharf
   4. Pulau Muara Besar Port
      (PMB)

   Airport

   1. Brunei Darussalam International
      Airport (BIA)

2. Cambodia

   Port

   1. Sihanoukville Port
   2. Phnom Penh Port
   3. Koh Kong Port

   Airport

   1. Phnom Penh International Airport
   2. Angkor International Airport
   3. Sihanoukville International Airport

3. Indonesia

   Port

   1. Tanjung Priok
   2. Sabang
   3. Benoa
   4. Pontianak
   5. Banjarmasin
   6. Balikpapan
   7. Panjang
   8. Ambon
   9. Belawan
   10. Telukbayur
   11. Palembang
   12. Jayapura
   13. Bengkalis
   14. Tanjung Emas
   15. Makasar
   16. Manado
   17. Tanjung Perak
   18. Malaka

   Airport

   1. Soekarno-Hatta International
      Airport
   2. Husein Sastranegara International
      Airport
   3. Juanda International Airport
   4. Ahmad Yani International Airport
   5. Adisumarmo International Airport
   6. Adisucipto International Airport
   7. Ngurah Rai International Airport
   8. Sepinggan International Airport
   9. Syamsudin Noor International
      Airport
   10. Hasanuddin International Airport
   11. Sam Ratulangi International
       Airport
   12. Minangkabau International Airport
   13. Frans Kaisepo International
       Airport
   14. Pattimura International Airport

4. Lao

   Airport

   1. Wattay International Airport
   2. Luang Prabang International
      Airport
   3. Pakse International Airport

5. Malaysia

Port	*Airport*
1. Port Klang	1. Kuala Lumpur International Airport
2. Port of Tanjung Pelepas	2. Penang International Airport
3. Kuantan Port	3. Langkawi International Airport
4. Penang Port	4. Kota Kinabalu International Airport
5. Johor Port	5. Kuching International Airport
6. Kemaman Port	
7. Bintulu Port	

6. Myanmar

Port	*Airport*
1. Myanmar International Terminals Thilawa	1. Yangon International Airport
	2. Mandalay International Airport
	3. Myeik Airport
	4. Myitkyina Airport

7. Philippines

Port	*Airport*
1. South Harbor	1. Ninoy Aquino International Airport (NAIA)
2. Manila International Container Port (MICP)	2. Diosdado Macapagal (Clark) International Airport
3. Cebu	3. Subic
4. Batangas	4. Cebu
5. Davao	5. Davao
6. Subic	6. Zamboanga
7. Cagayan de Oro	7. General Santos
8. General Santos	8. Laguindingan
9. Zamboanga	9. Laoag
	10. New Iloilo of Ozamiz

8. Singapore

Port	*Airport*
Port of Singapore	Changi International Airport

9. Thailand

Port	*Airport*
1. Bangkok Port	1. Suvarnabhumi International Airport
2. Sriracha Port	2. Chiang Mai International Airport
3. Laem Chabang Port	3. Chiang Rai International Airport
4. Map Ta Phut Industrial Port	4. Hat Yai International Airport
5. Songkhla Port	5. Phuket International Airport
6. Phuket Port	

10. Vietnam

Port	*Airport*
1. Da Nang Port	1. Noibai International Airport
2. Hai Phong Port	2. Da Nang International Airport
3. Ho Chi Minh City Port	3. Tan Son Nhat International
4. Hong Gai Port	Airport
5. Qui Nhon (Qui Nhon Port)	
6. Nha Trang (Nha Trang Port)	

NOTES

1. Asian Development Bank (ADB), *Bridges Across Oceans: Initial Impact Assessment of the Philippines Nautical Highway System and Lessons for Southeast Asia* (Manila, Philippines: ADB, 2010).
2. The section has been drawn on Asian Development Bank (ADB) research.

REFERENCE

Asian Development Bank (ADB). *Bridges Across Oceans: Initial Impact Assessment of the Philippines Nautical Highway System and Lessons for Southeast Asia.* Manila, Philippines: ADB, 2010.

3

BUILDING GREATER CONNECTIVITY ACROSS ASEAN

Michael Yeoh, Ng Yeen Seen,
Tilottama Roy

Introduction

The new byword for ASEAN is "connectivity". In the current competitive environment, connectivity as a concept is of paramount importance to countries, and furthermore, to regions attempting to achieve collective economic success.

As has been stated before, connectivity among nations is *sine qua non* in the age of globalization.[1] For a region to succeed globally, connectivity and the resulting coherence in activity and goals within the nations is what will increase the ability to compete. Connectivity is important on various levels. From physical to institutional, to cultural and social, connectivity within a region is integral in order for a region to succeed.

ASEAN, as a region, has various goals. The most prominent of these is to achieve economic integration by 2015. In order to achieve this and ensure future success of the region, various measures have been taken. The ASEAN Master Plan on Connectivity has done a noteworthy job of mapping out the areas of concern and detailing the possible solutions to problems that may be encountered while building the hard and soft infrastructure. It also ensured the harmonization of frameworks and goals across the member countries.

Of the various levels of connectivity outlined in the Master Plan, physical connectivity forms the backbone, on which the other areas of connectivity can be build upon. Physical connectivity is essentially soft and hard infrastructure. Hard infrastructure would include the actual physical structures that bolster social and economic activities, whilst soft infrastructure consists of the intangible aspects such as frameworks and institutional regulations that aid the functioning of the physical infrastructure.

In the Master Plan, physical connectivity is composed of transport infrastructure (land, air, and maritime), energy infrastructure, and information and communications technology (ICT) infrastructure. This chapter will look at all three arms — transport, energy, and ICT — and will highlight the current problems in building the infrastructure. The chapter will conclude with concrete policy recommendations.

Importance of Good Infrastructure

Infrastructure development is very important for the region's growth prospects. Improved infrastructure would increase the rate of competitiveness of the ASEAN region. Various studies have proven that a country's infrastructure has a direct effect on its competitiveness. In the Global Competitiveness Index, the four pillars of the basic requirements sub-index group are institutions, infrastructure, macroeconomic environment, and health and primary education. Specifically, "extensive and efficient infrastructure is critical for ensuring the effective functioning of the economy, as it is an important factor determining the location of economic activity and the kinds of activities or sectors that can develop in a particular economy".[2] A solid, well developed infrastructure system reduces distances between regions, thereby reducing distances between national, international, and regional markets; and a well developed telecommunications and transport infrastructure allows access to economic activities for less developed communities.[3]

Improved physical infrastructure such as seamless transport networks help to reduce poverty. There are studies which have shown the positive impact of infrastructure spending have on poverty reduction and distribution of income. If the Latin American countries were to mimic the East Asian median countries' levels of infrastructure, they would lower their Gini coefficients by 0.02 to 0.10 and increase their long term growth per capita by 1.1 per cent to 4.8 per cent.[4]

In terms of the urban poor, it has been proven that increased spending on infrastructure reduces the level of urban poverty. What matters most is the real expenditure on infrastructure, i.e. the quantity built, such as kilometres of roads built. It is the real expenditure that shows a negative relationship between poverty and infrastructure.[5]

Finally, it is not merely the spending on infrastructure that is important, but also the efficiency with which the spending is made. The level of efficiency in infrastructure spending has been shown to be a key component in narrowing the development gap between high and low income countries by as much as 40 per cent.[6]

It is also very important to manage the infrastructure fund. Management of infrastructure funds and the efficiency of project management determine success of infrastructure development. This requires proper institutional frameworks. For example, in Africa, research has shed light on the fact that infrastructure financing by itself does not lead to poverty reduction. It must be bolstered with infrastructural reform, and the development of the appropriate markets and regulatory frameworks within which infrastructural spending could work efficiently.[7] In addition to the physical infrastructure, the social infrastructure is also important as it is together that makes a real difference in poverty reduction.

Challenges for ASEAN Infrastructure Development

ASEAN is seriously lacking in infrastructure in many areas. The challenges for an efficient infrastructure system in ASEAN are as follows:

- ASEAN, as a region, is made up of very diverse countries, both economically and culturally. Economically, ASEAN member countries are of different sizes and are at different levels of national income. While this diversity is good, it also hinders the dream of a seamless infrastructure framework in the region.

- As the member countries are at different level of development, infrastructure frameworks are also at varying stages of progress. This is one of the greatest challenges for ASEAN.
- Infrastructure needs are, again, not the same throughout the region. In this regard, harmonious infrastructure development is crucial. As a region, it is important to understand the infrastructure gaps, and then to ensure an appropriate plan. Although the Master Plan has detailed the stretches of roads that are needed for regional connectivity, it had missed the smaller details. The Master Plan did not discuss about rural connectivity. ASEAN plans must address the issue of rural-urban divide in terms of physical architecture. This will not only help to promote economic growth but will also help to distribute the benefits of growth more evenly among its people.
- Good governance is also necessary among ASEAN members. The regulatory frameworks have to be strengthened to make sure that the capital that the region garner for infrastructure development is used for the right purposes and is used in a manner that addresses everyone's needs.
- Till now, there is a tendency among the ASEAN countries to act on their self-interest. This is a big hindrance from experiencing the complete benefits of regional cooperation. Much more needs to be done in terms of cross-border initiatives, especially the individual member countries have to address infrastructure concerns within their own boundaries. Indeed, there are some accomplishments in terms of cross-border projects (ASEAN Highway Network and the Singapore–Kunming Rail Link), but this needs to be expanded to include collaboration on local and national infrastructure projects as well. The more developed ASEAN nations must assist the less developed members in transferring knowledge, human resources and technology in this respect.
- Finally, the most critical issue for ASEAN infrastructure is financing. For the region to grow and to develop effective infrastructure, it needs massive investments. Although ASEAN has in place the traditional methods of funding, one particular way becomes very important. This is the Public-Private Partnerships (PPP), which currently appears to be not fully utilized. PPPs bring together the best of the knowledge and expertise of the private sector, and the funds and institutional reach of the public sector.

Public-Private Partnership Initiative

It is stated in the Master Plan that

> a critical factor affecting the attraction of private sector finance for
> sub-regional projects is the lack of adequate project preparation which
> could deter public-private partnerships (PPPs). The lack of adequate and
> reliable technical and financial information on PPP projects can hamper
> the evaluation of risks, not only from the point of view of the private
> sector entity, but also from the point of view of the public sector.[8]

While the Master Plan acknowledges the problem, much more needs
to be done. There is an Infrastructure Fund Pool, and the existing
Public-Private Infrastructure Advisory Facility, but this is not solely
dedicated to overseeing PPP funding opportunities within ASEAN.
ASEAN should build a "go to" body for private sector participants who
will be interested in collaborating with the government on infrastructure
projects specifically within ASEAN. In this vein, it would be beneficial
if ASEAN involves more industrial heads and entrepreneurs during
project and financial decision-making processes. This would create more
awareness on ASEAN matters among private sector participants, both
locally and internationally.

The Master Plan mentions that pre-feasibility studies are of paramount
importance to PPP initiatives, and these are sometimes a hindrance for
securing the funding needed. One solution would be to actually outsource
the feasibility studies to private sector experts within the chosen industry.
The feasibility study is usually the domain of the member governments,
for it is up to them to identify possible projects and then test their
feasibility in order to attract funding. If the private sector is allowed to
identify these opportunities themselves and incentivize the process, the
feasibility studies could be prepared by companies who are willing and
capable to work on the projects that they themselves have proposed.

Finally, ASEAN needs to establish a regional coordinating body for
PPP that could seek to harmonize regulations and best practices on PPP.
It will also help to promote and consolidate private sector participation
in the region. It is also important for ASEAN to establish a regional
banking network, that could facilitate mergers and acquisitions among
banks in ASEAN countries so that there will be larger ASEAN banks
operating in many of the ASEAN countries. Such ASEAN banks can
have stronger balance sheets to finance large scale infrastructure projects.
In terms of capital market development, an ASEAN stock exchange can

be considered that can have ASEAN companies listed for fundraising purposes.

In the final analysis, it is people-to-people connectivity that will eventually create a greater sense of ASEAN consciousness to make ASEAN more relevant to the ordinary people of ASEAN. There is lot of room for improvement to foster closer linkages among the people of ASEAN. Exchange programmes can be developed among education institutions within ASEAN. An ASEAN Youth Parliament can be set up and ASEAN studies should be introduced into the school curricula. Once the people have an ASEAN sense of belonging and an ASEAN consciousness developed in the younger generation, the future of ASEAN will be more secure.

NOTES

1. A.B. Chakraborty, "Fostering Physical Connectivity in India's Look East Policy", *Journal of Infrastructure Development*, vol. 1, no. 1 (2009): 45–65.
2. *The Global Competitiveness Report 2010–2011*, The World Economic Forum, 2010.
3. *The Global Competitiveness Report 2010–2011*, The World Economic Forum, 2010.
4. Cesar Calderon and Luis Serven, "The Effects of Infrastructure Development on Growth and Income Distribution", *World Bank Policy Research Working Paper No. 3400* (2004).
5. T.P. Ogun, "Infrastructure and Poverty Reduction: Implications for Urban Development in Nigeria", *UNI WIDER Working Paper No. 2010/43*.
6. Charles Hulten, "Infrastructure Capital and Economic Growth: How Well You Use It May Be More Important Than How Much You Have", *NBER Working Paper 5847* (December 1996).
7. Afeikhena Jerome and Ademola Ariyo, "Infrastructure Reform and Poverty Reduction in Africa", *African Development and Poverty Reduction: The Macro-Micro Linkage*, Forum Paper 2004.
8. ASEAN Secretariat, *Masterplan on ASEAN Connectivity* (Jakarta: The ASEAN Secretariat, January 2011).

REFERENCES

ASEAN Secretariat. *Masterplan on ASEAN Connectivity*. Jakarta: The ASEAN Secretariat, January 2011.

Calderon, Cesar and Luis Serven. "The Effects of Infrastructure Development on Growth and Income Distribution". *World Bank Policy Research Working Paper No. 3400* (2004).

Chakraborty, A.B. "Fostering Physical Connectivity in India's Look East Policy". *Journal of Infrastructure Development*, vol. 1, no. 1 (2009): 45–65.

The Global Competitiveness Report 2010–2011. The World Economic Forum, 2010.

Hulten, Charles. "Infrastructure Capital and Economic Growth: How Well You Use It May Be More Important Than How Much You Have". *NBER Working Paper 5847* (December 1996).

Jerome, Afeikhena and Ademola Ariyo. "Infrastructure Reform and Poverty Reduction in Africa". *African Development and Poverty Reduction: The Macro-Micro Linkage*. Forum Paper 2004.

Ogun, T.P. "Infrastructure and Poverty Reduction: Implications for Urban Development in Nigeria". *UNI WIDER Working Paper No. 2010/43*.

II
Transportation, Telecom, ICT and Energy Infrastructure

4

THE DEVELOPMENT OF LOGISTICS INFRASTRUCTURE IN ASEAN: The Comprehensive Asia Development Plan and the Post-AEC Initiative

Fukunari Kimura

Importance of Physical Connectivity in ASEAN

Physical connectivity, together with institutional connectivity, is the key for economic development in ASEAN and East Asia. Production networks in ASEAN and East Asia, particularly those in the manufacturing sector, are the most advanced in the world. Baldwin (2011) introduces the concept of the "2nd unbundling" for international division of labour in terms of production processes or tasks that extend the boundary of corporate activities, beyond the national border. Connectivity backed up by physical logistics infrastructure and institutional economic integration is crucial to the development of production networks.

Both ASEAN and East Asia have substantial differences in development stages. Such diversity actually enhances opportunities to expand production networks. By effectively utilizing the mechanics of production networks, the regions can achieve both the deepening of economic integration and the narrowing of development gaps. In the process, it is important to identify the demand for logistics infrastructure by geographical location and stages of development.

At the East Asia Summit 2010, ERIA submitted the CADP, which presented ASEAN's logistics and other economic infrastructure development plans that were consistent with the process of industrialization and the extension of production networks. The applied conceptual backbone is the extended fragmentation theory and new economic geography. ERIA, in parallel, supported the ASEAN Secretariat to complete the Brunei Action Plan and the Master Plan on ASEAN Connectivity, both of which shared a common conceptual framework.

This chapter is organized as follows: the next section briefly explains the conceptual framework based on the extended fragmentation theory and new economic geography, which logically links logistics/institutional connectivity with overall development strategies. The three tiers in terms of the degree of participation in production networks are also introduced. The third section assesses the current status of logistics infrastructure and services in ASEAN, while the fourth proposes further logistics and supplementary economic infrastructure development by the three tiers of economic development. The fifth section concludes the chapter by addressing the significance of presenting a new development strategy and a pathway beyond 2015.

Production Networks and Three Tiers of Economic Development

The competitiveness of ASEAN and East Asian economies resides the development of production networks, particularly in the manufacturing sector, with logistics links playing an essential role in the functioning of such production networks.

The mechanics of production networks are analysed by the fragmentation theory and its extension.[1] The theory formalizes fundamental differences between intermediate goods trade and finished products trade, particularly in the flexibility of a firm's decision-making in cutting out production blocks and the existence of service link costs.

Figure 4.1 illustrates the original idea of fragmentation. Suppose that a firm originally produces a product from downstream to upstream in a big factory located in a developed country. The production processes in the factory, however, may have various characteristics; some would be capital or human-capital-intensive while others would be purely labour-intensive. Some would be capital-intensive, but need 24-hour operation under the close supervision of engineers. Hence, if the firm can separate some of the production processes, design production blocks, and locate them in other places, the final total cost may be reduced. This is the so-called fragmentation of production.

Fragmentation of production is economically viable if the saving of production costs per se in production blocks is large and incurred service link costs for connecting remotely located production blocks are small. Whether the first condition is met depends on the production processes being technically separable and the availability of different location advantages. The second depends not only on logistics and

FIGURE 4.1

The Fragmentation Theory: Production Blocks and Service Links

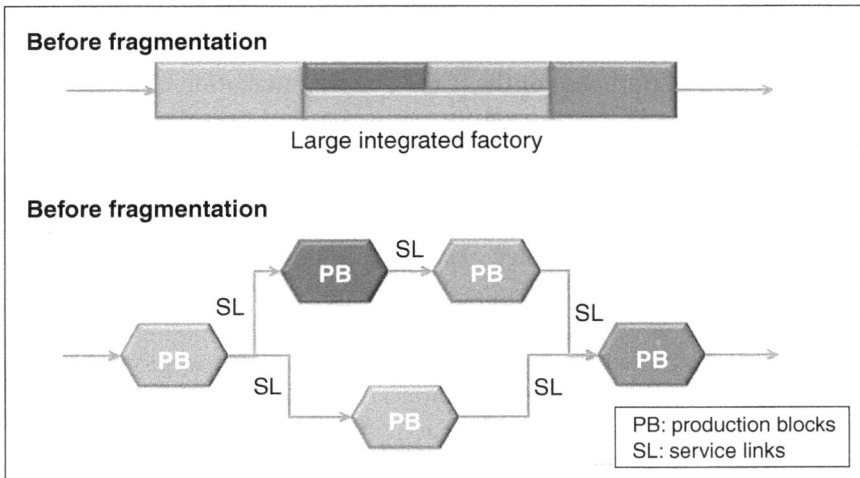

Source: ERIA (2010).

institutional connectivity, but also on various coordination costs, which make transactions in production networks relation-specific. In addition, service links often present economies of scale.

Production networks in ASEAN and East Asia have advanced further than simplistic fragmentation of production. Cross-border production sharing between the U.S. and Mexico, for example, has a relatively simplistic structure with back-and-forth, closed-loop, and intra-firm transactions (see Figure 4.2). On the other hand, in ASEAN and East Asia, there is open-ended "networks" of production-process-wise division of labour that cover a number of countries with a sophisticated combination of intra-firm and arm's length transactions. In some specific places, industrial agglomerations have begun to be created in which vertical, arm's length, and just-in-time transactions among multinationals and local firms occur.

Kimura and Ando (2005) propose the concept of two-dimensional fragmentation. In addition to fragmentation in the dimension of geographical distance, the extended framework introduces fragmentation in the dimension of disintegration, where a firm decides whether to keep some economic activities inside the firm or to outsource them to unrelated firms (see Figure 4.3). This framework explains the sophisticated nature of fragmentation in East Asia, where both intra-firm and arm's length (inter-firm) fragmentation of production processes flourish. By introducing the close relationship between geographical proximity and arm's length transactions, the framework can also neatly describe the simultaneous development of the firm-level fragmentation of production processes and the industry-level formation of agglomeration.

Lessons from new economic geography are important supplements in our conceptual framework. The fragmentation theory argues that a reduction in service link costs may be a trigger for participating in production networks. However, according to new economic geography, a reduction in trade cost generates two countervailing forces: agglomeration forces and dispersion forces (see Figure 4.4). Agglomeration forces make more and more economic activities be attracted to agglomerations. On the other hand, dispersion forces generated by congestion in agglomeration make some economic activities move from agglomerations to peripheries. To control these two countervailing forces, policies to enhance location advantages, which would work complementary to a

FIGURE 4.2

Production Networks: The U.S.-Mexico Nexus versus East Asia

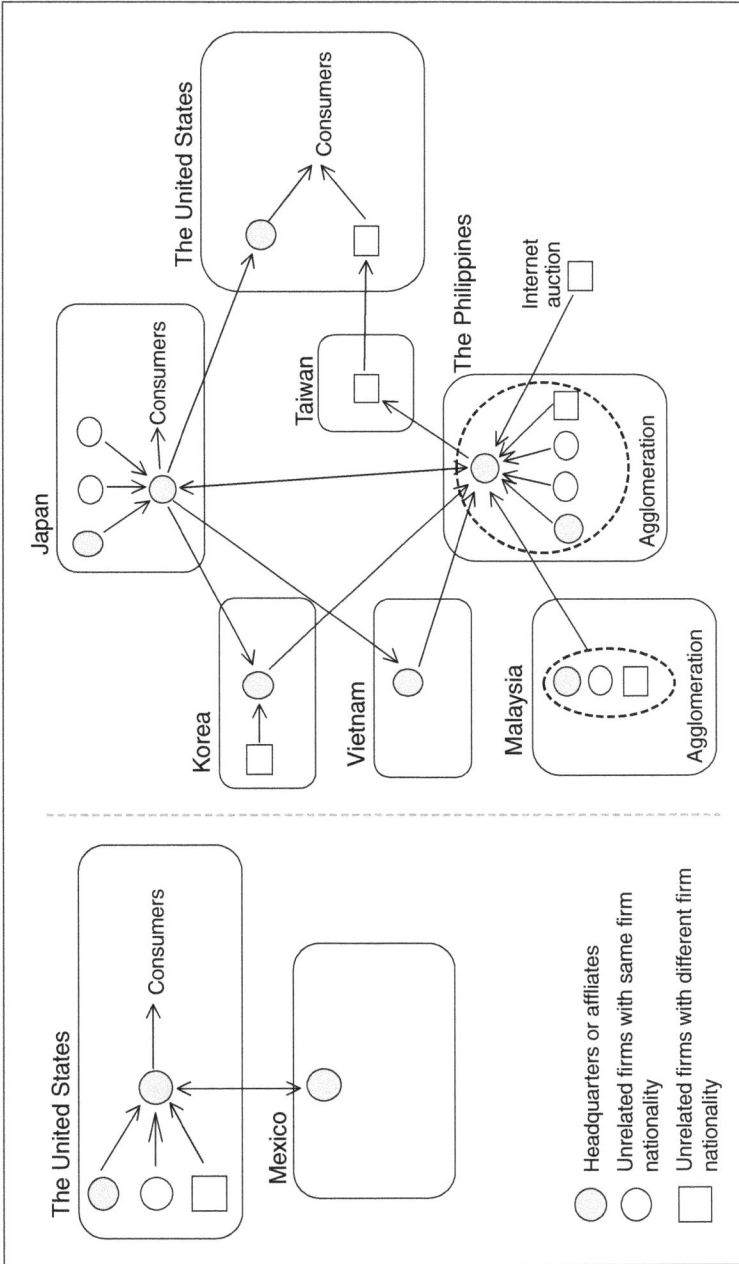

Source: ERIA (2010).

FIGURE 4.3
Two-Dimensional Fragmentation: An Illustration

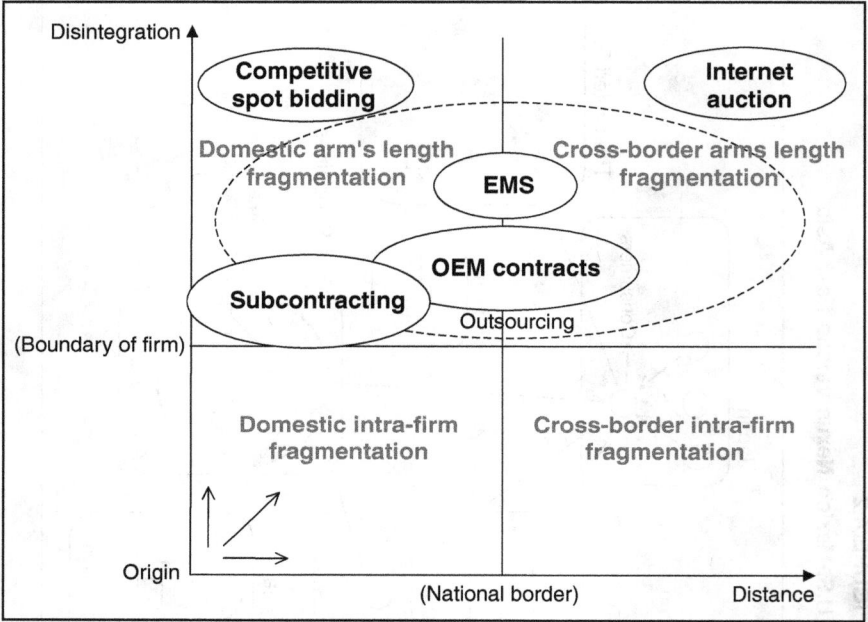

Source: ERIA (2010).

FIGURE 4.4
Agglomeration and Dispersion in New Economic Geography

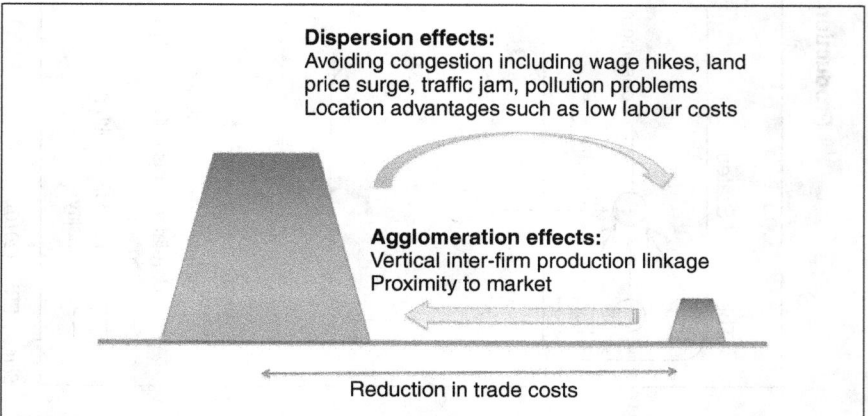

Source: ERIA (2010).

reduction in service link costs, are often required for attracting economic activities to countries/regions at lower stages of development.

Figure 4.5 presents the proportion of machineries in total exports and imports of manufactured goods with the world for East Asian countries (ASEAN+6), European countries (EU 27), and American countries (North American Free Trade Agreement and the Union of South American Nations (UNASUR) member countries. Red stacked bars indicate the percentage of machineries in total manufactured goods exports, and the blue bars do the same for the import side (see ERIA 2010). For both the red and blue bars, dark-coloured portions represent machinery parts and components, and the light-coloured portions denote machinery finished products. The bars are in the descending order of the percentage of machinery parts and components in total manufactured goods exports, from the left to the right. The percentages accounted for by exports and imports of machinery parts and components reflect active back and forth transactions in intermediate goods and are good proxies for the degree of a country's participation in the networks. Of course, machinery industries are not the only ones that utilize the mechanics of fragmentation. However, they develop the most extended, sophisticated production networks with quite frequent just-in-time transactions. Once a country or a region can come into production networks in machinery industries, other industries including services can also enjoy favourable environment for the "2nd unbundling".

Singapore, the Philippines, Malaysia, Japan, Korea, and Thailand present deep participation in international production networks. China (including Hong Kong) is also actively involved in the networks. Still, Indonesia, Vietnam, Australia, New Zealand, and India seem to be somewhat behind in their degree of participation in production networks, compared with other East Asian countries. There exist significant thresholds that countries or regions must surmount before they can enter production networks. This is, in fact, the other side of the coin of durability and stability due to the relation-specific nature of transactions.

Figure 4.6 maps the location of manufacturing sub-sectors in ASEAN, and parts of some other East Asian countries. At the provincial level, it first checks whether manufacturing value added occupies 10 per cent or more of the province's GDP. When the manufacturing share is 10 per cent or more, it then identifies the largest sub-sector amongst automotive, electrical and electronic, textiles and garment, food processing, and other manufacturing industries. The figure shows that only a

FIGURE 4.5

Shares of Machineries in Total Exports/Imports of Manufacturing Goods to the World in 2007

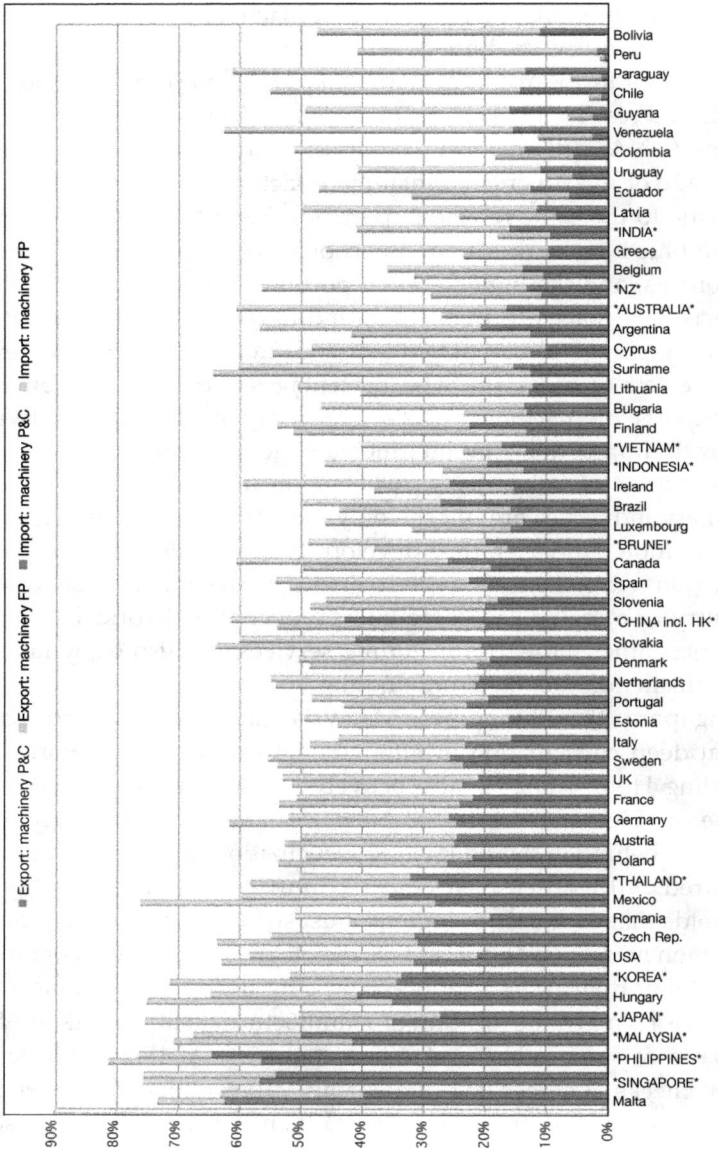

Legend: ■ Export: machinery P&C   ▨ Export: machinery FP   ■ Import: machinery P&C   ▨ Import: machinery FP

Countries (top to bottom): Bolivia, Peru, Paraguay, Chile, Guyana, Venezuela, Colombia, Uruguay, Ecuador, Latvia, *INDIA*, Greece, Belgium, *NZ*, *AUSTRALIA*, Argentina, Cyprus, Suriname, Lithuania, Bulgaria, Finland, *VIETNAM*, *INDONESIA*, Ireland, Brazil, Luxembourg, *BRUNEI*, Canada, Spain, Slovenia, *CHINA incl. HK*, Slovakia, Denmark, Netherlands, Portugal, Estonia, Italy, Sweden, UK, France, Germany, Austria, Poland, *THAILAND*, Mexico, Romania, Czech Rep., USA, *KOREA*, Hungary, *JAPAN*, *MALAYSIA*, *PHILIPPINES*, *SINGAPORE*, Malta

X-axis: 90%, 80%, 70%, 60%, 50%, 40%, 30%, 20%, 10%, 0%

Source: ERIA (2010).

FIGURE 4.6
Location of Manufacturing Sub-Sectors (2005)

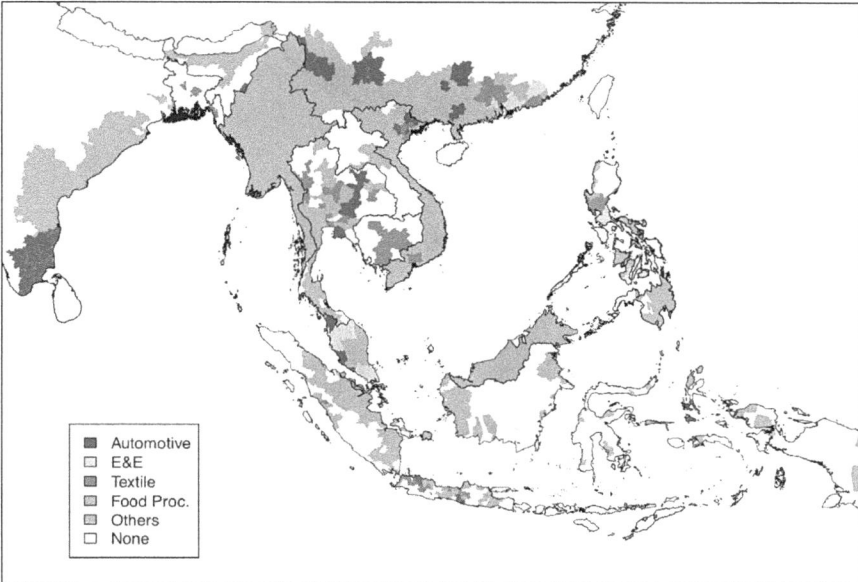

Source: ERIA (2010).

small number of provinces participate in the quick and high-frequency type of production networks, in the automotive and electric/electronic machinery sectors. Outside of such areas, some provinces have textiles and garment as well as food processing. Although these activities are sometimes connected to the world market, production networks are typically slow and low in frequency. Little manufacturing activity is found further from these provinces.

Figure 4.7 presents the level of per capita GDP by province in these countries. Income levels differ widely, not only across countries but also across regions within each country. This means that the differences in development stage are not fully utilized in extending production networks. The mechanics of fragmentation and agglomeration should be more aggressively explored in order to pursue both deeper economic integration and narrowing development gaps in these areas. Yellow circles indicate existing or possible industrial agglomerations in the region (see ERIA 2010).

FIGURE 4.7

Nominal GRDP Per-Capita (2005) and Industrial Agglomerations

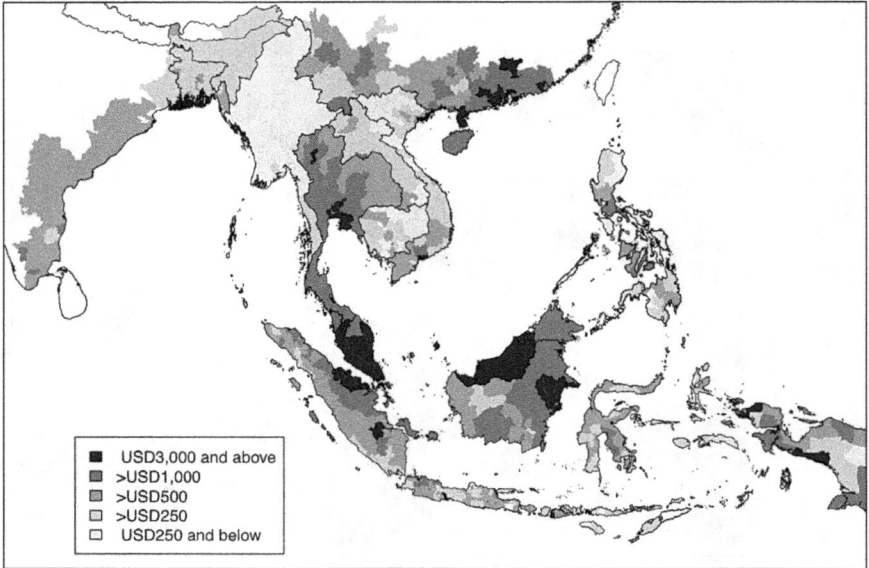

USD3,000 and above
>USD1,000
>USD500
>USD250
USD250 and below

Source: ERIA (2010).

To fully utilize the mechanics of production networks, it is crucial to strategically classify geographical location and the stages of development into three tiers in terms of the degree of participation in production networks.

Tier 1 includes countries/regions that are already in production networks and where industrial agglomerations have started to form. Issues and challenges to take care of are upgrading industrial agglomerations, increasing innovation, and climbing up the ladder from middle-income to fully developed countries/regions.

Tier 2 corresponds to countries/regions that are not yet fully integrated into quick and high-frequency production networks. Issues and challenges are how to participate in quick and high-frequency production networks by reducing service link costs and improving location advantages for production.

Tier 3 comprises countries/regions that are not likely to come into quick and high-frequency production networks in the short run, but would like to provide a new framework for industrial development with the development of logistics infrastructure as a trigger.

The conceptual framework of CADP provides comprehensive strategies for the spatial design of economic infrastructure and industrial placement based on the three-tier structure.

The Assessment of Logistics Infrastructure in ASEAN

In ASEAN and East Asia, the development of logistics infrastructure is closely linked with the degree of participation in production networks.

The World Bank compiled the Logistics Performance Index (LPI) as a multidimensional assessment of logistics performance. It uses numbers of assessments made by nearly 1,000 international freight forwarders to compare the trade logistics profiles of 155 countries in the world. LPI provides selected performance indicators with a scale from one (worst) to five (best), including information on the time, cost, and reliability of import and export supply chains, infrastructure quality, performance of core services, and the friendliness of trade clearance procedures. All ASEAN countries except Brunei are covered by LPI 2007 and 2010.[2]

The ranking of nine ASEAN countries is presented in LPI 2010. There are large gaps in ratings. Singapore is the highest in the ranking, i.e. 2nd out of 155 countries in the world, and is categorized together with Malaysia (29th) and Thailand (35th) into the first group of "logistics friendly countries". The Philippines (44th), Vietnam (53rd), and Indonesia (75th) are classified in the second group of "consistent logistics countries". Laos (118th), Cambodia (129th), and Myanmar (133rd) are still at the bottom group of "logistics unfriendly countries". These assessments closely reflect the countries' degree of participation in production networks.

LPI scores overall have a positive association with income levels. However, six ASEAN countries, a bit less so for Indonesia though, are actually way above the respective income groups. This is a partial indication of the relatively low service link costs for production networks in these countries. On the other hand, Laos, Cambodia, and Myanmar are located lower than the corresponding income group, which indicates ample room for the improvement of logistics infrastructure in order to participate in production networks.

The World Bank also conducts a huge undertaking called Doing Business. The 2010 version presents that ASEAN's average scores of six indicators including documents to export, time to export, cost to export, documents to import, time to import, and cost to import are higher than the world average.[3]

By transport modes, we also observe vast differences in stages of development for logistics infrastructure and logistics services across countries and regions. Highway networks in Singapore, Malaysia, and Thailand are well developed to support production networks, particularly for transactions in short to middle distances. Although traffic in North Java in Indonesia and Luzon in the Philippines are also large, there seems to be room for improvement. Roads in other islands in Indonesia and the Philippines as well as CLMV (Cambodia, Laos, Myanmar, and Vietnam) countries will eventually be confronted with large traffic though they are not yet ready for it. Roads are important for all three tiers of logistics infrastructure development.

ASEAN political leaders are enthusiastic for connecting railways across ASEAN as well as China and India. Indeed, filling gaps between Ho Chi Minh City and Phnom Penh, between Cambodia and Thailand, and between Thailand and Myanmar are assigned high priority in the Master Plan on ASEAN Connectivity (ASEAN Secretariat 2010*b*). However, we have to realize that railways are often economically unviable, particularly in cases of middle to long-distance passenger transportation, i.e., Tiers 2 and 3, even though they look environment-friendly. Railways are strong in transporting heavy and uninterrupted bulks; railways connecting mining sites and ports are the examples. Railways for urban transportation in Tier 1 are necessary even if they run deficit in order to counteract negative externalities of congestion. On the other hand, long-distance passenger railways have never been economically viable. Indeed, Shinkansen in Japan runs a surplus only in the part from Tokyo to Shin-Osaka.

Ports and marine transportation, particularly for container transportation, are crucial for production networks that connect industrial agglomerations in Tier 1. Singapore, Part Krang, and Laem Chabang are important ports for ASEAN's production networks. Tanjung Priok and Manila also handle large amounts of cargos, though there is room for improvement. Some other ports largely handle a bulk of natural resources. Ports and marine transportation, together with inland waterways, can also play important roles for Tiers 2 and 3.

Airports and air transportation are also essential to supporting production networks, particularly for transporting electronic parts and components as well as businessmen. The north-south corridor from Bangkok, Kuala Lumpur, Singapore, to Jakarta is by far the most important trunk line. Secondary lines are also flourishing due to the emergence of low cost carriers and open sky policy of ASEAN. Air transportation has a good potential for even expanding its role in connecting industrial agglomerations in ASEAN and East Asia.

Strategies for Logistics Infrastructure Development

Demand for logistics infrastructure as identified for Tier 1, Tier 2, and Tier 3 is as follows. Countries or regions in Tier 1 have already been successful in participating in production networks, and some of them have attracted a considerable number of production blocks. To step up from middle-income to the fully developed stage, we must construct an innovative society. Up until the middle-income level, industrialization has been fairly successful, but has been led predominantly by multi-national enterprises (MNEs). We observe the gradual penetration of local firms into production networks but cannot firmly conclude that it will result in the construction of an innovative society in which MNEs and local firms, entrepreneurs, and engineers will work together for active innovation. The next task is to take advantage of the positive agglomeration effects in developing arm's length (inter-firm) vertical division of labour in industrial agglomerations. Typical bottlenecks would be soft and hard logistics connections across national borders, metropolitan transport systems, electricity supplies, labour laws and practices, amongst others. Targets in logistics infrastructure development are summarized as follows:

1. Infrastructure to support efficient industrial agglomeration in spacious metropolitan areas;
2. Large-scale logistics infrastructure to connect with other industrial agglomerations;
3. Infrastructure for innovation basis and the nurturing of human capital; and
4. Infrastructure for intelligent and vigorous urban amenities.

Major sectors of infrastructure development are tabulated in Table 4.1.

TABLE 4.1
Infrastructure Development in Tier 1 by CADP

Logistics infrastructure	Other economic infrastructure	Urban and social infrastructure
1. **Road/bridges** Highway system, bridges, and bypasses roads in and around metropolitan areas Access roads/bridges to gateway ports/airports	1. **Industrial estates/special economic zones** High-tech park with private initiatives	1. **Water and sanitation, medical and others** Metropolitan and social infrastructure for urban amenity
2. **Railways** Urban public transport system (subway, LRT, MRT) and railways to connect urban and suburban areas	2. **Energy/power** Stable and ample supply of electricity and energy for both industries and residences	
3. **Ports/maritime** Sizable port facility to cater massive container transactions and specialized loading facilities	3. **Telecommunication** Infrastructure services for an innovative society	
4. **Airports** Sizable airport facility to cater to massive movements of passengers and freight		

Source: ERIA (2010).

Countries and regions in Tier 2 that do not yet participate in quick and high-frequency type production networks can utilize the mechanics of fragmentation to attract manufacturing activities. To participate in production networks, we must identify and solve major bottlenecks in three kinds of costs: (i) network set-up costs, (ii) service-link costs and, (iii) production costs per se. An overall improvement of the investment climate in the whole territory is not necessary at the initial stage. It is appropriate to provide an ideal investment climate at some specific place; to start with special economic zones (SEZs) is a good idea. By working in small specific areas, we should gain experience and accumulate both large and small troubleshootings. Together with soft logistics infrastructure, hard logistics infrastructure should be developed in order to link with neighbouring industrial agglomerations or the world market. Particularly for quick and high-frequency type production networks, logistics infrastructure must meet three-dimensional quality, i.e. quality in terms of monetary cost, time cost, and reliability. Targets in infrastructure development in Tier 2 are summarized as follows:

1. Reliable logistics links with neighbouring industrial agglomerations or the world market;
2. Other economic infrastructure such as electricity supply to solve bottlenecks in location advantages for manufacturing activities;
3. Industrial estates and SEZs, particularly at the initial stage of industrialization; and
4. Coordination with other policy modes to control agglomeration and dispersion forces.

Major sectors of infrastructure development are tabulated in Table 4.2.

Tier 3 covers countries or regions that are located far from urban centres and that often, but not always, have a small population size. In the case of ASEAN, the mountainous areas of Mekong, the islands of East Indonesia and the Southern Philippines are amongst those that fall into this tier. For these areas, the traditional view has taken static comparative advantage for granted and has often recommended the development of primary industries conditional on the existing poor status of logistics infrastructure. Such a conservative view, however, does not allow for a breakthrough in a vicious cycle of small logistics and slow industrial development. Although these countries/regions

TABLE 4.2
Infrastructure Development in Tier 2 by CADP

Logistics infrastructure	Other economic infrastructure	Urban and social infrastructure
1. **Road/bridges** Middle-distance roads for connecting industrial centres, logistics hubs, and neighbouring industrial agglomerations Sub-urban road system for avoiding congestions	1. **Industrial estates/special economic zones** SEZs in border areas and population centres	1. **Water and sanitation, medical and others** Improving water and sanitary conditions in urban areas
2. **Railways** Development of regional arterial railway networks	2. **Energy/power** Stable and ample supply of electricity and energy for industries	
3. **Ports/maritime** Upgrading major ports to enhance handling capacity	3. **Telecommunication** Development/upgrading of trunk telecommunication networks	
4. **Airports** Upgrading major airports for both passengers and cargos		

Source: ERIA (2010).

may not attract quick, high-frequency type production networks in the short run, we can provide new perspectives for industrial development by making middle to long distance logistics connections reliable. The demand for logistics infrastructure and logistics services is generated by industrial activity. Infrastructure and industrial activity can be said to have a "chicken and egg" relationship; if we simply extrapolated current demand for logistics infrastructure, nothing would happen. Logistics infrastructure should work as a trigger for new perspectives of industrial development. Targets in infrastructure development in Tier 3 are summarized as follows:

1. Credible small to medium scale logistics infrastructure to gain access to urban centres and the world market for creative business models;
2. Logistics infrastructure for mining and agricultural plantations to work as staples of economic development;
3. Effectively utilize green endowments; and
4. Seizing opportunities for manufacturing activities.

Major sectors of infrastructure development are tabulated in Table 4.3.

Our conceptual framework based on the extended fragmentation theory and new economic geography stresses the importance of interaction among the three tiers. The extended fragmentation theory calls for a reduction in service-link costs so that fragmentation of production occurs across tiers. New economic geography infers the importance of controlling agglomeration forces and dispersion forces by combining trade cost reduction with supplementary improvement of location advantages. To encourage interaction among the three tiers, the CADP introduces three broad sub-regions in ASEAN: Extended Mekong Sub-region, IMT[4]+ Sub-region, and BIMP[5]+ Sub-region (see Figure 4.8). Each sub-region is designed to cover a wider geographical range than the existing framework, in order to include Tier 1, Tier 2, and Tier 3 and pursue both the deepening of economic integration and the narrowing of development gaps. By developing efficient and innovative industrial agglomerations in Tier 1, the development of Tiers 2 and 3 can be accelerated. Development strategies for the three tiers must be cohesive and interactive.

CADP also conducts a simulation exercise on economic effects of improving logistics links by utilizing the Geographical Simulation

TABLE 4.3
Infrastructure Development in Tier 3 by CADP

Logistics infrastructure	Other economic infrastructure	Urban and social infrastructure
1. **Road/bridges** Long-distance road connection and rural road networks for various industrial development Sub-urban road system for avoiding congestions	1. **Industrial estates/special economic zones** Industrial estates in growth nodes 2. **Energy/power** Development of power plants taking advantage of location Local supply of electricity and energy	1. **Water and sanitation, medical and others** Improving water and sanitary conditions
2. **Railways** Middle-distance railways for resource-based industries	3. **Telecommunication** Local telecommunication networks	
3. **Ports/maritime** Upgrading of local ports		
4. **Airports** Upgrading/development of local airports		

Source: ERIA (2010).

FIGURE 4.8
Three Sub-Regions Proposed by CADP

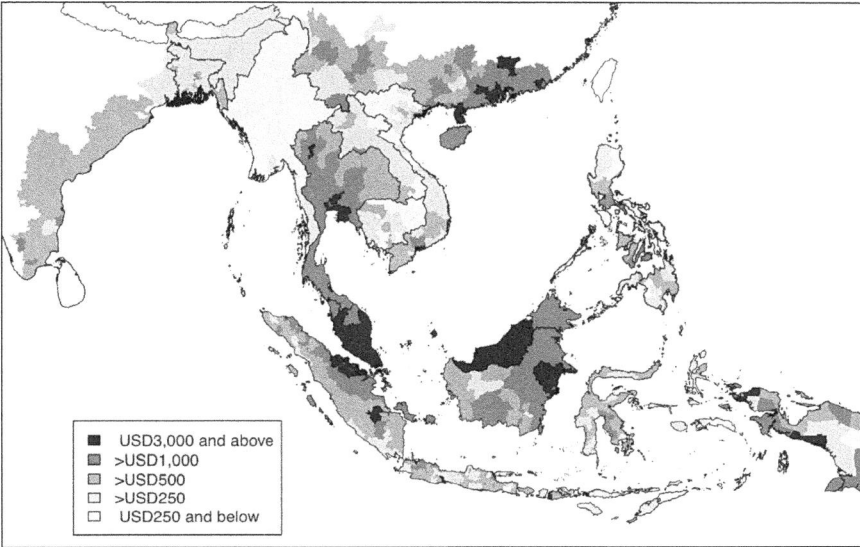

Legend:
- ■ USD3,000 and above
- ▦ >USD1,000
- ▤ >USD500
- ▢ >USD250
- ▢ USD250 and below

Source: ERIA (2010).

FIGURE 4.9
Simulation Results by GSM

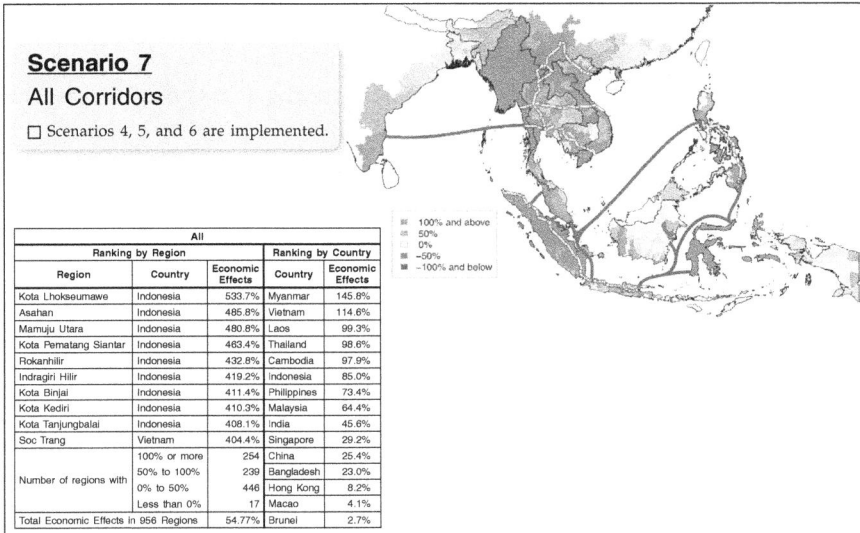

Scenario 7
All Corridors

☐ Scenarios 4, 5, and 6 are implemented.

Legend:
- ▦ 100% and above
- ▨ 50%
- ☐ 0%
- ■ −50%
- ■ −100% and below

All				
Ranking by Region			Ranking by Country	
Region	Country	Economic Effects	Country	Economic Effects
Kota Lhokseumawe	Indonesia	533.7%	Myanmar	145.6%
Asahan	Indonesia	485.8%	Vietnam	114.6%
Mamuju Utara	Indonesia	480.8%	Laos	99.3%
Kota Pematang Siantar	Indonesia	463.4%	Thailand	98.6%
Rokanhilir	Indonesia	432.8%	Cambodia	97.9%
Indragiri Hilir	Indonesia	419.2%	Indonesia	85.0%
Kota Binjai	Indonesia	411.4%	Philippines	73.4%
Kota Kediri	Indonesia	410.3%	Malaysia	64.4%
Kota Tanjungbalai	Indonesia	408.1%	India	45.6%
Soc Trang	Vietnam	404.4%	Singapore	29.2%
Number of regions with	100% or more	254	China	25.4%
	50% to 100%	239	Bangladesh	23.0%
	0% to 50%	446	Hong Kong	8.2%
	Less than 0%	17	Macao	4.1%
Total Economic Effects in 956 Regions		54.77%	Brunei	2.7%

Source: ERIA (2010).

Model (GSM). Figure 4.9 presents a part of the results where land links in yellow lines and sea links in blue lines are successfully speeded up (see ERIA 2010). Economic effects are calculated in percentage of incremental gross regional products, cumulative over ten years after the improvement of logistics links, *vis-à-vis* the benchmark case. It shows that ample room exists for the improvement of logistics connectivity.

Furthermore, CADP proposes prospective projects for logistics and other economic infrastructure in ASEAN and surrounding East Asia. Table 4.4 tabulates 695 projects to be implemented.

Beyond the Establishment of the ASEAN Economic Community

ASEAN and East Asia present a new development strategy charact- erized by aggressively utilizing foreign direct investment, participating in production networks, accelerating industrialization, and constructing industrial agglomerations. Stepping up from middle-income to fully developed economies is the next challenge. The advancement of Tier 1 stimulates the development of Tier 2 and Tier 3.

Connectivity is the key to further enhancing the competitiveness of the ASEAN economy. Institutional connectivity has been taken care of by the ASEAN Economic Community (AEC) initiative. Physical connecti- vity must be strengthened by the development of logistics and other economic infrastructure.

The year 2015 is not the final destination for the economic integration of ASEAN. Even if AEC is "established" in 2015, it would not be the end of economic integration. The pure definition of a "perfectly integrated economy" in economic theory is characterized by the equalization of prices of goods, productive factors, and other economic elements. Or, in the process towards a perfectly integrated economy, all sorts of economic elements including goods, productive factors, technologies, and others must become perfectly mobile across countries and regions. AEC is a brave effort heading for deeper economic integration. However, there still remain huge development gaps with far from perfect price equalization or perfectly mobile economic elements. The establishment of AEC in 2015 is a great accomplishment but just a beginning. As for logistics infrastructure development, connectivity for Tier 3, linkage for Tier 2, and innovation for Tier 1 should be promoted.

TABLE 4.4
Summary of the Numbers of Listed Projects

	Total	Mekong	BIMP+	IMT+	Brunei Darussalam	Cambodia	Indonesia	Laos	Malaysia	Myanmar	Philippines	Singapore	Thailand	Vietnam	China	India
Total	695	452	190	61	2	103	169	77	23	26	52	0	60	188	11	33
Priority																
Top Priority	170	133	51	14	1	15	33	1	3	8	25	0	26	57	1	18
Priority	166	87	56	23	0	19	53	6	7	6	17	0	7	48	1	10
Normal	359	252	83	24	1	69	83	70	13	12	10	0	27	83	9	5
Tier																
Tier 1	178	109	63	6	0	0	45	0	7	0	18	0	22	65	1	20
Tier 2	313	217	59	45	1	58	60	26	10	22	27	0	34	110	4	7
Tier 3	204	126	68	10	1	45	64	51	6	4	7	0	4	13	6	6
Type																
Public	541	358	146	45	2	95	121	71	21	25	45	0	54	125	11	17
PPP	154	94	44	16	0	8	48	6	2	1	7	0	6	63	0	16
Sector																
Logistics	443	279	128	44	2	60	106	55	13	18	46	0	39	100	8	18
:Road/Bridge	227	150	66	11	1	37	54	43	2	6	21	0	10	49	5	7
:Railway	66	51	6	9	0	6	9	3	5	2	0	0	19	19	0	4
:Port/Maritime	99	44	41	22	1	8	34	1	5	9	18	0	7	23	0	6
:Airport	36	28	6	2	0	6	4	7	1	1	3	0	2	8	3	1
Other Economic	201	146	45	10	0	32	45	22	7	8	3	0	21	78	3	9
:Industrial Estate/SEZ	56	56	0	0	0	8	0	7	0	3	0	0	8	28	0	4
:Energy/Power	135	80	45	10	0	17	45	13	7	3	3	0	11	47	2	5
:Telecommunication	12	11	1	0	0	8	1	2	0	2	0	0	2	3	1	0
Urban and Social	49	25	17	7	0	11	18	0	3	0	3	0	0	10	0	4
Others (soft)	2	2	0	0	0	0	0	0	0	0	0	0	0	0	0	2

Source: ERIA (2010).

NOTES

1. The seminal work of the fragmentation theory is Jones and Kierzkowski (1990).
2. The major results provided by LPI are found in ASEAN Secretariat (2010*a*).
3. Also see ASEAN Secretariat (2010*a*).
4. Indonesia-Malaysia-Thailand
5. Brunei-Indonesia-Malaysia-Philippines

REFERENCES

ASEAN Secretariat. *Brunei Action Plan (ASEAN Strategic Transport Plan) 2011–2015*. Jakarta: The ASEAN Secretariat, November 2010*a*. <http://www.aseansec. org/25790.htm>.
―――. *Master Plan on ASEAN Connectivity*. Jakarta: The ASEAN Secretariat, December 2010*b*. <http://www.aseansec.org/>.
Asian Development Bank. *Key Indicators for Asia and the Pacific 2011*, p. 250.
Baldwin, Richard. "21st Century Regionalism: Filling the Gap between 21st Century Trade and 20th Century Trade Rules". Centre for Economic Policy Research, Policy Insight No. 56, May 2011. <http://www.cepr.org>.
Economic Research Institute for ASEAN and East Asia (ERIA). *Comprehensive Asia Development Plan*, 2010. <http://www.eria.org>.
Gartner. Mobile Devices Worldwide Forecast, 2003–14, 1Q10 Update.
Jones, Ronald W. and Henryk Kierzkowski. "The Role of Services in Production and International Trade: A Theoretical Framework". In *The Political Economy of International Trade: Essays in Honor of Robert E. Baldwin*, edited by Ronald W. Jones and Anne O. Krueger. Oxford: Basil Blackwell, 1990.
Kimura, Fukunari and Mitsuyo Ando. "Two-dimensional Fragmentation in East Asia: Conceptual Framework and Empirics". *International Review of Economics and Finance* (special issue on "Outsourcing and Fragmentation: Blessing or Threat", edited by Henryk Kierzkowski), 14, issue 3 (2005): 317–34.
Lakaniemi, Ikka. "Connectivity Scorecard and Broadband Impact Study". LECG and NokiaSiemens Networks, 2009.
Lehr, William H., Carlos A. Osorio, Sharon E. Gillett, and Marvin A. Sirbu. "Measuring Broadband's Economic Impact". <http://www.itu.int/wsis/ stocktaking/docs/activities/iii/MIT_Carnegie.pdf>.
McKinsey & Company. "Broadband for the people: Policies that support greater access". Recall No. 15: Monetizing Data, pp. 40–43.
Waverman, Leonard, Meloria Meschi, and Melvyn Fuss. "The Impact of Telecoms on Economic Growth in Developing Countries". Vodafone Policy Paper 2 (2005).

5

CHALLENGES FOR BUILDING BETTER TRANSPORTATION INFRASTRUCTURE LINKAGES ACROSS ASEAN:
Indonesia's Perspectives Towards an Integrated Asian Economic Community

Bambang Susantono

Introduction

To meet the challenges in a global marketplace, ASEAN needs to integrate its member countries and achieve a more dynamic economy, which is inclusive and sustainable. ASEAN leaders are conscious of the increasing interdependence of their economies within the region as well as the rest of the world, and hence aim to implement the ASEAN Economic Community (AEC) by 2015. This vision requires a well-connected ASEAN that will lead to a more competitive and resilient ASEAN. This is expected to be realized through ASEAN connectivity. ASEAN leaders agreed on the concept of ASEAN Connectivity during the 15th ASEAN Summit in Cha-am Hua Hin on 24 October 2009. The country leaders observed that the strategic location of ASEAN has the potential to physically anchor itself as the transportation, information and communication technology, and tourism hub of the region. The Master Plan on ASEAN Connectivity was subsequently adopted one year later by the ASEAN Heads of State at the 17th ASEAN Summit on 28 October 2010.

The Master Plan is expected to accomplish the following goals within the region: 1) enhance trade, investment, tourism, and development; 2) narrow development gaps; and 3) facilitate people-to-people contacts. Furthermore, the connectivity is expected to enhance the attractiveness of ASEAN as a foreign direct investment (FDI) destination and to encourage better integration of production and innovation networks in the region.

A well-connected ASEAN may be achieved through three kinds of connectivity, i.e. physical, institutional, and people-to-people connectivity. Physical connectivity entails an enhanced physical infrastructure (including transport infrastructure, i.e. road, rail, air, and sea linkages), while institutional connectivity refers to effective institutions, mechanisms, and processes. Finally, people-to-people connectivity is meant to empower people.

To realize ASEAN connectivity, it is important to emphasize that the development gaps among the ASEAN member countries is a major issue that needs attention and immediate action. Less developed countries should be given a chance to catch up with their more developed counterparts. This requires a concerted effort in ASEAN in form of new policies that could support strong and sustainable growth in the region. In the transportation sector, in particular, infrastructure networks that connect the entire ASEAN region are of high importance. However, to attain such connectivity is a challenge for ASEAN member countries.

This chapter aims to discuss how regional and domestic connectivities are interrelated and how the success of regional connectivity would depend on domestic connectivity of individual countries in the region. Conscious effort is essential to improve transport linkages in the ASEAN region and narrow the development gap between less and more developed ASEAN members. Finally, this chapter provides policy directions that will be useful in planning and accelerating regional connectivity.

How Regional Connectivity Improves Local Economy

To have an efficient ASEAN connectivity, each country in the region needs to strengthen its domestic connectivity as it is important in supporting the national economy. Poor domestic connectivity can jeopardize the developments in the national economy.

Poor domestic connectivity limits local economic growth and even distribution of economic wealth. In the context of ASEAN, domestic connectivity must support all efforts to narrow the development gaps among its member countries and to reduce pockets of poverty. Most of the bigger ASEAN countries have areas that are still isolated, both economically and geographically. As a result, the potential of these areas cannot be fully exploited. Domestic connectivity needs to be increased through, inter alia, the development of ICT for better flow of information to all areas of the country. National connectivity may also be improved through a better transport infrastructure network.

Table 5.1 shows the positive impacts of connectivity on the poor. Better roads can directly improve the poor's access to employment and public services. Urban mass transit increases the access to employment opportunities as it gives them freedom of mobility. ICT helps the poor through better access of knowledge, enabling them to be involved in the wider community.

As ASEAN connectivity aims to narrow the development gap, the local economy should be aligned with the regional economy. Local economy's alignment will enable smoother flow of labour and capital, so that the gap between lagging regions and developed regions can be reduced, as shown in Figure 5.1. It seeks to justify how interregional flows of labour and capital can help the lagging regions in catching up on disparities with advanced regions. With connectivity, the flows of labour and capital will be unrestricted between the regions. As labour flows out from the lagging region, it will be able to increase productivity and this will result in an increase of remuneration for labour. Capello (2007) argues that this dynamic process will come to an end when both regions reach the same remuneration, the same productivity, and therefore the same levels of income, thus accomplishing the goal of growth equity.

With an objective of narrowing the development gap among all ASEAN country members, the poverty level in the region can be simultaneously reduced. There are three ways where regional connectivity may help in reduction of poverty. First, domestic connectivity should

TABLE 5.1

Potential Positive Impacts of Connectivity on the Poor

Sector	Direct impact on Poor	Indirect impact on Poor
Roads	• Access to employment and markets • Access or services (health, education)	• Reduced transport cost and improved market access for enterprises and service providers, lowering cost of serving remote communities
Railways	Limited	• Reduced cost and improved market access for enterprises
Urban Mass Transit	Access to employment opportunities	• Employment creation from more efficient labour markets
Ports	Limited	• Reduced transport cost encouraging employment creation
Airports	Limited	• Reduced transport cost encouraging employment creation
ICT	Better communication access, aiding migration, information on opportunities, access to knowledge and potential engagement in wider communities	• Employment creation through improved knowledge of markets, reduced management supervision cost, access to wider knowledge base

Source: Jones (2004a), quoted from Connecting East Asia, ADB-JBIC-World Bank (2005)

FIGURE 5.1

Modified Scheme of Interregional Flows of Production Factors

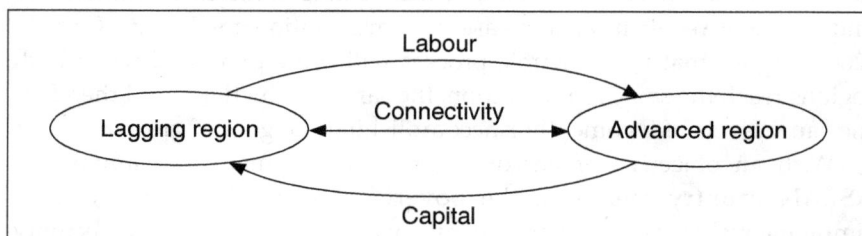

Source: Capello (2007).

help decrease poverty measured by income and livelihoods; for example, that of the "dollar a day" poverty line. In this definition, poverty could be alleviated as the real incomes of the poor increase, employment opportunities open up, and productive assets on which the poor depend are enhanced by the better infrastructure. All would be made possible with better connectivity. Second, access to education and health services are improved when connectivity has been realized. Third, poverty may be reduced when people's ability to engage in collective activities or to access wider sources of information and opportunities is expanded with better connectivity, allowing them better social inclusion, human capabilities, and freedom.

It should be understood, however, that the development gap and poverty reduction will not take place if the domestic connectivity (especially that of the less developed countries) is not strong enough. When a city in a less developed country is connected to another city in a more developed country, under an ideal condition (i.e. when domestic connectivity has been well built in both countries), it will reach equilibrium, closing the development gap. However, if the domestic connectivity of a less developed country is not strong, a resource drain could take place. This entails that labour or other resources are moving freely to the more advanced country, leaving behind the lagging country, and as such the latter country will remain poor. This, of course, would be plausible because it would be easier for people to travel or for goods to move to the more advanced country than it would be to other cities in the lagging country due to poor domestic connectivity. For example, Jakarta will increase its per capita GDP when it is seamlessly connected to Singapore. However, Jayapura will still be lagging behind Jakarta if the domestic connectivity is poor, thus widening the development gap.

It is natural for regional connectivity to be perceived with scepticism from several countries because of the perceived threats of a potential resource drain. Regional connectivity may come with positive and negative implications. Negative implications possibly occur in the early periods of a well-connected region. It is possible that the larger economies will crowd out the smaller economies. However, regional connectivity could create an accelerated positive effect after some period when the initial resistance has faded away and acceptance by the wider public has been achieved. Negative effects could be subsequently diminished, when smaller economies reorganize themselves around their larger counterparts. Both positive and negative effects could take place together, starting with negative effects in the early period and gradually becoming positive at a later time.

When all country members are well connected, ASEAN will become a single market and production base where there is free flow of goods and services, factors of production, investment and capital. Together with the elimination of tariffs for trade between ASEAN countries and through mutually beneficial cooperation, it is then expected that ASEAN connectivity will reduce economic inequality among member countries. Also, under these conditions, ASEAN's bargaining position in the global economy will become stronger and ASEAN will become a group of countries with a stable regional economy. Countries which are still economically lagging behind can take advantages of the free flow of goods, labour, and capital, accompanied by technology, to improve their business cultures and production capacity and quality.

Another challenge to the free flow of goods is the absence of equal product quality and technical regulations in the industry of each country member. For this reason, ASEAN country members have to improve the quality of products and production processes. With the free flow of goods and labour, less developed countries have to be very well prepared. Foreign workers could be more qualified than local workers and many foreign products could be cheaper and of higher quality than locally produced ones. This could be a challenge for the less developed countries in ASEAN, where local workers may not be as well-trained or highly educated, businesses are weak due to the lack of entrepreneurial skills, and the quality of local products are less competitive.

With the free flow of investment, funding imbalances in ASEAN countries are also expected to be resolved. Strengthening the bargaining position of ASEAN, as an integrated economic community, requires channelling Foreign Direct Investment (FDI) into ASEAN so that all member countries, including the developed, emerging economies and the less developed countries, can reap the benefits of these investments.

1. Challenges in Regional Connectivity

For ASEAN countries that are developed and have well-connected transport infrastructure networks, further investment in infrastructure alone will not have a significant effect on economic growth. For such countries, further investment in transport infrastructure is only a complementary programme, which should be implemented to advance economic development (Banister and Berechman 2000).

For less developed countries, good transportation infrastructure is necessary to be able to compete internationally in new regional markets. With reduced trade barriers and new open markets in the ASEAN region, less developed countries need to have a high accessibility to enter these markets, so that they can pursue their efforts to reduce the development gap with those that have advanced in the region.

Banister and Berechman (2000) argue that in planning investment in infrastructure projects, less developed countries need to consider specific issues that may affect the potential impact of such investment on their economic growth. The first consideration is that any investment in transportation projects must be within the framework of local, national, and even regional networks. The second consideration is that economic growth must occur at the network level rather than at the project level. Finally, the third consideration is related to prioritizing objectives and criteria, including: a) most of the benefits must be related to transport, b) no double counting in measuring non-transportation benefits, and c) there is a functional relationship between transportation benefits and the potential impact on economic growth.

To implement infrastructure projects, ASEAN countries will face several challenges. These challenges include: 1) the lack of adequate financial funding, 2) the lack of institutional coordination, and 3) the lack of planning integration among subsectors. The lack of adequate financial funding for transport infrastructure projects is a common problem in many developing countries. The limited state budget is usually inadequate or in some cases, uncertain. ASEAN member states should cooperate in providing necessary adjustments in policies and priorities. At the national level, member states need to seek innovative financing mechanisms and responsive policies to attract and sustain the infrastructure in transport (ASEAN 1999). In order to meet the large transport infrastructure financing need in this connectivity effort, current means of financing must be strengthened and other new innovative mechanisms need to be employed. There are commitments for funding and loans from international institutions and several Dialogue Partners. In addition, private financing and other means such as PPP, particularly those from within the region, need to be encouraged. The lack of institutional coordination among the member states is also a major factor for the inefficient and ineffective management of transport infrastructure and services. Public institutions do their own planning that is often independent of each other. A lack of focus on transport infrastructure development strategy is then apparent. This problem is caused by overlapping responsibilities in the transport-related development and different modal planning and development. The lack of institutional coordination then often creates the problem of transport planning. Different modes of transport often do not receive equal attention, resulting in uncoordinated transport planning.

2. Grow Together in Harmony

A growth process that is market-oriented would be more profitable for ASEAN member countries which are more developed, since such countries already have adequate infrastructure and human resources. For the less developed countries, special programmes would be required to accelerate infrastructure provisions and human resource development to enable them to yield economic growth.

Infrastructure development can greatly contribute to economic growth through job creation and improved access to economic activities and social services. Meanwhile, economic growth will boost the demand for labour, which in turn will expand economic opportunities, increase worker productivity and raise wages. It also would increase government revenues, and the funds acquired by the government can be used to finance basic education, health care, and infrastructure development. All of these will increase the quality of the labour force, as required by markets.

When the ASEAN Economic Community is realized, there will be more employment opportunities in the region which require a greater labour force. The positive potential impact of this is that poverty could be alleviated, provided that the labour force has met the market requirements.

The private sector, as the engine of growth, can play a direct role in poverty reduction, since it can participate in the provision of physical and social infrastructures, including the provision of basic services that will provide benefits for the poor. In order for the private sector to participate in the provision of such services, certain guidelines should be set as well as the development of a financial sector. Also, when the role of the private sector develops, the role of government should be shifted, namely from the owner and producer to a facilitator and regulator. This will require an effective regulatory framework to ensure fair competition, good practice, fair standards, and that basic services can be reached by the poor.

The data of per capita GDP and economic growth of ASEAN countries can be seen in Figure 5.2. In general, ASEAN countries are divided into three groups, namely: 1) countries with a GDP per capita higher than average and have an economic growth rate lower than average, 2) countries with both a GDP per capita and economic growth rate lower than average, and 3) countries with a GDP per capita lower than the average but have an economic growth rate higher than average. The countries included in the first group are Singapore and Brunei Darussalam, in the second, Thailand, and in the third, the Lao PDR, Vietnam, Indonesia, Myanmar, Cambodia, Malaysia, and the Philippines.

FIGURE 5.2

ASEAN GDP per capita and growth in 2008–2010, analyzed

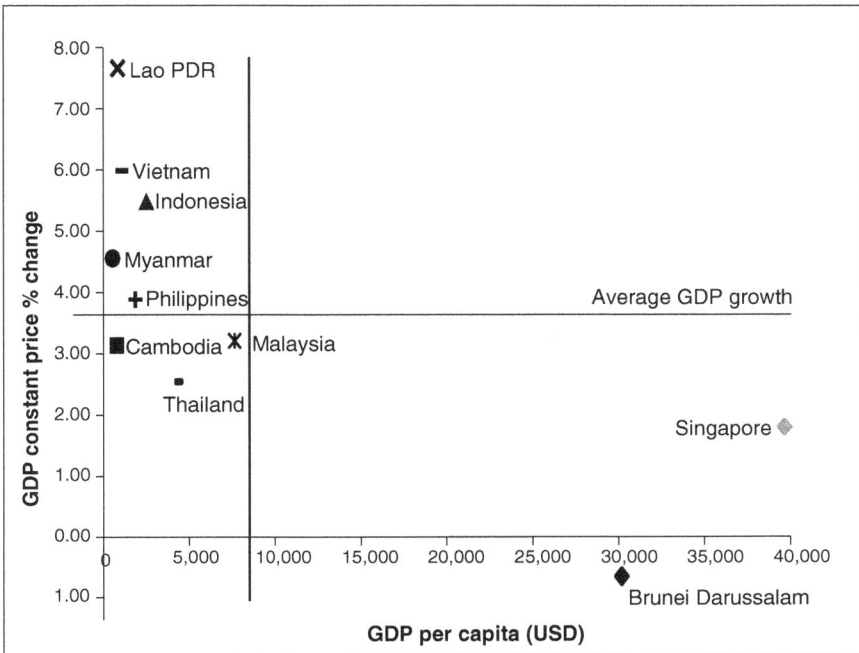

Source: IMF, 2010.

CLMV (Cambodia, Laos, Myanmar, and Vietnam) economies in general have grown faster than the other six ASEAN countries. Their collective share to ASEAN GDP has increased from less than 6 per cent in 1998 to around 9 per cent in 2008. However, there is evidence of rising inequality within the member countries and incomes per capita across the region shows no sign of converging. Great disparities exist. The gaps among these three groups are huge and that among individual member countries within each group is also significant. For example, in 2008, the average GDP per capita of the more developed member states is almost 14 times that of the less developed member states.

ASEAN countries should grow and develop together in harmony. Countries in the first group (Singapore and Brunei Darussalam), which already have a GDP per capita higher than the average should provide opportunities for other countries with a lower GDP per capita to reduce the welfare gap in the region. Singapore and Brunei could participate in infrastructure investments in countries belonging to the second and third groups. These investments would help countries in these groups to reduce the development gap that exists in the region.

Countries that are in the second and third groups should try to catch up on regional economic growth by increasing their GDP per capita. Although this needs further research, improving the quality and quantity of infrastructure in the countries in the second group could possibly increase their economic growth and GDP per capita. Similar policies could also be made for countries within the third group. Besides additional transport infrastructure, these countries need to improve the skills, knowledge, and competence of labour needed by the global market. This can be achieved through the development of infrastructure so that people have better access to basic socio-economic needs, namely education, health, and employment.

In the Master Plan on ASEAN Connectivity, there are a number of key actions and priority projects that will be realized to facilitate inter-connectivity within the ASEAN region. Currently there are missing links in the AHN (ASEAN Highway Network), as well as the SKRL (Singapore Kunming Railway Link). The AHN is targeted for completion in 2015, while the completion of the SKRL will extend to 2020. The building of these links will connect mainland ASEAN. This connectivity will also extend beyond ASEAN, with plans to extend the AHN to China and India.

Observing Figure 5.4, it is apparent that there are still transport gaps between the mainland and archipelagic states of ASEAN. To connect the mainland to the archipelagic states of ASEAN (Philippines and Indonesia), a study for the ASEAN RORO network and Short-Sea Shipping is ongoing and due to be completed in 2012 for implementation thereafter. This is a very important strategy to enhance the connectivity of archipelagic ASEAN through efficient and reliable shipping routes. The RORO approach has been able to bring down the cost of shipping among the Philippine islands by 30–40 per cent (The Asia Foundation 2010). It is expected that the RORO network will give similar benefits to shipping intra-ASEAN which will then increase regional trade. This network is expected to cover areas which have limited or no access

FIGURE 5.4
Transport Network in ASEAN

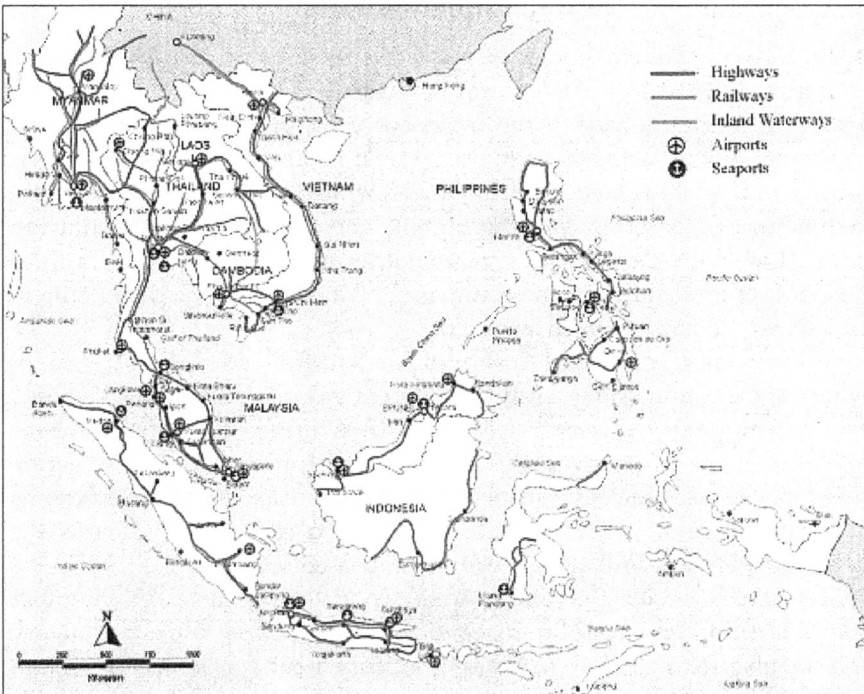

Source: ASEAN, 1999.

to international trade lanes, thus giving them the ability to participate in regional trade or, in other words, allowing these areas to grow and therefore narrowing the development gap with the more advanced regions.

The establishment of the ASEAN Single Aviation Market (ASAM) and liberalization of passenger and cargo air services are also due to be ratified and implemented by all member countries by 2015, to support the establishment of a well connected ASEAN towards an ASEAN Economic Community (AEC).

To facilitate an integrated transport system in ASEAN, both "hardware" and "software" are inevitably crucial. Physical transport infrastructure is necessary, as well as the capacity building programmes. ASEAN member countries will also need capable human resources who will then maintain the built infrastructure, with further emphasis on capacity building for the less developed nations.

3. Conclusions and Recommendations

ASEAN connectivity should increase the welfare of ASEAN member countries. Regional growth cannot be measured solely by the economic growth of each country in the region. Robust regional growth should also concern narrowing development gaps. It can be achieved when the growth of less developed countries is accelerated. These countries should be the most prepared in catching up with the more developed countries, or else they would experience a potential resource drain, domestically, as deeper economic integration occurs. In such a situation, the development gap would remain or even widen.

Policies among countries should be harmonized and synergized, where each country may assume different roles in enhancing regional growth, holding and developing their own niche. One of the means to decrease the disparity is through enhancing transport infrastructure services, because efficient transportation will increase the competitiveness of a country, and will help the less developed countries to narrow the development gap with their more advanced counterparts.

To avoid the lack of institutional coordination, ASEAN member states should form a solid institutional framework. This framework should also govern the sustainable arrangement for long-term maintenance and management of transport infrastructure. It should also include a systematic approach in the provision of transport services and more involvement of the private sector and users in infrastructure financing.

Integrated transport planning requires a good transport management information system to allow comprehensive planning and precise decision making. The member states should share the same format and modalities so that other regional planners may review and compare the planning across countries and make informed decisions.

Because each ASEAN member country has different characteristics, the development of infrastructure and determining appropriate strategies to reduce poverty for each country will vary as well. It is, therefore, recommended to undertake deeper studies related to the local characteristics possessed by each ASEAN member country so that the development of infrastructure in each country can be better planned.

REFERENCES

ASEAN. *ASEAN Transport Cooperation Framework Plan*. Jakarta: The ASEAN Secretariat, 1999.

————. *Master Plan on ASEAN Connectivity*. Jakarta: The ASEAN Secretariat, 2010.

Asia Foundation, The. *Philippines Spearheads ASEAN Effort to Establish Regional RO-RO Sea Transport Network*. <http://asiafoundation.org/in-asia/2010/09/22/philippines-spearheads-asean-effort-to-establish-regional-ro-ro-sea-transport-network/> (accessed 20 April 2011).

Asian Development Bank, Japan Bank for International Cooperation, and World Bank. *Connecting East Asia: A New Framework for Infrastructure*. Manila, 2005.

Banister, D. and J. Berechman. *Transport Investment and Economic Development*. London: UCL Press, 2000.

Capello, R. *Regional Economics*. New York, NY: Routledge, 2007.

Hoyle, B. and R. Knowles. *Modern Transport Geography, Edition 2*. West Sussex: John Wiley & Sons, 1998.

International Monetary Fund. *World Economic Outlook, October 2010*. <http://www.imf.org/external/pubs/ft/weo/2010/02/weodata/index.aspx> (accessed 25 April 2011).

Katz, B., ed. *Reflections on Regionalism*. Washington, D.C.: R.R. Donneley and Sons., 2000.

Scott, A., ed. *Global City-Regions: Trends, Theory, Policy*. Oxford: Oxford University Press, 2001.

6

CONNECTING SOUTHEAST ASIA THROUGH BROADBAND

Arne Jeroschewski, Andre Levisse,
Lorraine Salazar, Robert Tesoriero, and
Shaowei Ying[1]

Introduction

As the average global mobile phone penetration rate approaches 83 mobile phones per 100 people,[2] it is increasingly clear that ubiquitous broadband access provision is the next frontier in information and communication technologies (ICT) for all developing countries.

Broadband access is a key driver of economic and social development. Its effects are profound and pervasive. The direct economic benefits of broadband stem from the immediate value of the investments made in building the network through increased expenditures in industries such as construction and equipment supply. This, in turn, creates a multiplier effect in industries — such as telecommunications and media — that rely on the network. Indirectly, an investment in a broadband network has three major benefits. First, foreign investors — including multinational companies — are more likely to gravitate toward markets that are supported by a solid, fast, and reliable broadband infrastructure. Second, in the long term, greater broadband connectivity can lead to improvements in economic productivity and business efficiency (i.e., economic transformation towards the services sector). Third, investment in broadband infrastructure facilitates human capital formation by easing access to and the transfer of knowledge. This, in turn, promotes the development of a more highly-skilled workforce, leading to further improvements in efficiency and productivity.

Estimates show that if broadband penetration in emerging markets reaches approximately 50 per cent (the average level of European penetration), it would generate approximately 10 to 15 million jobs and create an estimated US$400 billion in GDP. In Asia alone, projections suggest that roughly 5 to 8 million new jobs would be created and that approximately US$150 to 180 billion would be added to the GDP (equivalent to a 1 per cent increase in GDP).[3]

People in ASEAN Want to be Online

ASEAN member states can be categorized into three groups in terms of their mobile, broadband, and PC penetration levels, as shown in Figure 6.1. The groupings reflect the different levels of development within ASEAN. The more economically affluent member states — Brunei, Malaysia, and Singapore — belong to the first group and have high levels of mobile, broadband, and PC penetration. Group 2 is comprised of middle-income countries Indonesia, the Philippines, Thailand, and Vietnam, which are characterized by high levels of mobile penetration, but low levels of broadband and PC penetration.[4] Finally, Group 3 is comprised of Cambodia, Laos, and Myanmar, which have low levels of mobile, broadband, and PC penetration.

Despite low household broadband penetration levels, consumer demand for Internet access and services is strong in Southeast Asia. The number of Internet users is growing faster than the total number of Internet subscriber accounts. Affordable public access points, such as Internet cafes, fill the gap, as shown in Figure 6.2. In Indonesia, for instance, about 7,500 "Warnets" or Warung Internets provide Internet access to people living in Java for around US$0.60 cents per hour, or 0.2 per cent of monthly household disposable income. In the Philippines,

FIGURE 6.1

Varying Degrees of Telecom Development Across ASEAN Countries

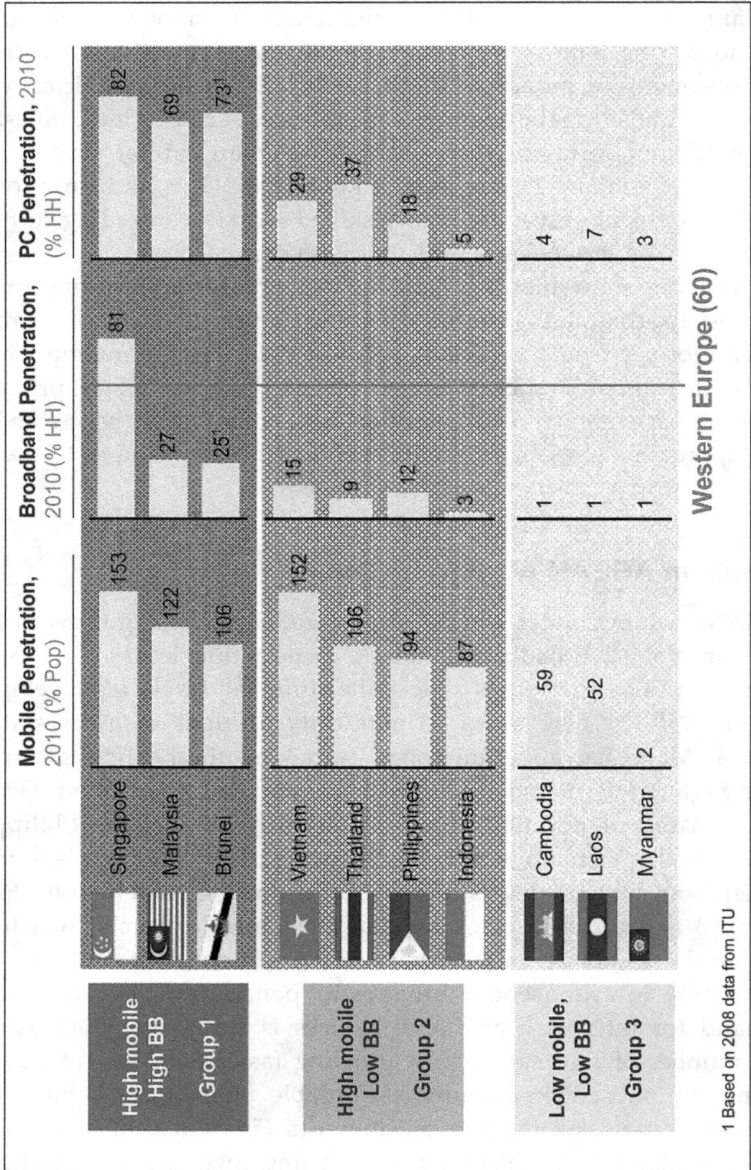

Source: Informa Telecoms and Media, World Cellular Information Service, October 2011.

1 Based on 2008 data from ITU

FIGURE 6.2

Despite Low Household Broadband Penetration, Demand for Internet Services is Evident by Wide Use of Internet Cafes

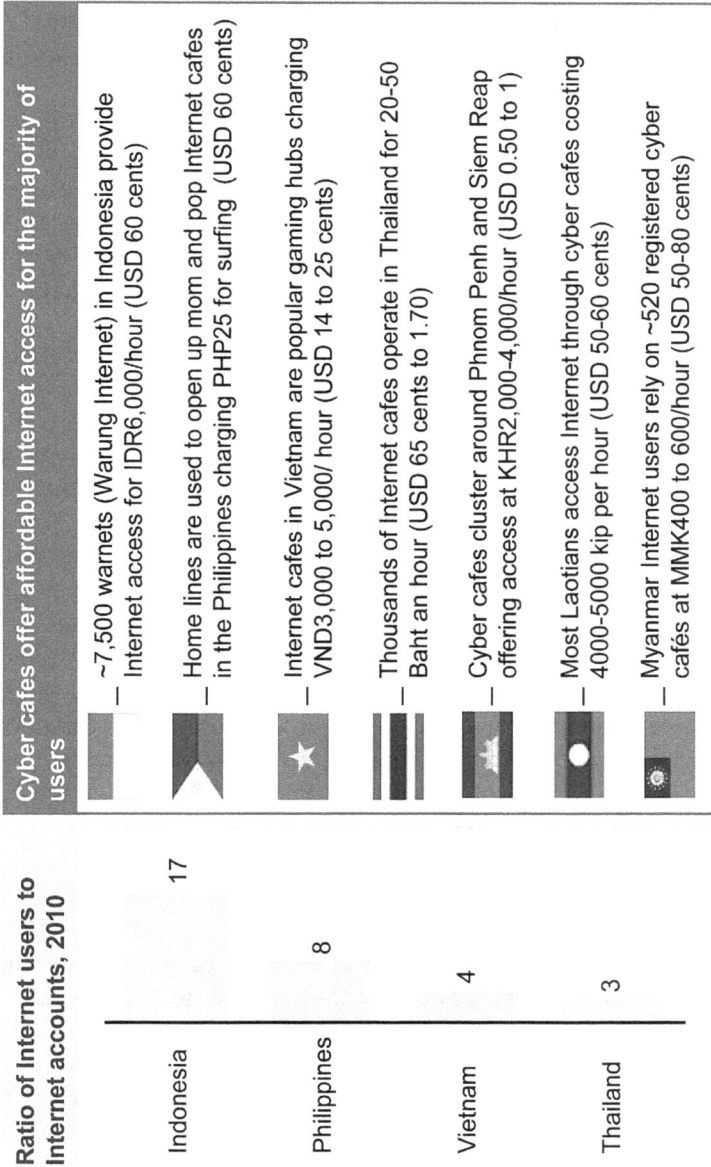

Ratio of Internet users to Internet accounts, 2010	Cyber cafes offer affordable Internet access for the majority of users
Indonesia — 17	— ~7,500 warnets (Warung Internet) in Indonesia provide Internet access for IDR6,000/hour (USD 60 cents)
	— Home lines are used to open up mom and pop Internet cafes in the Philippines charging PHP25 for surfing (USD 60 cents)
Philippines — 8	— Internet cafes in Vietnam are popular gaming hubs charging VND3,000 to 5,000/ hour (USD 14 to 25 cents)
Vietnam — 4	— Thousands of Internet cafes operate in Thailand for 20-50 Baht an hour (USD 65 cents to 1.70)
	— Cyber cafes cluster around Phnom Penh and Siem Reap offering access at KHR2,000-4,000/hour (USD 0.50 to 1)
Thailand — 3	— Most Laotians access Internet through cyber cafes costing 4000-5000 kip per hour (USD 50-60 cents)
	— Myanmar Internet users rely on ~520 registered cyber cafés at MMK400 to 600/hour (USD 50-80 cents)

Source: Pyramid Q1 2011; Press; Freedom House.

Internet cafes charge about US$0.60 cents per hour (about 0.09 per cent of monthly household disposable income). Finally, the same is true in Thailand where Internet cafes charge between US$0.65 to US$1.70 per hour, comprising about 0.3 per cent of monthly household disposable income.[5]

What do Southeast Asian consumers do when they go online? Interestingly, people in Southeast Asia are some of the world's most frequent users of popular social networking sites like Facebook and Twitter. In 2010, as Figure 6.3 shows, Indonesia, the Philippines, and Singapore were among the top ten Twitter users. Similarly, the Philippines and Indonesia are among the top ten markets of unique Facebook users, ranking third and fourth, respectively.

With the rising number of Internet users in Southeast Asia, there is significant opportunity for local companies to enter the market. However, the success of local online service and content companies in ASEAN varies, with global players heavily dominating the markets.[6] Local companies are most successful in Vietnam and Indonesia, where 35 and 22, respectively, of the top 50 most visited sites are local websites. In the Philippines, only 6 of the top 50 websites belong to local companies, and the country ranks the lowest of all Southeast Asian countries in this regard. Because English language proficiency is more common in the Philippines, Malaysia, and Singapore, local sites in those countries can compete with international sites to offer attractive content. However, there is room for local companies to offer distinct local content that caters to local cultures, demands, and tastes. Successful examples of companies that have done so are Kaskus in Indonesia, Mudah in Malaysia, and Zing in Vietnam (see Figure 6.4).

Barriers to Broadband adoption

The popularity and proliferation of Internet cafes indicates that Southeast Asian consumers want affordable access to broadband. However, there are key challenges that prevent a more widespread adoption of broadband in the region.

Fixed line broadband penetration is limited in most parts of Southeast Asia for three key reasons: first, the existing fixed line telecommunications infrastructure in most countries (with the exception of Singapore and Malaysia) is poor. This is due to the lack of historic public, or

FIGURE 6.3

Southeast Asians are Some of the Top Users of Facebook and Twitter

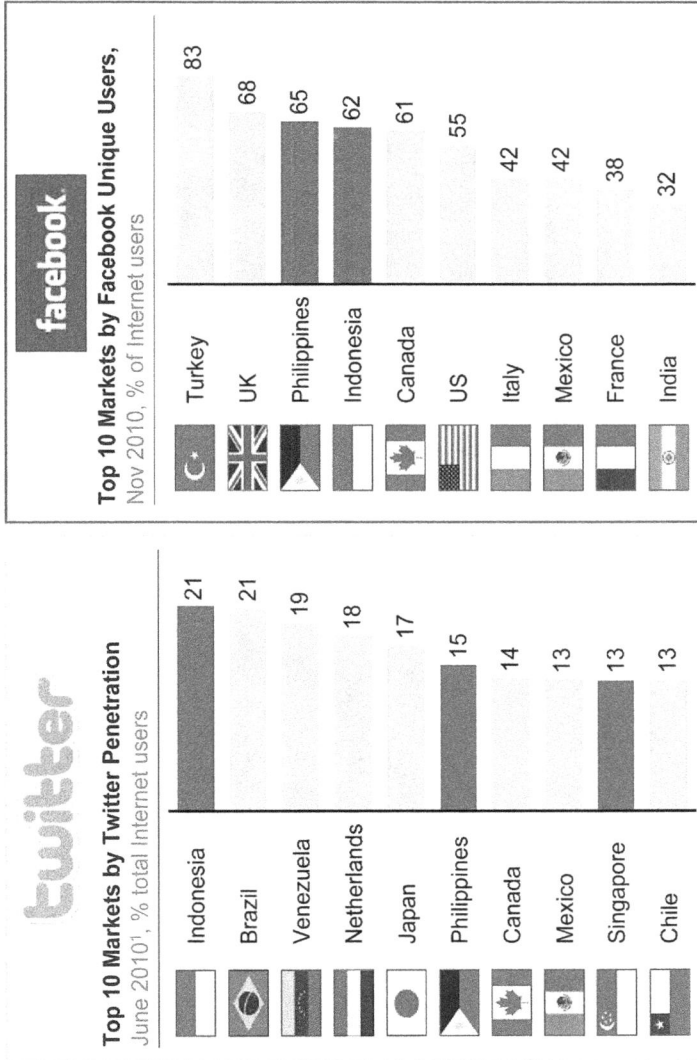

twitter

Top 10 Markets by Twitter Penetration
June 2010[1], % of total Internet users

Country	%
Indonesia	21
Brazil	21
Venezuela	19
Netherlands	18
Japan	17
Philippines	15
Canada	14
Mexico	13
Singapore	13
Chile	13

facebook

Top 10 Markets by Facebook Unique Users,
Nov 2010, % of Internet users

Country	%
Turkey	83
UK	68
Philippines	65
Indonesia	62
Canada	61
US	55
Italy	42
Mexico	42
France	38
India	32

1 Total audience age 15+, home and work locations

Source: Comscore; Inside Facebook.

FIGURE 6.4

Unique Tastes and Culture of ASEAN Provide Opportunities for Local Online Companies to Develop and Offer More Localized Content

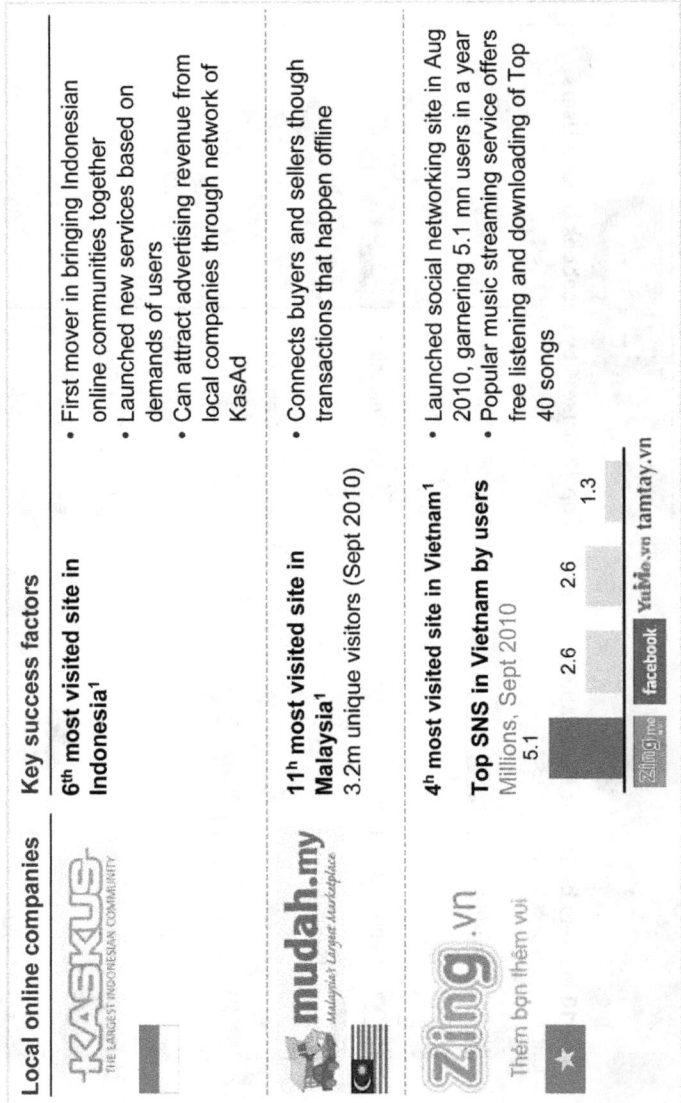

Local online companies	Key success factors
KASKUS THE LARGEST INDONESIAN COMMUNITY	**6th most visited site in Indonesia[1]** • First mover in bringing Indonesian online communities together • Launched new services based on demands of users • Can attract advertising revenue from local companies through network of KasAd
mudah.my *Malaysia's Largest Marketplace*	**11th most visited site in Malaysia[1]** 3.2m unique visitors (Sept 2010) • Connects buyers and sellers though transactions that happen offline
Zing.vn Thêm bạn thêm vui	**4th most visited site in Vietnam[1]** **Top SNS in Vietnam by users** Millions, Sept 2010 5.1 2.6 2.6 1.3 Zing me facebook YuMe.vn tamtay.vn • Launched social networking site in Aug 2010, garnering 5.1 mn users in a year • Popular music streaming service offers free listening and downloading of Top 40 songs

1 Alexa.com September 2010

Source: iResearch Lit Search; Alexa; Press.

private investment in the sector as well as consumers' low levels of capacity and willingness to pay for services. While liberalization of the industry has increased competition, most new entrants have invested in mobile rather than fixed networks, which has left the fixed infrastructure underdeveloped and with limited reach. Also, poor electricity infrastructure in countries like Myanmar, Laos, and Cambodia limits PC usage. Cambodia has the lowest number of households with access to electricity at 21 per cent. Comparatively, in Laos and Myanmar, 46 per cent and 47 per cent of households, respectively, have access to electricity.[7] Second, future fixed line infrastructure rollout is expensive and likely not commercially viable for the underserved areas. Under-penetration typically occurs in rural areas, where both demand and disposable income are lower. As a result, rolling out a fixed network is uneconomical. Finally, fixed networks are expensive to operate and require large numbers of field technicians. For these reasons, relying on fixed networks to drive broadband access across all parts of Southeast Asia is unrealistic.

With regard, to mobile broadband, three key factors limit its proliferation. The first is awareness and affordability. Many people are neither informed about nor familiar with the broadband products available, much less their benefits. The second issue — which is linked to the first — is the issue of affordability, which is critical in developing markets where the total cost of ownership (which includes the cost of a PC or a mobile handset device, the upfront cost of signing up for a service or buying a SIM card, and the ongoing cost of subscription) typically accounts for a substantial portion of a family's disposable income.

Another barrier to the further adoption of mobile broadband in Southeast Asia is a lack of smartphones in the majority of ASEAN countries. As represented in Figure 6.5, basic and enhanced phones are still the predominant types of handsets available in ASEAN countries. Meanwhile, data-capable smartphones and PDAs, while increasing in number, comprised only 10 per cent of handset sales in 2010.[8] Although smartphones comprise 25 per cent of handset sales in Singapore, the percentage of smartphones sold to end users in other ASEAN countries ranged from 6 per cent in Vietnam and the Philippines to 7 per cent in Indonesia, 10 per cent in Thailand, and 12 per cent in Malaysia. Regional smartphone penetration is expected to increase by 25 per cent by 2014, as handset prices decline. Southeast Asia benefits from its proximity to China as well as from the proliferation of non-branded, affordable

FIGURE 6.5

Further Barrier to Broadband Adoption is the Lack of Smartphones in Most ASEAN Countries

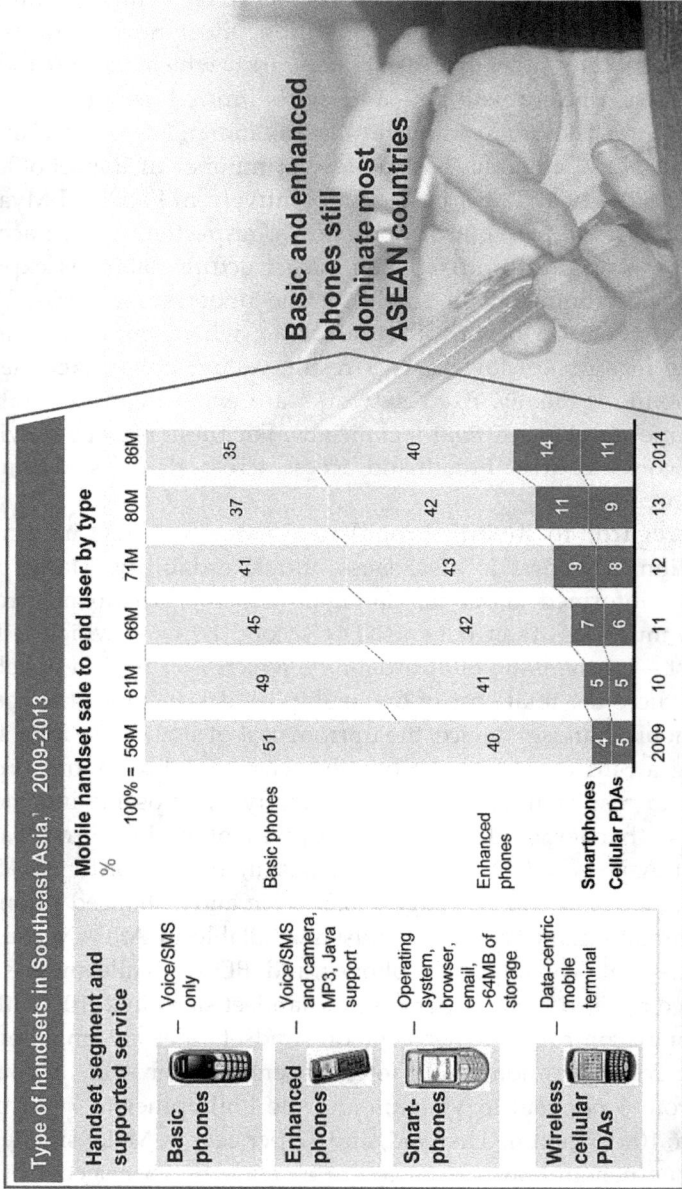

Type of handsets in Southeast Asia.[1]   2009-2013

Basic and enhanced phones still dominate most ASEAN countries

Handset segment and supported service	
Basic phones	— Voice/SMS only
Enhanced phones	— Voice/SMS and camera, MP3, Java support
Smartphones	— Operating system, browser, email, >64MB of storage
Wireless cellular PDAs	— Data-centric mobile terminal

Mobile handset sale to end user by type

%

100% =	56M	61M	66M	71M	80M	86M
Basic phones	51	49	45	41	37	35
Enhanced phones	40	41	42	43	42	40
Smartphones	4	5	7	9	11	14
Cellular PDAs	5	5	6	8	9	11
	2009	10	11	12	13	2014

1 Data only available for Indonesia, Malaysia, Philippines, Singapore, Thailand, and Vietnam

Source: Gartner; Yankee.

smartphones. Such products provide competition for the traditional American, European, and North Asian handset manufacturers, and help reduce handset prices.

Finally, network capacity and quality for mobile broadband in many emerging markets are still not meeting expectations, and this is negatively shaping the customer experience.

Increasing connectivity

Despite these challenges, there are various opportunities for increasing broadband connectivity in Southeast Asia — including solutions that can be developed through regulation, government leadership, and public-private sector partnership.

Fixed and mobile networks are the two primary technological choices for broadband service provision. Generally speaking, the level of fixed and mobile network penetration in most developed countries is significant. For emerging economies, however, the low levels of fixed network development mean that investments in mobile broadband networks offer the greatest potential for extending broadband service.

Regulatory levers for appropriate technology choices

Given this situation, developed and developing countries are faced with different challenges and policy choices in encouraging the roll-out of broadband infrastructure. Developed nations are looking into an optimal means for replacing their old, fixed copper networks with faster fiber networks, as well as simultaneously seeking a means to accommodate the growing demand for data capacity and speed in their mobile networks. In emerging markets, the debate revolves more around how access to mobile broadband can be universalized and how the timely deployment of advanced mobile networks can be fostered. In both cases, substantial industry investment is necessary. The European Union recently calculated that achieving the target of providing 50 per cent of the region's households with 100 Mbps speeds and another 50 per cent with 30 Mbps speeds will cost EUR 180 to 270 billion.

In order for broadband service provision to remain economical, appropriate broadband infrastructure should be selected based on population density. In urban and suburban areas with high population densities, fiber or digital subscriber lines (DSL) and/or cable networks are the most appropriate choice. However, for most rural locations in ASEAN, mobile broadband is the most affordable solution, since it is the technology with the lowest incremental costs per user (see Figure 6.6).

Regulators have several levers at their disposal to help facilitate mobile broadband rollout. First, they can free up and assign broad spectrum allocation to operators (e.g. 20 MHz per player) at a low frequency (e.g. 700 MHz) range for mobile broadband usage. Doing so helps reduce the capital expenditure necessary for network coverage as unit cost of capacity is lesser at lower frequencies. However, this lever has to be carefully considered in light of their potentially negative effects on competition in the future mobile broadband market. Second, regulators can stimulate investment by providing incentives for rural rollout via spectrum auctions instead of extracting spectrum license fees. In addition, they can also provide complementary public funding for coverage in remote, underserved areas to achieve service penetration targets. Finally, regulators can selectively reconsider their restrictive position on network sharing, in order to foster economic investments in otherwise underserved areas with less favourable economics.

Regulation also plays a critical role in supporting fixed network roll-out. Decision-makers must experiment with different approaches to address the fundamental economics of new infrastructure as consumers' willingness to pay for the service is insufficient to warrant a viable business case for infrastructure investment. Several regulatory models have been implemented around the world to stimulate the development of next generation broadband networks in this environment. Currently, there are two models that could result in increased fiber network deployment: targeted regulatory relief and government tenders accompanied with subsidies.

Regulatory relief on new investments provides the investing operator with exclusive rights to use their own network and enables investment benefits to be more readily extracted. This provides incentives to invest, and it can help stimulate efforts to provide coverage in areas that would otherwise have been considered uneconomical for operators competing in an open-access regime.

The United States is a good example of a country that has adopted a regulatory relief strategy. It adopted an open access regime — embodied in the Telecommunications Act of 1996 — in which strong unbundling requirements were placed on existing copper networks. However, in 2004, the U.S. regulator, the Federal Communications Commission, proposed

FIGURE 6.6

For Rural Areas of Emerging Markets with Moderate Throughput, Mobile Broadband is the only Affordable Solution

Technologies with the Lowest Incremental Costs/User/Month

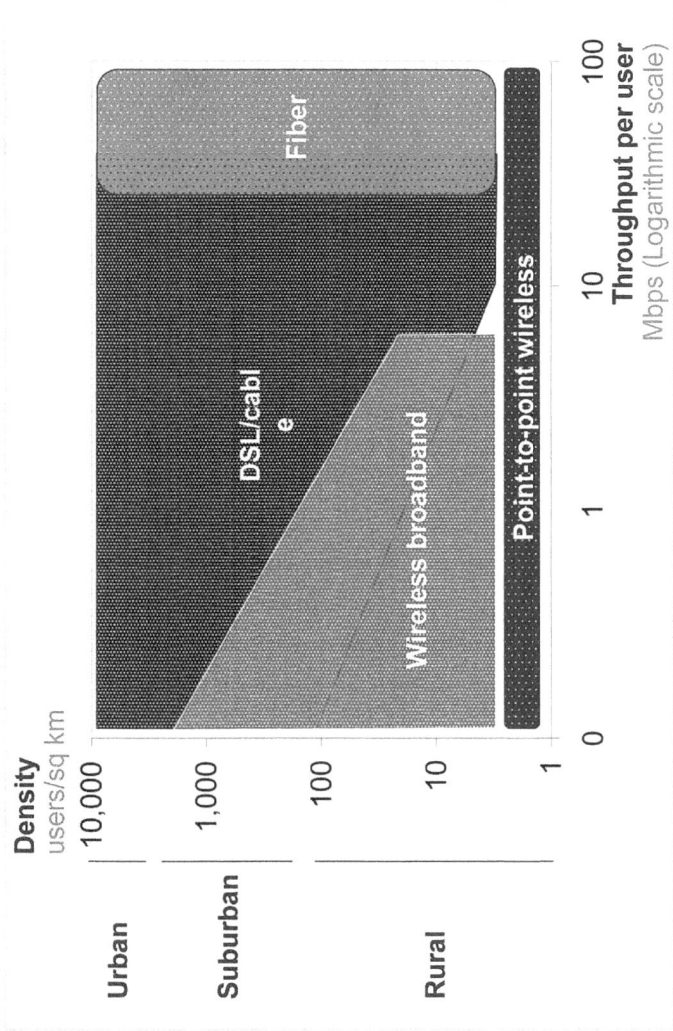

Source: Vendor interviews; Analyst reports; McKinsey Analysis.

that new fiber networks servicing the mass market would not, with the exception of voice service, be required to provide unbundled access to competitors. The FCC's rationale was that the strength of existing competition between cable and copper infrastructure warranted a weaker access regime to stimulate the construction of a new parallel network infrastructure. This form of regulatory relief, along with competitive pressure from cable operators that were rolling out their own broadband networks (e.g. using cable broadband technologies such as DOCSIS 3.0), was supportive of the roll out of fiber to the premises (FTTP) by Verizon and fiber to the node (FTTN) by AT&T in 2004. By 2009, 15 per cent of American households (or about 17.2 million homes) had access to FTTP and another 17 million households had the option to access broadband via AT&T's FTTN option.

The alternative model, in which government tenders are accompanied by subsidies, allows shared wholesale access to next generation networks, accompanied by government subsidies for investments in otherwise uneconomical areas. Although both Malaysia's and Singapore's next generation broadband network plans fall under this regulatory model, Japan exemplifies this model. Japan has the second fastest average broadband speeds in the world and the second highest fiber to the home penetration rate (next to Korea) at 40 per cent of households.[9] The majority of the fiber rollout was carried out by the incumbent NTT, which took advantage of a package of tax incentives from the government. Incentives included low-cost loans and accelerated depreciation and deductions for business users. Copper access was mandated in 1999, and prices were set low to reflect the low costs of operating and maintaining a fully depreciated network. The action spawned strong competitors in the DSL market and Japan's broadband penetration rate increased from less than 1 per cent in 1999 to 66 per cent in 2009.

Competitive pressure from DSL, cable operators, and new, smaller fiber players compelled NTT to roll out its FTTP network. In mid-2008, fiber overtook DSL as the dominant broadband technology in Japan, and it has retained its position ever since. NTT is required to grant access to its fiber network, and the regulated prices are high enough to guarantee return on investment and prevent competitors from undercutting NTT's retail price. Presently, the Japanese regulator is reassessing the access regime as well as prices, to ensure they are set at an appropriate level.[10]

Both models have proven to be successful in fostering fiber rollout in their respective countries. However, both models could also adversely affect industry competitiveness. Regulatory relief could limit consumer choice and competitiveness of next generation of broadband, if insufficient competition is in place. Government tenders and subsidies must be contextualized in a balanced open access regime and assessed in light of the potential alternative uses or trade-offs in the use of government funding.

Public sector investment leadership

The public sector can take the lead in encouraging private investment in telecommunications infrastructure by co-investing in networks. Singapore and Malaysia are leading the way for the other ASEAN countries in this regard.

Singapore's government has actively promoted the development of broadband infrastructure by providing subsidies directly to private companies that are investing in the construction of the national fiber network. The Next Generation Nationwide Broadband Network aims to provide ultra-high-speed broadband access at speeds of about 1 gigabyte per second (Gbps) nationwide. By the end of 2010, 60 per cent of Singaporean homes had broadband coverage. The current target is achieving coverage for 95 per cent of Singapore's 1.1 million residences by 2012. Singapore's government has also co-funded the construction of a wireless broadband network. The project, called Wireless@SG, provides free access to users in public places until 2013.

The Malaysian government is co-investing in a similar initiative with Telekom Malaysia to fund the construction of a high-speed broadband (HSBB) network. The government is investing RM 2.4 billion (US$805 million) in the ten-year project, and Telekom Malaysia is co-investing RM 8.9 billion (US$3 billion). The Malaysian HSBB project aims to provide speeds of 1 Gbps to 1.3 million households by end of 2012, with initial deployment in the Klang Valley, Kuala Lumpur; Iskandar in the Johor State of Malaysia; and key industrial zones throughout the country. Broadband speeds of up to 1 Gbps are expected to enable a new digital lifestyle for consumers and to accelerate productivity and knowledge-based growth for Malaysian enterprises.

Governments can also actively encourage the development of a digital media ecosystem that cuts across various industries. For

FIGURE 6.7

Governments can also actively encourage the development of a Digital Media Ecosystem

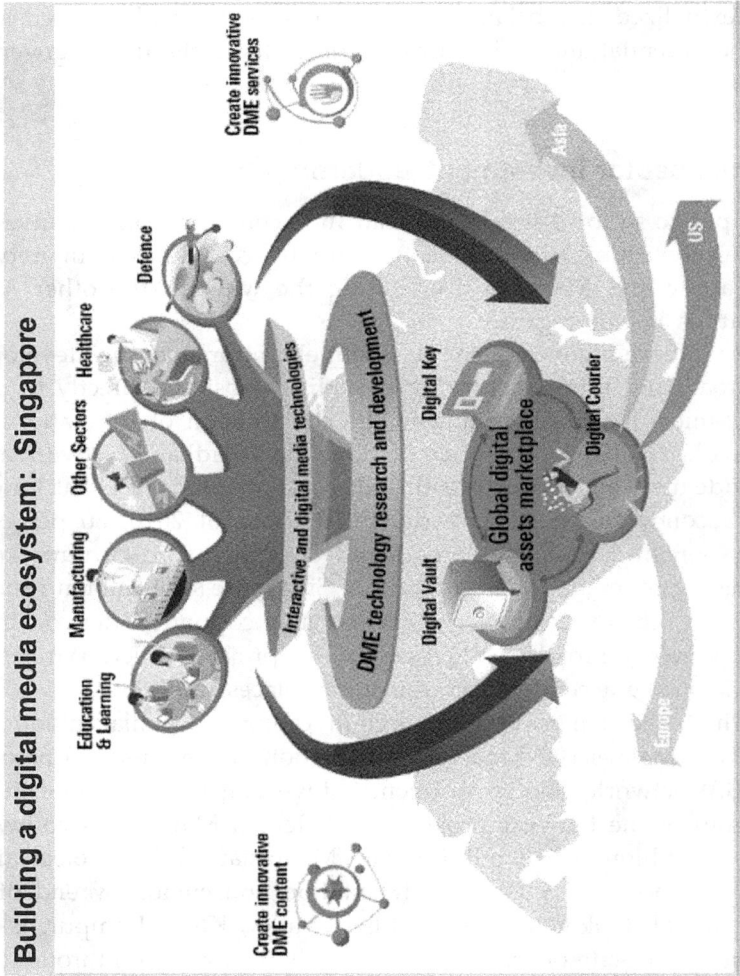

Building a digital media ecosystem: Singapore

Source: Media Development Authority (<www.mda.gov.sg>) and Infocomm Development Authority (<www.ida.gov.sg>).

instance, as shown in Figure 6.7. Singapore's government proactively encourages transparency in content development; provides greater and more affordable access to content; and reduces entry barriers to ensure the growth of a dynamic information and communication technologies (ICT) industry. It also supports the private sector by providing grants and financing that promote growth and innovation. Finally, it actively nurtures and attracts local and global talent and equips enterprises with necessary business competencies.

Public and private sector initiatives and partnerships

Governments can also increase Internet connectivity by pushing more e-services and providing broadband access to educational institutions. Many good examples of these types of efforts exist, including:

- Thailand's 2020 ICT Masterplan to create a Smart Thailand was launched in January 2011 to provide 30,000 schools and community education centres and 90 per cent of the population with broadband access by 2020.[11]
- Vietnam's National Program on IT applications (2011 to 2015) aims to open e-portals for online public services for all state agencies. Already, the programme has digitized about 5,700 administrative procedures and generated cost savings.[12]
- The Philippine government's Personal Computers for Public Schools project aims to develop knowledge workers and promote IT culture in classrooms by providing 3,714 primary schools with 47,000 computer packages.[13]

Governments can also partner with the private sector to promote broadband access. Already, there are various examples of private sector initiatives that were created to increase broadband connectivity and access. For instance:

- In Indonesia, mobile telecommunications company XL has launched the Computers for Schools programme to provide computing facilities and Internet connections to 100 educational institutions and schools throughout Indonesia. The aim of the project's creators is to provide assistance for 60 schools and up to 300 students per year.[14]
- In Malaysia, in support of the Malaysian Government's Vision 2020 plan, the Intel Corporation launched a teacher training programme

at institutions such as the Institut Perguruan Perempuan Melayu (IPPM or the Institute of Female Malay Teachers) to enable female teachers to regularly and effectively use new technology in their teaching.[15] Female teachers comprise 70 per cent of the total teaching force in Malaysia's primary and secondary schools.[16]

- In the Philippines, GILAS (Gearing up Internet Literacy and Access for Students) is a multi-sector project created by private sector and non-profit organizations to improve Internet access for and the literacy of secondary school students. Established in 2001, the project has connected almost 50 per cent of the country's 6,800 high schools.[17]

- In Vietnam, the Intel Corporation partnered with Vietnam's Ministry of Education and Training, twelve local PC system integrators, and two local banks, to offer affordable desktop and laptop systems bundled with discounted ADSL broadband services. The programme offers one-year, interest-free bundles to families who are buying their first PC. A second project, called Smart PC, Smart Business, aims to increase PC and Internet use among small- and medium-size businesses by offering hardware and software with ADSL broadband. Finally, a third project was created to equip 200 community centres in the Bac Ninh Province with Internet access, in order to provide farmers with access to critical information on market prices, what products to grow and how best to grow them, and where to sell their produce.[18]

Conclusion

Broadband is a key enabler of economic and social development. While the use of mobile telephony technology is now successfully embedded in the culture of many ASEAN nations, broadband is still at a nascent stage of development in most of the mid- to low-income ASEAN member states. Despite this, demand among Southeast Asian consumers is evident — as demonstrated by the frequent use of social networking sites and the booming Internet cafe business.

Poor infrastructure, the high level of capital investment required for network rollout, issues of awareness and affordability, poor mobile network quality and the market dominance of basic handsets are some of the key barriers to the increased adoption of broadband in Southeast Asia. Nevertheless, there are solutions to these challenges, and some solutions are already being implemented by ASEAN governments and companies and being used as best practices and models for the rest of the region to emulate or learn from. First, there are regulatory levers for promoting the deployment of fixed and mobile networks that regulators in the region can adopt in order to promote the development of broadband networks. Second, governments can take action on broadband deployment's supply side by co-investing in infrastructure. Finally, governments, in partnership with the private sector, can stimulate demand for broadband by promoting online services, providing broadband access to schools and communities, and building digital ecosystems.

By supporting the rollout of broadband infrastructure, governments and companies in the region will not only be providing what the population needs, they will also be providing much-needed infrastructure that would underpin regional connectivity and economic integration.

NOTES

1. The authors would like to thank Nida Khafiyya for her research support for this article.
2. Average mobile penetration for Africa, the Americas, Asia and the Pacific, and the Middle East reached 82.5 per cent in October 2011. Asia and the Pacific's mobile penetration was 74 per cent. See Informa Telecoms and Media, World Cellular Information Services, October 2011.
3. These estimates were based on the following key assumptions: (1) mobile broadband penetration will reach the present level of fixed broadband penetration in Western Europe (approximately 54 per cent); (2) fixed and mobile broadband are assumed to be similar or interchangeable goods; (3) the economy is able to absorb and leverage the broadband infrastructure for economic growth and that key economic sectors like manufacturing and services can utilize the broadband infrastructure; and (4) the level of education allows and facilitates the effective adoption of broadband. Various econometric analyses suggest that every 10 per cent increase in broadband leads to a 0.5 per cent increase in GDP and 0.5 per cent employment elasticity. See Leonard Waverman, Meloria Meschi, and Melvyn Fuss, "The Impact of Telecoms on Economic Growth in Developing Countries", Vodafone Policy Paper 2 (2005); Ikka Lakaniemi, "Connectivity Scorecard and Broadband Impact Study", LECG and NokiaSiemens Networks, 2009; and William H. Lehr, Carlos A. Osorio, Sharon E. Gillett, and Marvin A. Sirbu, "Measuring Broadband's Economic Impact", <http://www.itu.int/wsis/stocktaking/docs/activities/iii/MIT_Carnegie.pdf>.

4. Vietnam, which was commonly considered part of CMLV (Cambodia, Myanmar, Laos, and Vietnam) or the least developed members of ASEAN, should now be rightfully considered a mid-level ASEAN member country. Vietnam's fast rate of development is a testimony to the country's strong economic growth in the past decade.
5. Monthly disposable incomes calculated from data from the Economist Intelligence Unit.
6. See <Alexa.com>.
7. The latest available data from Cambodia is from 2005, and for Laos and Myanmar, 2002. For mid-income level countries in ASEAN, the rate of electrification is as follows: Indonesia, 91 per cent of households (2007); the Philippines, 83 per cent (2008); and Vietnam, 96 per cent (2005). Data is not available for other ASEAN countries. See Asian Development Bank, *Key Indicators for Asia and the Pacific 2011*, p. 250.
8. See Gartner, Mobile Devices Worldwide Forecast, 2003–14, 1Q10 Update.
9. Ministry of Information and Communication, Japan.
10. See McKinsey & Company, "Broadband for the people: Policies that support greater access", Recall No. 15: Monetizing Data, pp. 40–43.
11. See <http://www.mict.go.th/download/Master_Plan.pdf>.
12. See <http://www.egov.com.vn>.
13. See <http://www.dti.gov.ph>.
14. See <http://www.xl.co.id>.
15. See <http://www3.intel.com/cd/corporate/csr/apac/eng/education/casestudies/casestudies4/359544.htm>.
16. Malaysian Ministry of Education.
17. See <http://www.gilas.org>.
18. See <http://www3.intel.com/cd/corporate/csr/apac/eng/community/countries/vn/394513.htm>.

REFERENCES

Asian Development Bank. *Key Indicators for Asia and the Pacific 2011*, p. 250.
Gartner. Mobile Devices Worldwide Forecast, 2003–14, 1Q10 Update.
Lakaniemi, Ikka. "Connectivity Scorecard and Broadband Impact Study". LECG and NokiaSiemens Networks, 2009
Lehr, William H., Carlos A. Osorio, Sharon E. Gillett, and Marvin A. Sirbu. "Measuring Broadband's Economic Impact". <http://www.itu.int/wsis/stocktaking/docs/activities/iii/MIT_Carnegie.pdf>.
McKinsey & Company. "Broadband for the people: policies that support greater access". Recall No. 15: Monetizing Data, pp. 40–43.
Waverman, Leonard, Meloria Meschi, and Melvyn Fuss. "The Impact of Telecoms on Economic Growth in Developing Countries".

7

THE CURRENT STATE OF ICT SYSTEMS ACROSS ASEAN

Lee Yu Kit

Introduction

ASEAN is a tremendously diverse region, encompassing within its borders some 4 million square kilometres, 600 million people, 32,000 islands, 900 different languages and a diversity of development that ranges from US$800 per capita to US$49,000 per capita from its least to its most developed member countries.[1] This diversity extends to ICT adoption across ASEAN. As discussed in the next section, Internet usage has a relation to a country's development. The world average Internet penetration rate is 23.8 per cent.[2] The internet penetration rates for developed countries are: United States — 77.3 per cent, Japan — 78.2 per cent, South Korea — 81.1 per cent, Australia — 80.1 per cent.[3] Compared to this, the rate of Internet penetration of the ASEAN member states is shown in Table 7.1.[4]

TABLE 7.1

Internet Penetration in ASEAN

ASEAN Countries	Penetration (%)
Singapore	67.4
Malaysia	62.8
Brunei	46.2
Vietnam	24
Philippines	21
Thailand	20
Indonesia	10.5
Laos	1.5
Cambodia	0.5
Myanmar	N/A

Source: Internet World Statistics.

Data varies widely depending on the source, how the measurement is derived, and when it was taken. For consistency, the data for Table 7.1 is taken from a common source.

A Broader Measure

Internet penetration is a gross measure as it does not sample other quantitative or qualitative criteria such as quality of Internet access, legal framework, and other infrastructural issues. A more compound measure is a country's readiness for Internet-based opportunities. The Economist Intelligence Unit (EIU), collaborating with IBM, publishes an annual E-readiness ranking.

E-readiness is defined as an indicator of how amenable a national market is to Internet-based opportunities. The ranking evaluates the technological, economic, political and social assets of sixty-eight countries and their cumulative impact on respective information economies. The rankings are based upon nearly 100 quantitative and qualitative criteria, organized in six distinct categories: Connectivity and Technology Infrastructure, Business Environment, Consumer and Business Adoption, Legal and Policy Environment, Social and Cultural Environment, and Supporting e-services.[5]

TABLE 7.2
E-readiness Ranking

ASEAN Countries	Rank
Singapore	13
Malaysia	37
Thailand	47
Philippines	56
Indonesia	62
Vietnam	67
Others	Not rated

Source: Economist Intelligence Unit (EIU) and IBM.

For 2010, the No. 1 country is Denmark, followed by the United States and Sweden as No. 2 and No. 3 respectively. The ASEAN countries' rankings are shown in Table 7.2.

The measure of adoption of technology follows a curved, rather than linear path. As countries adopt broader measures of ICT, the ecosystem develops in tandem, bringing with it increasing innovation, new service providers and new ideas. In this respect, the maturity of ICT adoption can be argued to be an indirect measure of human capital development. It is no coincidence that the ICT centres the best known being Silicon Valley and Bangalore, are also hotbeds of innovation.

The accelerated pace of change of technology and its increasing sophistication suggests that member states who are behind the adoption curve will find it hard to keep up. The indirect corollary to this argument is that the "digital divide" is indeed widening — and it is a measure of the development of human capital and innovativeness for that country.

ICT as an Enabler

To understand how greater connectivity can contribute to the ASEAN Economic Community, it is necessary to understand what is meant by ICT and the implications of greater connectivity.

"ICT" which stands for "Information and Communications Technology" encompasses the use of IT and telecommunications, so it is the convergence of these two technologies in the handling and dissemination of information. A survey in 2003 by the ITU, the UN Agency for ICT, found that in many countries, there was no formal definition of the term "ICT"[6] although the concept is well understood.

It is no exaggeration to say that the "information age" marks a new era in the development of civilization, just as the Industrial revolution before that ushered in a new age, replacing an era when humans were dependent on agriculture. For the foreseeable future, information is the new currency of human knowledge, and it is one that is exciting and still in its relative infancy.

ICT as Accelerator of Economic Activity and Productivity

ICT is recognized as an accelerator of economic activity. International estimates indicate that every 10 per cent increase in broadband penetration contributes to a growth of 1.3 per cent in GDP.[7] Research from the Brookings Institution and Criterion Economics suggest an increase in employment from 0.2–0.3 per cent for every 1 per cent increase in broadband penetration.[8]

In tandem with the development of physical infrastructure, ICT plays a crucial role in the development of a nation or a region. This is due to the "multiplier" effect used in economics, where every dollar spent on ICT is "multiplied" by new consumer behaviour, supporting services and downstream industries.

ICT increases productivity. Between 1995 and 2002, ICT was responsible for two-thirds of productivity growth and almost all labour productivity increase in the United States. Between 2000 and 2005, it was responsible for over 1 per cent labour growth in productivity in the United States.[9]

As a Foundation for New Service Models

ICT is the required backbone to the development of new applications and services. With the availability of ICT, new business models arise, driving the growth of innovation. Businesses develop an online presence, taking advantage of lower transaction costs online. They become more competitive and have higher profit margins.

Small businesses can participate in the digital economy, and in turn, providers of services such as web developers, ISPs, supporting technical services develop in response to the market. All these activities contribute to the economic vitality of a nation or region.

Equalizer: Resetting the Social Status Quo

ICT is a great equalizer, not respecting social strata just as it does not respect national borders. Barring intentional restrictions such as censorship, anyone with a connected computer has the same access to information to anyone else, wherever they are located.

ICT provides a historic opportunity to less developed communities or countries, and that is access to the same information as anyone else in any other part of the world. This implies that for the first time in human history, a person living in a remote part of the world has instant access to other humans, to instant, up-to-date information, to all the vast resources of the interconnected world, and can participate in that world.

Driving Adoption: Device Convergence

Technology is evolving rapidly and the pace of change is accelerating. TIME magazine recently estimated that computing power increases more in a single hour than in the last ninety years combined,[10] and that rate of change is only increasing. In tandem with this, the unprecedented mobility of the human race is contributing to device convergence that further accentuates the trend towards connectivity and puts connected machines in the hands of more people than ever before.

On the one hand, where there was the traditional desktop PC, itself a revolution compared to the mini-systems and mainframes, the desktop PC has quickly evolved into more mobile forms, first the Laptop, the Notebook, and then the Netbook, each smaller and more mobile than the last form factor.

On the other hand, fixed line telephones have been largely relegated to a supporting role by the worldwide explosion in adoption of the mobile phone, which has evolved rapidly into the increasing popularity of the Smartphone and now the computing Tablet.

Device convergence: is the Tablet a convergence of the mobile phone with the traditional PC of yet another transitory form?

PC > Notebook > Netbook > Tablet > ? < Tablet < Smartphone <Handphone < Telephone

In the last quarter of 2010, for the first time ever, smartphones outsold PCs.[11] Device convergence allows more people than ever to participate in the digital economy. This trend will continue to accelerate, bringing people who previously never used ICT into the fold of the digital world.

Virtual Communities

Connectivity provides the ability to organize and mobilize large groups of people who have never met, who are unknown to each other, and who may be geographically very distant from each other.

This is a phenomenon made possible only by ICT. People can be bound by any common cause, wherever they may be. This is the rise of the global virtual community. Any topic can garner a worldwide following of people in the hundreds of thousands or millions, something the campaign office of President Barack Obama fully understood in harnessing the online community during the presidential campaign.

Online communities take a number of forms, such as Weblogs, bulletin boards, even virtual reality (such as Second Life). Many of these are projects started as volunteer efforts which have since snowballed with the momentum of sheer numbers. One such example is Wikipedia, the online encyclopaedia, which has millions of contributors.

Online pressure groups, interest groups, massively multi-player games, are expressions of the virtual community. An example of the virtual community is the social network, which has proven to have the power of very real, physical action to move people to action, to reshape the geopolitics of the world. Many movements arise on social media sites such as Facebook and Twitter. Connectivity thus has multiple dimensions: social, economic, political, and cultural.

How can Greater Connectivity Promote Economic Activity across ASEAN?

We live in an interconnected world. Countries are connected to each other through trade, cultural, social, and financial ties. The strength of this coupling was well illustrated in the regional financial crisis of 1997 and again in the global financial crisis of 2007–08. Although the latter was caused by the lack of financial oversight in the U.S. economy, it quickly threatened to become a global phenomenon. The EU acted en bloc to tighten regulation, boost economies and provide assurance to the market. Country economies, most notably that of Iceland, failed.

Many Asian countries thought they were sufficiently decoupled from the Western economies to escape the global malaise, but had the financial markets of the developed countries experienced a meltdown, Asian economies would have been severely affected.

Asian countries, including ASEAN, produce goods and services consumed in other parts of the world, and vice-versa. What affects large Asian economies such as India and China have a knock-on effect on ASEAN economies, currencies and financial markets. In a globalized economy, ICT enables the flow of instantaneous information, for the vast flow of funds, provides electronic links that can cause economies to rise and fall, and for information to be disseminated across the world almost in real time.

How does ASEAN leverage on ICT to promote economic activity? ICT by and of itself is an important enabler, but it is only one of several enablers, needed to create a vibrant economic climate within the region.

ICT can be used to connect buyers and sellers of goods, to negotiate prices and terms, but goods still need to be physically delivered, and this can only happen if there are good roads, ports, and the supporting physical infrastructure to enable physical delivery in good condition — such as refrigerated trucks for perishable goods.

ICT is not separate and discrete from other infrastructure prerequisites: the two are intimately connected. Physical transport of goods is dependent on the supply chain management, the tracking of goods, knowing where they are and in what condition they are, having just-in-time processes so that they clear borders quickly and efficiently.

ICT thus works symbiotically with the physical world, and as we shall see later, is becoming more and more integrated with it.

ASEAN as a region is very much a work-in-progress compared to the more mature economies. This provides opportunity, to be able to avoid the costly mistakes and the step-by-step progression of trying out new ideas and technologies. The exchange and flow of ideas and information is so globalized that the idea of leap-frogging to achieve quantum leaps in productivity is not only possible, it is necessary for rapid progress in a world where the pace of change continues to accelerate.

The effective use of ICT can replace manual labour-intensive processes, dramatically shorten lead times, and boost productivity. Along the way, new roles and skills are created, new organizational structures realized, new business models created, and innovation can arise.

Before ICT can be applied cross-border, it must be applied and widely available within a country itself. The countries already on the adoption path will adapt and change faster than those who are further behind. This is due to the momentum and nature of ICT: the rate of adoption is not linear, but curved upwards.

The Interconnected Nature of Economies

On regional matters, all countries have a degree of coupling. We can draw some lessons from similar blocs, as illustrated in the EU, which shares common regulation, policy and a common currency. When a member country such as Greece or Ireland is in danger of default, the whole community acts to protect its interests as the economies have interdependence. Similarly, the global financial crisis of 2007–08 was an illustration of how regionally-connected governments acted in order to drive common policy to avoid the worst effects of the contagion.

The level of interconnectedness between private and public interests was also evident: through the danger of large banks defaulting on loans, country economies were affected through tax revenues, country debt and investments.

Although the crisis was a financial one, it illustrates the role played by ICT and the connected nature of governments with private enterprise. This extends to social or cultural trends as well, as discussed above. A news item posted on the Internet becomes common worldwide know-ledge in a matter of hours, spreading at speeds much faster than would be possible without the underlying infrastructure of ICT.

The benefits of connectivity can be broadly grouped into three areas:

- Strengthening internal processes
- Connecting to collaborate
- Connecting for the future

Strengthening Internal Processes

Countries need to achieve a certain degree of ICT self-sufficiency before they can reap the benefits of connectivity with other nations.

(a) Internal Efficiencies: Creating Value in Governments

A large contributor to promoting economic activity is in creating efficiencies in the delivery of government services. ICT is the catalyst to streamline processes, re-skill workers, and collaborate more effectively within government and with businesses and citizens.

Many countries already embrace the Government portal concept, as the one-stop shop for citizens and businesses to connect to government services. These can be further enhanced to promote online services to businesses and citizens which reduce process turnaround times, reduce manual intervention, provide greater convenience and thereby increase overall productivity.

Over time, an online presence can migrate to higher value services. Typically, information only websites migrate towards download of forms, and then mature to providing online services. Online payments, online applications, online status checking, online renewal of licenses, and permits should continue to drive down the costs of doing business, increase efficiency and reduce waste and waiting time.

In Saudi Arabia, interaction between citizens and government were transformed with the implementation of systems which automated business processes, increased agency collaboration and provided citizens with online, voice and mobile access. Response time for some services were reduced from several days to several minutes, and interagency collaboration improved, making for a more efficient and productive government.

In Malaysia, the introduction of online tax returns for individuals and corporations by the Inland Revenue Board has been a contributory factor in the increase in government revenue, with an average 30 per cent year-on-year increase in the take-up of e-filing,[12] due to the convenience of online services over paper filing.

The cost of doing business online is well documented as being a fraction of providing the service over the counter, which is a strong incentive for governments to provide online services. For example, a banking transaction involving a teller averages US$1.07, a telephone transaction costs US$0.54, an ATM transaction costs US$0.27, banking with PC-based software costs US$0.015, and an Internet-based transaction costs US$0.01.[13]

The online presence can be further enhanced by collaboration between ASEAN member states: there are already moves in this direction, as evidenced by the intent to establish an ASEAN Single Window[14] for customs clearance. This would connect the individual member countries' national Single Windows to facilitate trade across ASEAN.

(b) Internal Security

A secure environment is needed for trade to flourish. Citizens must feel "safe" to move freely about to conduct their business. Collaboration between law enforcement agencies takes many forms, including sharing information on known criminals, tip-offs on cross-border smuggling, gangland activity and cross-border intrusions.

Borders are potential weak points for revenue leakage. The estimated loss in unpaid duties to the Malaysian government is estimated at US$65 million in the first five months of 2010[15] alone. In addition, the smuggling of banned or contraband goods such as firearms can constitute a threat to national security.

ICT has panoply of tools to strengthen policing and border controls. Sophisticated criminal syndicates can bypass manual checks and processes, while the use of sophisticated ICT such as biometrics, pattern and risk analysis allow law enforcement agencies to be more effective in the use of resources to arrest or reduce crime, which in turn, promote security and provide an environment more conducive to economic growth.

As examples, the UK Border Agency uses advanced analytics to form data collected in advance from carriers so that they have the information to make decisions before the passengers even arrive at their border.

The Polish National Police is equipped with a remote information access system, giving direct access to the Schengen Information System-Visa System, enabling it to check identity, visa status and vehicles entering Poland.

(c) Identifying Risks and Reducing Graft

Corruption and graft discourages investors and increases the cost of doing business — 45 per cent of businesses report not entering a market[16] because of graft. The revenue leakage from graft can be very substantial. Although accurate data is hard to come by, the World Bank estimates the cost of corruption as being US$1 trillion per annum worldwide.

Well designed ICT systems eliminate or minimize the opportunities for graft, especially where process weaknesses allow fraud or corruption to be committed.

Digital surveillance systems linked to analysis software can spot and alert instances of improper handling or procedure at sensitive points such as border control. Automation of processes eliminates opportunities for manual intervention or subvention of processes, such as approvals or processing of applications where applicants may be incented to seek "shortcuts".

ICT also allows quick analysis of data, such as spotting risk areas for enforcement efforts from trolling through vast amounts of data. The use of analytics can be applied to any area where there are large amounts of data, in which there may be patterns of behaviour that make for more effective application of efforts in arresting fraud or addressing areas of concern. Data can also be shared across different agencies between countries. ICT allows privacy concerns to be addressed by masking or anonymising sensitive data. Thus, region-wide data across ASEAN can be interrogated to spot regional criminal activity, and put in place effective and collaborative plans.

The New York City Department has driven down the crime rate over the past decade, thanks in part to an advanced analytics system that integrates data from various sources, and allows them to see crime trends as they occur. The efficient data-gathering and crime-analysis also allows for a faster and higher rate of crime-closing.

The implementation of ICT systems for policing also provides the infrastructure for governments to share information on cross-border transgressions. The sharing of "blacklists" on a real-time or near real-time basis through the application of ICT is an example of how law enforcement between countries can be improved by closing a potential loophole in update of security information between member states.

The reduction of corruption increases the confidence of businesses, increases investment, increases employment and thus boosts government revenues.

(d) Revitalizing Rural Communities

For the developing countries, much of the economy is based on agriculture and fishing. Rural communities living in remote regions are often subject to a middleman who exploits an information gap by being the intermediary between buyer and seller.

Producers are often small communities who live close to the source of production. They are often disadvantaged by receiving low prices for their produce. The village cooperative is a mechanism that seeks to equalize the information gap, through organization and reducing or eliminating the middleman. Village cooperatives are not uncommon throughout ASEAN, especially in the crafts and arts industries.

Through ICT, producers can advertise their goods, find buyers, transact through trusted payment channels, and employ reliable delivery services. The net result is faster and more direct goods to market, more money in the hands of the producers, and the preservation of traditional village lifestyles. The Fair Trade and Direct Trade movements are manifestations of this phenomenon.

Government operated cooperatives or agricultural initiatives have a major role to play in connecting communities of producers and ready buyers, by creating the virtual marketplaces, rules between buyers and sellers, connecting third party delivery services and establishing secure payment channels.

This provides an opportunity to bring rural communities into the digital age, by increasing living standards, economic activity and buying power and affecting social trends such as urban migration.

Connecting to Collaborate

The interconnected nature of the ASEAN member states provides for a number of areas of mutual benefit through connecting by ICT.

(a) Healthcare

Healthy populations are essential to healthy economies. The cost of providing healthcare services and the cost to the economy in lost productivity can be significant. The ASEAN countries, being in the same regional geography, share some common characteristics in terms of communicable diseases and outcomes.

Data shared across countries allows a larger pool of data for analysis and research purposes. This approach is a tried and tested one in clinical trials where large data pools allow observations not apparent in smaller sample populations. Similarly, research efforts into common tropical diseases can be a collaborative effort between countries rather than each country conducting its own research and tests. Overall, this drives down costs and spreads benefits, with ICT being the common enabler to share test results, data and coordinate and organize efforts.

For example, a transnational agency for the prevention of infectious diseases deployed an information exchange platform that offers near real-time access to disease data, granting access to local and national health authorities while respecting privacy and security requirements. Users can forecast and analyse health risks better, allowing more time for hospitals and countries to prepare for potentially disastrous disease outbreaks.

Telemedicine is a tried and tested concept in bringing healthcare expertise to areas where it may not be available. For example, IBM worked with partners to bring modern and expert healthcare to the remote island of Tristan da Cunha in the Atlantic Ocean where the population is served by a single physician. The use of ICT techniques allows healthcare experts from various specializations and various parts of the world participate in real time in assessing medical cases.

Similarly, in ASEAN, such a model could serve members of the public in remote areas where expert healthcare is not readily available.

(b) Increasing Collaboration

The ability to exchange and share information can result in better decision-making for governments, increase collaboration between agencies, facilitate cross-border, intra-regional ASEAN trade and greater market efficiencies.

Accurate data sharing between governments provides for consistency of data, more uniform policy and better decision-making that benefits the community as a whole. Regional-interest data such as demographics, healthcare, public security, and population movement help governments to plan and to provision as appropriate in order to stimulate economies.

The reduction of trade barriers, thereby enlarging the business possibilities of the region as a whole, is also required to lower the costs of doing cross-border business, to increase trade flow between countries and to facilitate the movement of people across borders.

The clear need for collaboration, information sharing and dissemination through the use of ICT emphasizes the connected nature of the regional member states and the need to improve ICT infrastructure for mutual economic benefits.

(c) Responding to Regional Crises

Crises that affect the region as a whole, such as the 2003 SARS epidemic, and later the bird flu epidemics, illustrate the cross-border nature of certain threats.

These crises illustrated the need for ASEAN governments to exchange information in order to arrest the spread of the diseases, to educate the public, to assess the nature and extent of the threat, and to protect their individual economies. During this period, travel to and within the region was curtailed, causing an economic impact to the airline and service industries (hotels, restaurants, tourism) and attendant loss in revenue to governments.

On 29 April 2003, a Special ASEAN Leaders meeting was convened in Bangkok, Thailand, to tackle the regional crisis.

It became apparent for the need for governments and healthcare institutions to share and exchange information, both within individual countries and between countries. The movement of infected people also needed to be tracked to contain the diseases.

The use of ICT in such scenarios is crucial in the collection, analysis and dissemination of information as well as updates, advisories and policy. The tools of ICT which provide for modelling "what-if" scenarios allow governments to take preventive actions. Countries which are "cut-off" from the information flow are severely disadvantaged in terms of how to cope with the crisis, with resultant damage to their economies and well-being of populations.

(d) Reducing Cross-Border Costs

Country economies are strengthened by increases in cross-border trade (CBT). This is because suppliers can seek out lower-cost providers of goods and services, producers can find the best prices for their goods and producers can look for source materials that are lower in cost or not available locally.

The use of ICT expands the reach of suppliers and buyers, allowing access to hitherto inaccessible markets. The ability to communicate with foreign buyers via email, for example, greatly facilitates communication and trade.

Furthermore, ICT provides an avenue for secure payments and other transactions, such as the setting up of agreements between interested parties and intermediaries, such as banks or guarantors. Already, the

Internet provides a degree of technology neutrality that disguises the complexity of originating or destination ICT systems.

Electronic means can similarly facilitate trade with other countries outside the ASEAN bloc; this in turn increases the overall revenue generation within the member states, contributes to employment and revs up the economic engine.

The success of online shopping in developed countries indicates that cross-border trade can be increased through this means if other regulatory barriers are removed. The increase of overall trade between countries contributes to governmental revenue, thus contributing to the ASEAN Economic Community.

Connecting for the Future

ASEAN member states share common resources and common interests in a shared environment.

(a) Measuring the Physical World

The deadly tsunami on 26 December 2004 demonstrated that a natural disaster in one country can have regional consequences. In ASEAN, we share resources and common interests in ample and clean water supply, flood mitigation, and so on. One country's actions — such as constructing a dam across a river — can have downstream effects on fisheries and agriculture in another country.

It is in the interests of ASEAN to monitor critical shared interests in resources such as water supply, fishing grounds, wildlife, forest cover and pollution as these are cross-border. Physical ecosystems such as these are usually monitored by land observers or satellite, but these can also be monitored in real time using ICT.

The use of embedded sensors connected to computers allows the condition of common-interest resources to be monitored and for collective action to be taken. The tsunami alert system put in place after the 2004 tsunami is an example of such a system, but the technology is evolving for even remote, unpopulated areas to be monitored and for alerts to be sent to monitoring stations if out-of-range conditions are encountered.

In Venice, Italy, tourists can access an application called TagMyLagoon which provides information on tourist sites, traffic, and accommodation. The application is enabled with passive sensors located at points of interest in the city, which interact with wireless devices using the city's existing network.

As regional initiatives, these have the potential to avoid the worst effects of natural catastrophes, for governments to take preventive action, and to forge plans to manage shared resources in the future for shared economic benefits.

Summary and Moving Forward

This chapter has set forth the heterogeneous nature of ASEAN and how this is true with regards to ICT. It has provided what ICT means in this context, and the implications of ICT as an enabler to various outcomes including phenomena that arise with the use of ICT, such as social media being a tool for organization of human populations allied to common causes.

It has examined some of the benefits to ASEAN of greater connectivity, although it should be emphasized that this is by no means exhaustive. Some of these are visionary in nature and that is as it should be, for as ASEAN continues to progress, there will be initiatives it can embark upon to distinguish itself as members of the international community.

There are many challenges in the future but it also abounds in opportunities. Governments of the ASEAN countries should continue to emphasize ICT within their countries, especially in education, and actively collaborate to mutually benefit from the intelligent use of ICT by connecting across the community.

NOTES

1. *Jakarta Post*, 16 March 2011.
2. Internet World Statistics, <http://www.internetworldstats.com/list4.htm>.
3. Internet World Statistics, <http://www.internetworldstats.com/top25.htm>, quoting ITU, UN Agency for ICT, June 2010.
4. Internet World Statistics, <http://www.internetworldstats.com/list4.htm>.
5. The Economist Intelligence Unit, "Digital Economy Rankings 2010: Beyond E-Readiness".
6. <http://www.itu.int/ITU-D/ict/partnership/material/05-42742%20GLOBAL %20ICT.pdf>.

 7. Address by the Prime Minister of Malaysia, January 2011 to the 10th ASEAN Telecommunications and Information Technology Ministers Meeting (TELMIN) in Kuala Lumpur.

 8. Information Technology and Innovation Foundation report, 2008 on Stimulus Plan to Obama administration.

 9. Information Technology and Innovation Foundation report, 2008 on Stimulus Plan to Obama administration.

10. *TIME Magazine*, 21 February 2011.

11. IDC Market Research.

12. *Bernama*, 21 March 2011.

13. <www.msmoney.com>.

14. ASEAN Secretariat, <www.aseansec.org>.

15. Deputy Finance Minister Datuk Dr Awang Adek Hussein, quoted in Malaysian digest.com.

16. <http://www.apec.org/en/Press/Features/2009/0618_anti-corruption.aspx>.

8

ASEAN AND ICT: A TALE OF TWO CITIES?

Emmanuel C. Lallana

The story of ASEAN and ICT may well be a tale of two ASEANs — the "Young ASEAN" and the "Official ASEAN".

Young ASEAN is comprised of "digital natives" — tech-savvy, digitally-nimble, and multi-tasking individuals who are fluent in digital devices and the Internet. Official ASEAN, on the other hand, is composed of "digital immigrants" who are learning to adapt to their new environment but still "retain, to some degree, their 'accent,' that is, their foot in the past".[1]

The Young ASEAN

The youth of Southeast Asia are at the forefront of the global social network revolution. In the first quarter of 2011, there were an estimated 131.3 million Facebook (FB) users in Asia.[2] The top five countries in Asia in terms of FB users are Indonesia (35.2 million), India (23 million), the Philippines (22.4 million), Malaysia (10.1 million), and Taiwan

(9.1 million). A recent study showed that the Philippines posted the highest FB penetration rate across the globe, making Filipinos "the world's heaviest users of social media".[3] In fact, Asia is FB's fastest-growing region.[4] In the last two years, FB has seen 1,000 per cent growth in Malaysia and 4,000 per cent growth in Thailand (4,000 per cent!). As Patrick Winn notes, "As of 2010, the largest Facebook population outside America is no longer the United Kingdom. It's Indonesia, an archipelago where 80 per cent still lack Internet access."

Young ASEAN is also at the forefront of Twitter use. A 2009 report revealed that two ASEAN countries are in the top twenty global list of those with the largest share of Twitter users.[5] They are Indonesia (ranked 6th) and the Philippines (ranked 15th). In terms of Twitter activity, Indonesia is 6th (accounting for 2.3 per cent of the world's tweets), Singapore is 12th (with 0.88 per cent), the Philippines is 13th (with 0.85 per cent), and Malaysia is 18th (with 0.47 per cent).

Young ASEAN is multi-taskers too. A recent study revealed that 8–24 year olds in Asia fit 38 hours' worth of activities in a 24-hour period.[6] Of these 38 hours' worth of activities that Asia's youth manage to squeeze in a day, 10 hours are spent on some form of media. The heaviest media users are Malaysians (12.9 hours per day) and Thais (12.8 hours per day). This covers time spent on the Internet, watching TV or DVD/VCD/videos, reading newspapers or magazines, and listening to the radio.

In the same study, 31 per cent of "older" Asian youth (15–24 year old bracket) pay 100 per cent attention to the Internet when they are online and a further 38 per cent give the Internet 75 per cent of their attention. Television is the next most involving medium, with 18 per cent of the 15–24 year olds giving it their full attention and 31 per cent giving it 75 per cent of their attention.

The study also shows that 37 per cent of the youth connected to information and communications technology (ICT) in the region said that they could not live without the Internet and that 29 per cent would be unable to function without their mobile phones. Overall, the Internet was seen as the best source for staying up-to-date and having access to useful information, entertainment, and enjoyment.

The device of choice for Asian youth is the mobile phone.[7] According to a survey, personal ownership of mobile phones by Asian youth increased from 60 per cent in 2008 to 64 per cent in 2010.[8] The highest gainers include Singapore where youth mobile phone ownership moved from 80 per cent to 85 per cent in two years.

Among the youth surveyed who own a mobile phone in Asia, the average number of contacts on their mobiles is 77 people, which is more than the average number of their instant messaging buddies (74 people) and email contacts (55 people). Topping the chart with the most contacts on their mobile phones are Indonesians (131 contacts), Singaporeans (108 contacts), and Filipinos (102 contacts).

Among Asian youth who own mobile phones, about half use their mobiles to listen to music, play games, and take photos. One in five (21 per cent) uses this device to record videos.

The Official ASEAN

While the Young ASEAN is flourishing in the digital world, Official ASEAN is still struggling with it. On numerous occasions, ASEAN leaders have underscored the importance of ICT in ASEAN. As early as November 2000, ASEAN leaders signed the e-ASEAN Framework Agreement which sought to achieve "digital readiness" through activities in the areas of: 1) connectivity, 2) local content, 3) providing a seamless environment for electronic commerce, 4) providing a common marketplace for ICT goods and services, 5) human resource development, and 6) e-governance. A decade later, the ASEAN Heads of States/Government adopted the Master Plan on ASEAN Connectivity during the 17th ASEAN Summit on Hanoi. For its part, the ASEAN Telecommunications and IT Ministers, through its Senior Officials Meeting, is preparing an ASEAN ICT Master Plan 2010–2015. The vision of this ICT Master Plan is "Towards an Empowering and Transformational ICT: Creating an Inclusive, Vibrant, and Integrated ASEAN".

Compared to the holistic approach of the e-ASEAN Framework, recent ASEAN ICT initiatives seem to be focused on infrastructure development. For instance, the ASEAN ICT Master Plan does not pay enough attention to the development and/or use of "applications" or "apps". Applications are what will ultimately make the development of infrastructure useful or meaningful to the citizens of ASEAN member states. Applications are as important as infrastructure and capacity building. A failure to address these three aspects of ICT equally will lead to a sub-optimal use of ICT for development.

The bias for ICT as infrastructure is also apparent in the Master Plan on ASEAN Connectivity (MPAC). The MPAC is deemed "both a strategic document for achieving overall ASEAN Connectivity and a plan of action for immediate implementation for the period 2011–2015 to connect ASEAN through enhanced physical infrastructure development (physical connectivity), effective institutions, mechanisms and processes (institutional connectivity), and empowerment of people (people-to-people connectivity)."[9]

In the MPAC, ICT is discussed under "physical connectivity" together with transport and energy.[10] ICT infrastructure is seen as "fundamental to supporting trade, facilitating investment and enlarging markets through its ability to facilitate information exchange, to connect people, to support delivery of services and reduce the cost of business and trade and trade-related transactions".[11] The objective of physical connectivity is "to develop an integrated and well-functioning intermodal transport, ICT and energy networks in ASEAN and the wider region".[12]

ICT did not rate high in the priority strategies of the MPAC. ICT is only one of the seven Key Strategies to Enhance Physical Connectivity. The key actions for "Strategy 6: Accelerate the development of ICT infrastructure and services in each of the ASEAN Member States" are to:

- Establish an ASEAN Broadband Corridor by identifying and developing locations in each ASEAN member state to offer quality broadband connectivity. This will enable seamless usage of broadband services and applications across ASEAN to further connect and enhance the development of ICT and other sectors by 2014;
- Promote the diversity of international connectivity among ASEAN member states by 2015;
- Establish an ASEAN Internet Exchange Network to facilitate peering amongst ASEAN Internet access providers to reduce latency and increase speed as well as lower costs by 2013;
- Promote network integrity and information security, data protection and Computer Emergency Response Team (CERT) cooperation by developing common frameworks and establishing common minimum standards where appropriate, to ensure a level of preparedness and integrity of networks across ASEAN by 2015;

- Review Universal Service Obligations and/or similar policies to ensure that infrastructure covered under these policies are broadband Internet capable by 2015;
- Prioritize and expedite roll-out of broadband Internet capable infrastructure to schools by 2015;
- Conduct feasibility study on developing an ASEAN Single Tele-communications Market after 2015, in the context of free flow of products, services, investment, and skilled human resources by 2015.[13]

The key challenges identified in the MPAC in developing the ASEAN ICT infrastructure are: 1) the digital divide, 2) the insufficient coordination to ensure connectivity among National Information Infrastructure, 3) the need to nurture technological innovation, 4) the lack of financing for infrastructure projects, and 5) the ability of ASEAN member states to develop and harmonize ICT regulations necessary for the connectivity project and to encourage national and private investments in ICT infrastructure and services.[14] MPAC seems unaware that government can influence ICT development not only through policy and regulatory environments, but also through its purchase and use of ICT goods and services. The MPAC argues that "enhanced institutional connectivity in the ASEAN region raises the effectiveness of physical connectivity by easing the flow of goods and services (from the elimination of barriers to trade), reducing the cost of moving goods and services (from improved transport and trade facilitation services), and ensuring greater economic and social returns from greater physical connectivity and deeper economic linkages (through higher investments)."[15]

ICT is not seen as playing any role in enhancing institutional connectivity in ASEAN. This may be due to the fairly narrow definition of "institutional connectivity" used in the MPAC. In this document, institutional connectivity is defined as "... linking various international or regional agreements and protocols to facilitate international transactions of goods and services as well as movement of natural persons across borders".[16] A broader view of institutional connectivity would include enhancing connections within and between "any structure or mechanism of social order and cooperation governing the behaviour of a set of individuals within a given human community".[17] Had

MPAC used this broader definition, ICT would include a discussion and recommendations on how the "organizations" of ASEAN — the ASEAN Summit, ASEAN Coordinating Council, ASEAN Community Councils, ASEAN Sectoral Ministerial Bodies, Committee of Permanent Representatives, National Secretariats, and the ASEAN Secretariat — could facilitate international transactions of goods and services and movements of natural persons.

Another area where ICT could play an enhanced role is in people-to-people connectivity. In the MPAC, people-to-people connectivity is seen as "the socio-cultural glue that supports and anchors the various initiatives toward greater physical connectivity as well as the regulatory and institutional reforms that are needed to ensure institutional connectivity in the ASEAN region."[18]

The MPAC identified two key strategies to enhance people-to-people connectivity: 1) to promote deeper intra-regional social and cultural understanding, and 2) to encourage greater intra-ASEAN people mobility.[19]

The first key action identified to promote deeper inter-regional social and cultural understanding is to "establish coordinated but distributed Virtual Learning Resource Centres on the People, Culture, History, Places of Interest, and Economy of each ASEAN Member State by 2012". The rationale given was that "the advent of Internet presents an opportunity for each ASEAN member state to share information through dedicated website(s) about its people, culture, history, economy, and places of interest. The websites are interlinked and coordinated through the ASEAN Committee on Culture and Information (COCI)."

The idea of using websites to share information is also outmoded. With the evolution of the original World Wide Web (Web 1.0) to Web 2.0, we now have sites that "allows users to interact and collaborate with each other in a social media dialogue as creators (prosumers) of user-generated content in a virtual community, in contrast to websites where users (consumers) are limited to the passive viewing of content that was created for them".[20] While Young ASEAN is leading the global Web 2.0 charge, Official ASEAN is still thinking in terms of Web 1.0.

Key action (ix) seeks to "promote understanding of common cultures and history of ASEAN through regular cultural events" gives a nod to virtual learning resource centres.[21] However, it was explained that "apart from the curricular offerings/education modules and virtual learning resource centres, the building of a sense of community in the region is best facilitated by direct people-to-people interaction and cooperative endeavours. There are many possible areas for such people-to-people cooperative endeavours."

Not only is building a community of half a billion through face-to-face interaction a very large task, this perspective also runs counter to an important sociological point: "Our conceptions of revolution, and of social integration itself, remain shaped too much by experiences in directly interpersonal relations and give too little attention to the growing importance of indirect relationships mediated by technology and complex organizational structures."[22]

Another ICT related proposal is key action (x) where it seeks to "optimise the use of ICT as a tool to promote ASEAN people engagement and empowerment in the context of ASEAN Community building and identity by 2015". It is explained that "ICT can be harnessed to assist ASEAN in facilitating policy coordination, enhancing its coordination with stakeholders, and creating a regional identity. Through the use of ICT, ASEAN member states can facilitate communication among and between their peoples and stakeholders and effectively manage information regarding ASEAN and its initiatives in a manner that is not bounded by physical restrictions such as distance."

Bridging the Two ASEANs

For the two ASEANs to meet, it is imperative that Official ASEAN go beyond its view of ICT as merely facilitating infrastructure. It must see ICT as a transformational tool.

Manuel Castells, who espouses the "network society" perspective, believes that we "have entered a new technological paradigm, centred around microelectronics-based, information/communication technologies, and genetic engineering".[23] What makes this new paradigm different and unique is:

> ... the use of knowledge-based, information technologies to enhance and accelerate the production of knowledge and information, in a self-expanding, virtuous circle. Because information processing is at the source of life, and of social action, every domain of our eco-social system is thereby transformed.[24]

ASEAN's success in regional integration and community building is partly dependent on its ability to harness ICT in the following areas: 1) horizontal and vertical policy coordination, 2) deepening stakeholder participation, and 3) helping create a regional identity, particularly among the youth.

ICT and Policy Coordination

ASEAN has created new bodies to enhance its policy coordination efforts. The ASEAN Coordinating Council and the three ASEAN Community Councils were created to enhance horizontal policy coordination — procedures and offices that are established ensure that the overall goal of community-building is served and that there are no overlaps or inconsistencies in the output of the various sectoral bodies and processes. On the other hand, the ASEAN Sectoral Ministerial bodies, the (new) Committee of Permanent Representatives to ASEAN (CPR), and the ASEAN National Secretariat of each member state may be seen as bodies to enhance vertical policy coordination.

I believe that the work of these bodies, including that of the ASEAN Secretariat, would be greatly enhanced if they use ICT more intensively. At present, ICT use in these bodies is limited to the use of office productivity tools (email, word processing, and spreadsheets) and web browsers.

I also believe that the use of conferencing and collaboration tools would significantly enhance the coordination capacities of these bodies.

ASEAN should examine the new software-based conferencing solutions for audio and web conferencing and continued face-to-face conferencing via video. Private sector companies who use these capabilities have achieved increased efficiencies, total cost savings, and environmental footprint reductions.

Another ICT application that ASEAN can use to respond to the challenge of horizontal and vertical policy cooperation is collaborative software. Collaborative software refers to applications that support interaction among individuals in the decision-making process. Collaborative software are designed to transform the way documents and rich media are shared in an organization, in order to enable more effective team collaboration. Collaborative software facilitate and manage group activities such as electronic calendars, project management systems, workflow systems, and knowledge management systems.

Like conferencing, collaborative software can make ASEAN more efficient and even reduce the length and/or frequency of ASEAN Working Groups and Senior Officials and Ministerial Meetings.

ICT and a More Inclusive Regionalism

An inclusive institution of governance has been one of ASEAN's goals and during the 38th anniversary of ASEAN, Indonesia's President Yudhoyono underscored the need to enlist the people into the cycle of planning, implementation, monitoring, and re-planning of programmes and projects.

Three non-state actors (business community, research community, and the non-governmental organizations/civil society organizations) have had varying degrees of success in terms of participating in ASEAN processes. Their success points to the important role that entities associated with ASEAN could play in developing ideas and proposals for ASEAN consideration. It is time for ASEAN to explore using ICT to enhance its policy dialogue with civil society organizations, academia and research institutes, and interested citizens of ASEAN member countries.

eParticipation, or using ICT as another medium for participation in policy making for selected entities, can be used to enhance ASEAN's policy dialogue. One of the interesting initiatives of the U.S. government in engaging a broader public in government decision-making is the "Peer to Patent" project. According to its main proponent, the goal is to "transform (the Patent Office's) closed, centralized process and construct architecture for open participation that unleashes the 'cognitive surplus' of the scientific and technical community". The heart of the Peer to Patent project is a website aimed at soliciting information from technical and scientific experts that would help the patent examiner do a more thorough assessment of the claims of patent applicants.

Creating a Regional Identity

The ASEAN Charter declared the commitment of the peoples of Southeast Asia to intensify community building through enhanced regional cooperation and integration, in particular by establishing an ASEAN Community composed of the ASEAN Political-Security Community (APSC), the ASEAN Economic Community (AEC) and the ASEAN Socio-Cultural Community (ASCC).

However, ASEAN has been least successful in its socio-cultural community (and identity) building efforts. Among the concerns identified by ASEAN observers in designing the ASEAN Socio-Cultural Blueprint are: 1) the ASCC's lack of concrete drivers, 2) the possibility of needing two types of scorecards in the implementation of ASCC's initiatives, since they need to be done at national and regional levels, 3) the possibility of ASEAN member countries not having a common understanding of social issues, and 4) ASEAN, as an organization, not having the institutional capacity to translate these social issues into legislation.

ICT can help create and/or promote a regional identity by enabling the citizens of member countries, particularly the youth, to "imagine" an ASEAN community through social networking tools.

ASEAN could make use of blogs to reach out to its constituencies. The ASEAN Secretariat could publish "policy blogs" where it could discuss present policy initiative issues related to the community. A good example of using blogs to enhance a sense of community is the blog of former Singaporean Foreign Minister George Yeo.

Policy Recommendations

ASEAN faces the challenge of evolving into a more institutionalized organization capable of effectively and efficiently realizing its goal of greater regional integration. ICT can help ASEAN achieve this goal through:

- ASEAN's adoption of appropriate, robust, and cost efficient conferencing and/or collaborative software to be used by various ASEAN bodies or at meetings. The ASEAN Secretariat could evaluate and make recommendations on the specific tools/software;
- ASEAN's (through the Secretariat) development and/or adoption of appropriate eParticipation tools and initiatives to enhance the engagement with "entities associated with ASEAN" and other stakeholders;

- ASEAN's (through the Secretariat) studying of the use of a social networking strategy aimed at the ASEAN youth, in order to develop a sense of ASEAN identity;
- The ASEAN Secretariat's use of blogs and policy wikis in its information dissemination strategy; and
- ASEAN's appointing of a Chief Information Officer (CIO) to the ASEAN Secretariat, who will provide leadership for developing and implementing ICT initiatives in the Secretariat as well as the various ASEAN bodies. Initially, the ASEAN CIO can undertake these activities of:
  - Conducting an ICT audit within the Secretariat;
  - Developing an Interoperability framework within ASEAN;
  - Developing an Information Security policy; and
  - Developing an Enterprise Architecture for ASEAN, including the notion of an ASEAN Community Cloud.

NOTES

1. Marc Presnky, "Digital Natives, Digital Immigrants", <http://www.twitchspeed.com/site/Prensky%20-%20Digital%20Natives,%20Digital%20Immigrants%20-%20Part1.htm> (accessed 24 April 2011).
2. Yung-Hui Lim, "Latest Estimates for Facebook Users by Country — Asia (Quarter 1 2011)", <http://www.greyreview.com/2011/04/05/latest-estimates-for-facebook-users-by-country-asia-quarter-1-2011/>.
3. "PH ranked as top social networking nation", <http://newsbytes.ph/2011/03/25/list-ranks-ph-as-top-social-networking-nation/> (accessed 20 April 2011).
4. Patrick Winn, "In Asia, more users signing on to Facebook", 11 January 2011, <http://www.globalpost.com/dispatch/china/110110/facebook-growth-asia>.
5. <http://asiancorrespondent.com/37057/indonesia-officially-the-twitter-capital-of-asia/>. Subsequent information on Twitter is taken from this report.
6. "Survey shows young Asians fit 38hrs of activties into one day (but still manage eight hourse of sleep)", <http://asiamedianotes.wordpress.com/2008/06/18/survey-shows-young-asians-fit-38-hours-of-activities-into-one-day-but-still-manage-eight-hours-sleep/> (accessed 28 April 2011).
7. The countries included in this study are China, Hong Kong, India, Indonesia, Korea, Malaysia, Philippines, Singapore, Taiwan, Thailand and Vietnam.

8. "Singaporean youth top in Asia who couldn't live without phone", <http://www.synovate.com/news/article/2010/08/singaporean-youth-top-in-asia-who-couldn-t-live-without-their-mobile.html>.

9. ASEAN Secretariat, *Master Plan on ASEAN Connectivity*, Executive Summary (Jakarta: ASEAN Secretariat, January 2011), p. i.

10. Master Plan on ASEAN Connectivity, p. 2.

11. Ibid., p. 15.

12. Ibid., p. 7.

13. Ibid., p. 42.

14. Ibid., p. 15.

15. Ibid., p. 43.

16. Ibid., p. 18.

17. "Institution", <http://en.wikipedia.org/wiki/Institutions>.

18. Ibid., p. 52.

19. Ibid.

20. <http://en.wikipedia.org/wiki/Web_2.0> (accessed 26 April 2011). For a more technical discussion, see "What is Web 2.0?", <http://oreilly.com/web2/archive/what-is-web-20.html>.

21. MPAC, p. 53.

22. Craig Calhoun, "Community without Propinquity Revisited: Communications Technology and the Transformation of the Urban Public Sphere Sociological Inquiry (68:4) August 1998", p. 379, <http://www.nyu.edu/ipk/calhoun/files/calhounCommunityWithoutPropinquity.pdf>.

23. Manuel Castells, "Materials for an exploratory theory of the network society", *British Journal of Sociology*, vol. 51, no. 1 (January/March 2000): 9–10.

24. Ibid., p. 10.

REFERENCES

ASEAN Secretariat. *Master Plan on ASEAN Connectivity*. Executive Summary. Jakarta: ASEAN Secretariat, January 2011.

Calhoun, Craig. "Community without Propinquity Revisited: Communications Technology and the Transformation of the Urban Public Sphere Sociological Inquiry (68:4) August 1998". <http://www.nyu.edu/ipk/calhoun/files/calhounCommunityWithoutPropinquity.pdf>.

Castells, Manuel. "Materials for an exploratory theory of the network society". *British Journal of Sociology*, vol. 51, no. 1 (January/March 2000): 9–10.

Lim Yung-Hui. "Latest Estimates for Facebook Users by Country — Asia (Quarter 1 2011)". <http://www.greyreview.com/2011/04/05/latest-estimates-for-facebook-users-by-country-asia-quarter-1-2011/>.

"PH ranked as top social networking nation". <http://newsbytes.ph/2011/03/25/list-ranks-ph-as-top-social-networking-nation/> (accessed 20 April 2011).

Presnky, Marc. "Digital Natives, Digital Immigrants". <http://www.twitchspeed.com/site/Prensky%20-%20Digital%20Natives,%20Digital%20Immigrants%20-%20Part1.htm> (accessed 24 April 2011).

"Singaporean youth top in Asia who couldn't live without phone". <http://www.synovate.com/news/article/2010/08/singaporean-youth-top-in-asia-who-couldn-t-live-without-their-mobile.html>.

"Survey shows young Asians fit 38hrs of activties into one day (but still manage eight hourse of sleep)". <http://asiamedianotes.wordpress.com/2008/06/18/survey-shows-young-asians-fit-38-hours-of-activities-into-one-day-but-still-manage-eight-hours-sleep/> (accessed 28 April 2011).

Winn, Patrick. "In Asia, more users signing on to Facebook", 11 January 2011. <http://www.globalpost.com/dispatch/china/110110/facebook-growth-asia>.

9

INTEGRATION OF ENERGY INFRASTRUCTURE TOWARDS ASEAN'S CONNECTIVITY

Nguyen Manh Hung and Beni Suryadi

ASEAN's Energy Situation

ASEAN is one of the fastest growing economic regions in the world and has a fast growing energy demand driven by economic and demographic growth. In 2010, its combined nominal GDP had grown to US$1.8 trillion. If ASEAN were a single entity, it would rank as the ninth largest economy in the world. The region's population of approximately 600 million people is 8.8 per cent of the world's population.

The region's economic and population growth had a consequential increase in primary energy consumption, which was registered at an average 3.6 per cent per annum from 1995 to 2007. Total primary energy consumption increased from 339 MTOE (million tonnes of oil equivalent) in 1995 to 511 MTOE in 2007. Among the energy sources consumed in the region, coal had the fastest growth rate increasing at an annual rate of 13.0 per cent mostly due to the installation of coal-fired power plants in the region. This is followed by natural gas which grew by 6.5 per cent per annum, increasing its share from 16.4 per cent in 1995 to 21.4 per cent in 2007. Oil remains as the major energy source in ASEAN but its growth was relatively slower than other sources of energy at 2.2 per cent per annum.

Electricity production increased from 157 TWh (Terawatt-hour) in 1990 to 504 TWh in 2005 and 571 TWh in 2007. This is equivalent to an average annual growth rate of 7.9 per cent over the 1990 to 2007 period.

The region as a whole is a net energy exporter while five of the member states are large energy importers. Although from 1990 to 2007 the region still has substantial net exports on coal and natural gas, in terms of oil, however, it has become a net importer since 1995 as the rapid increase in oil demand was not matched by oil production.

With the assumed GDP growth rate of 5.2 per cent per annum from 2007 to 2030, final energy consumption in ASEAN will grow at an average annual rate of 4.4 per cent from 375 MTOE to 1,018 MTOE in the business-as-usual scenario during the same period (ACE and IEEJ February 2011). This is very much higher than the world's average growth rate of 1.4 per cent per year in primary energy demand for 2008–2035 (IEA 2010).

For ASEAN, which has demonstrated a high economic growth and a high need for energy supply, the challenge to ensure a secure supply is an overriding concern. Energy is crucial to the transformation of ASEAN into a stable, secure, prosperous, rules-based, competitive, resilient, and integrated economic community by 2015 — ASEAN Economic Community (AEC) 2015. One way to face this challenge is by the integration of energy infrastructure in the region.

ASEAN Economic Community (AEC) 2015

The AEC is the realization of the end goal of economic integration as espoused in the ASEAN Vision 2020, which is based on a convergence of interests of ASEAN member countries to deepen and broaden economic integration through existing and new initiatives with clear timelines. The AEC will establish ASEAN as a single market and production base, making ASEAN more dynamic and competitive with new mechanisms and measures to strengthen the implementation of its existing economic initiatives; accelerating regional integration in the priority sectors, facilitating movement of business persons, skilled labour and talents, and strengthening the institutional mechanisms of ASEAN. The AEC envisages the following key characteristics: a) a single market and production base, b) a highly competitive economic region, c) a region of equitable economic development, and d) a region fully integrated into the global economy. These characteristics are inter-related and mutually reinforcing. Incorporating the required elements of each characteristic in one Blueprint shall ensure the consistency and coherence of these elements as well as their implementation and proper coordination among relevant stakeholders.

Energy cooperation is named under point B — Competitive Economic Region, B4. Infrastructure Development — of the AEC Blueprint that was declared by ASEAN SOE Leaders on the occasion of the 40th Anniversary of ASEAN and the 13th ASEAN Summit in Singapore. Regional collaboration, through interconnection of energy infrastructure, Trans-ASEAN Gas Pipeline (TAGP) and the ASEAN Power Grid (APG) Projects, allows the optimization of the region's energy resources for greater security. These projects also provide opportunities for private sector involvement in terms of investment, including financing, and technology transfer. Interconnected networks of electricity grids and gas pipelines offer significant benefits both in terms of security, flexibility, and quality of energy supply.

ASEAN Plan of Action for Energy Cooperation (APAEC) 2010–2015

At the 27th AMEM (ASEAN Ministers on Energy Meeting) on 29 July 2009, the ASEAN Ministers for Energy developed the ASEAN Plan of Action for Energy Cooperation (APAEC) 2010–2015 under the theme "Bringing Policies to Actions: Towards a Cleaner, more Efficient and Sustainable ASEAN Energy Community". The Plan aims to enhance sustainable energy supply through accelerated implementation of interconnecting arrangements for electricity and natural gas, judicious utilization of coal and renewable energy sources (including nuclear energy) as an option, and promotion of energy efficiency and conservation to stimulate regional economic growth and environmental protection. APAEC 2010–2015 is the third series of the implementation plan, a continuation of the two previous energy plans, namely: APAEC 2004–2009 completed on 30 June 2009 and APAEC 1999–2004 completed on 30 June 2004. It supports the realization of the ASEAN Community towards 2015 and beyond. In addition, it also covers the energy component of the ASEAN Economic Community Blueprint 2015, such as ensuring a secure and reliable energy supply for the region through collaborative partnerships in the ASEAN Power Grid (APG) and Trans-ASEAN Gas Pipeline (TAGP), including the promotion of cleaner coal use, energy efficiency and conservation, and renewable energy (with biofuels as well as nuclear energy as an option), to support and sustain economic and industrial activities.

The APAEC 2010–2015 contains strategic programmes with some quantitative, aspirational goals or targets that are expected to move the region towards enhancing greater energy security and strengthen international cooperation, including financial institutions and dialogue partners, to tap their resources and expertise. It recognizes the available facilities of the ASEAN Economic Community and other instruments and avenues of ASEAN cooperation including the ASEAN Infrastructure Financing Mechanism to move the plan of actions to reality by 2015.

In spite of the current status and speculations on the energy market, the APAEC 2010–2015 presents many opportunities and challenges, as outlined in this chapter, to stimulate investment, trade, and cooperation in the energy sector in ASEAN. Moreover, this situation will be further cushioned by the physical integration of energy infrastructures such as the APG and the TAGP. This provides an optimal solution for stimulating and strengthening the economy of the ASEAN region.

The APG and TAGP are flagship programmes mandated in 1997 by the ASEAN Heads of State/Government under the ASEAN Vision 2020 towards ensuring regional energy security through promoting the efficient utilization and sharing of resources. As such, ASEAN leaders called for cooperation to establish interconnecting arrangements for electricity and natural gas within ASEAN through the APG and a TAGP.

ASEAN Power Grid (APG)

Currently, electricity accessed by roughly 67 per cent of the ASEAN peoples is made available through grid power supply, stand-alone, and distributed power generation systems. The region's electricity is produced through a mix of oil, gas, coal, hydro, geothermal, and other renewable resources. Electricity production increased from 157 TWh in 1990 to 504 TWh in 2005 and 571 TWh in 2007. This is equivalent to an average annual growth rate of 7.9 per cent over the 1990 to 2007 period. In the future, electricity production is projected to increase to almost 2,414 TWh in the BAU scenario or at average annual growth rates of 6.5 per cent.

To continuously and reliably meet the growing demand for electrical energy, however, capital investments for the installation of additional generating capacities and transmission lines are necessary. It was found that one effective way to lower the requirements for capital investments is to interconnect the power systems via transmission lines between neighbouring countries, so that the energy resources of the countries can be optimally harnessed. Enhancing electricity trade across borders, through integrating the national power grids of ASEAN member states, is expected to provide benefits — enabling the region to meet rising energy demands and improving access to energy services.

The Electricity Generation Authority of Thailand (EGAT), a member of the Heads of ASEAN Power Utilities/Authorities specialized body for ASEAN Power Grid, describes the grid as a win-win economic relationship among ASEAN countries. Those countries with abundant natural resources but with little requirement for electricity supply can generate income from their surplus power. Countries with high power demand can meet their electricity shortfalls with power import from neighbouring countries at reasonable prices. The ASEAN power grid will provide cheaper electricity supply for all members and ensure sustainability of energy resources as well as energy efficiency, which will enable ASEAN to be more competitive in the world markets.

To pursue the programme, ASEAN adopted a strategy, as stated in the APAEC 2010–2015 Program Area No. 1 ASEAN Power Grid, which encourages interconnections of fifteen identified projects (see Figure 9.1); first on cross-border bilateral terms, then gradually expanding to a sub-regional basis and finally to a completely integrated Southeast Asian or ASEAN power grid (APG) system.

FIGURE 9.1

Map of ASEAN Interconnection Grid

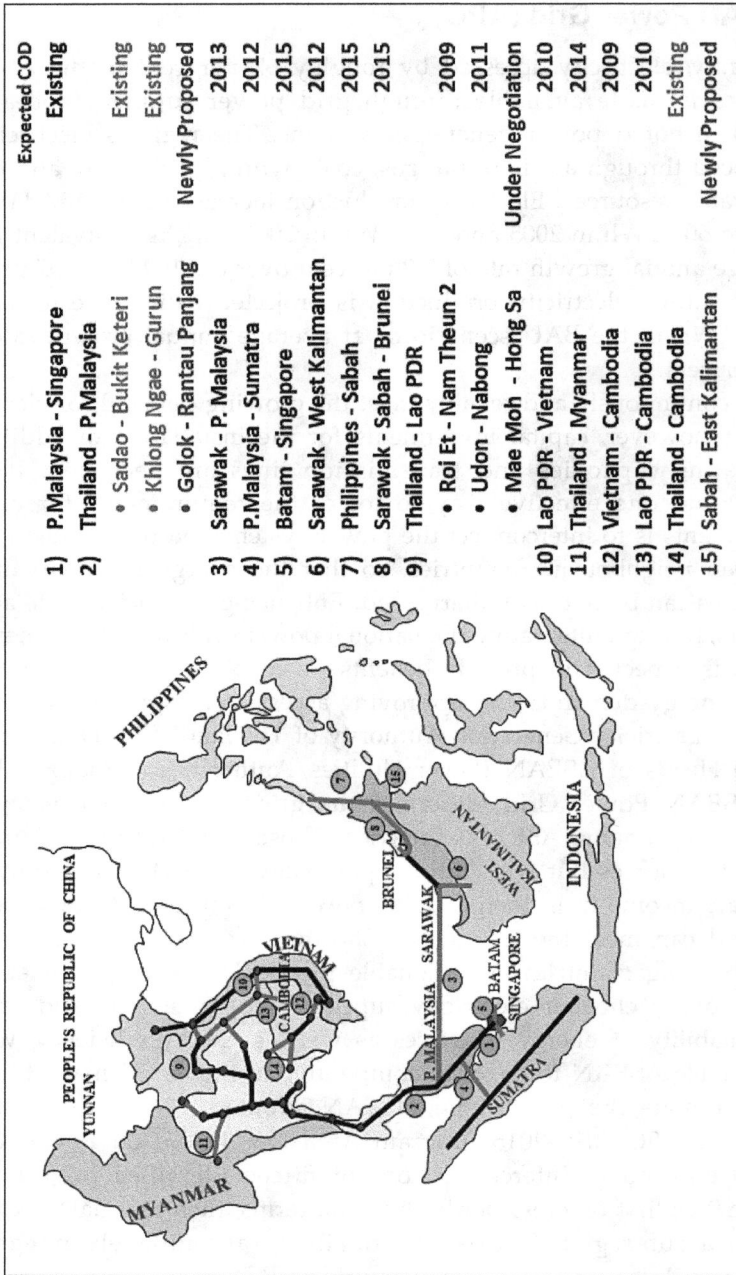

		Expected COD
1)	P.Malaysia - Singapore	Existing
2)	Thailand - P.Malaysia	
	• Sadao - Bukit Keteri	Existing
	• Khlong Ngae - Gurun	Existing
	• Golok - Rantau Panjang	Newly Proposed
3)	Sarawak - P. Malaysia	2013
4)	P.Malaysia - Sumatra	2012
5)	Batam - Singapore	2015
6)	Sarawak - West Kalimantan	2012
7)	Philippines - Sabah	2015
8)	Sarawak - Sabah - Brunei	2015
9)	Thailand - Lao PDR	
	• Roi Et - Nam Theun 2	2009
	• Udon - Nabong	2011
	• Mae Moh - Hong Sa	Under Negotiation
10)	Lao PDR - Vietnam	2010
11)	Thailand - Myanmar	2014
12)	Vietnam - Cambodia	2009
13)	Lao PDR - Cambodia	2010
14)	Thailand - Cambodia	Existing
15)	Sabah - East Kalimantan	Newly Proposed

Source: HAPUA Report on the 9th Regional Energy Policy and Planning–Sub Sector Network (REPP-SSN) Meeting, Singapore, 6–7 July 2010.

Currently, the APG is in progress with four ongoing interconnection projects and additional eleven projects are being planned for interconnection through 2015 (see Annex 1). The investment requirement of the APG is estimated at US$5.9 billion. A potential savings of about US$662 million dollars in new investment and operating costs is estimated — resulting from the proposed interconnection projects.

APAEC 2010–2015 for APG

The key objective of APG under APAEC 2010–2015 is to facilitate and expedite the implementation of the ASEAN Interconnection Master Plan and to further harmonize technical standards and operating procedures, as well as regulatory and policy frameworks among the ASEAN member states.

The strategies are:

1. To achieve long-term security, availability, and reliability of energy supply, particularly in regional cooperation on electricity through the Trans-ASEAN Energy Network;
2. To optimize the region's energy resources towards an integrated ASEAN Power Grid System; and
3. To further harmonize all aspects of technical standards and operating procedures as well as regulatory frameworks among member countries.

The ASEAN Interconnection Master Plan Study (AIMS) II

AIMS II proposed a comprehensive plan of regional transmission network that links ASEAN power systems. The first study (AIMS I) was completed and adopted in 2003 and now ASEAN adopted AIMS II that was completed in 2010.

This study concluded that the ASEAN region as a whole has abundant energy resources with great diversity. There are large hydropower potentials as well as huge oil, natural gas, and coal resources. This provides vast opportunities to exploit these energy resources collectively within ASEAN, thereby reducing the need and dependency on imported fuel from other regions. It is expected that interconnection will give rise to the following benefits: greater economic generation and transmission of electricity, greater reliability and security of electricity supply in member countries, and the provision of a platform for future energy trade.

AIMS-II confirmed that the power interconnection is economically and technically feasible within the region and identified at least fourteen generic interconnection projects for economic energy exchange and power import/export. The results of AIMS-II also identified significant savings in the investment of new power projects and operating costs within member countries. By 2025, there will be up to 19,576 MW (megawatt) of cross-border power purchase and 3,000 MW of economic exchange through the cross-border interconnections. The integration of ASEAN Network resulted in a net saving of 788 MUSD and a reduction in installed capacity by 2,013 MW.

Trans-ASEAN Gas Pipeline (TAGP)

TAGP aims to interconnect the gas pipeline infrastructure of ASEAN member states and to enable gas to be transported across borders of member states. The full adoption of the TAGP is being led by the ASEAN Council on Petroleum (ASCOPE) to enhance greater energy security for the region.

The original TAGP aims to develop a regional gas grid by 2020, linking the existing and planned gas pipeline networks of ASEAN member states. The updated ASCOPE-TAGP Master Plan 2000 involves the construction of 4,500 kilometres of pipelines mainly undersea, worth US$7 billion (see Figure 9.2). Eight bilateral gas pipeline interconnection projects, with a total length of approximately 2,300 km, are currently in operation (see Annex 2). They are: 1) Malaysia–Singapore in 1991, 2) Yadana, Myanmar to Ratchaburi, Thailand in 1999, 3) Yetagun, Myanmar to Ratchaburi, Thailand in 2000, 4) West Natuna, Indonesia to Singapore in 2001, 5) West Natuna, Indonesia to Duyong, Malaysia in 2001, 6) South Sumatra, Indonesia to Singapore in 2003, 7) Malaysia–Thailand Joint Development Area to Malaysia via Songkla in 2004, and 8) Malaysia–Singapore in 2006. These interconnections form part of the backbone of energy security and sustainability of the supply objectives of ASEAN to be accelerated by 2015, simultaneously serving as a key driver of growth to the various energy consuming sectors of the ASEAN economies.

FIGURE 9.2
Trans-ASEAN Gas Pipeline Infrastructure

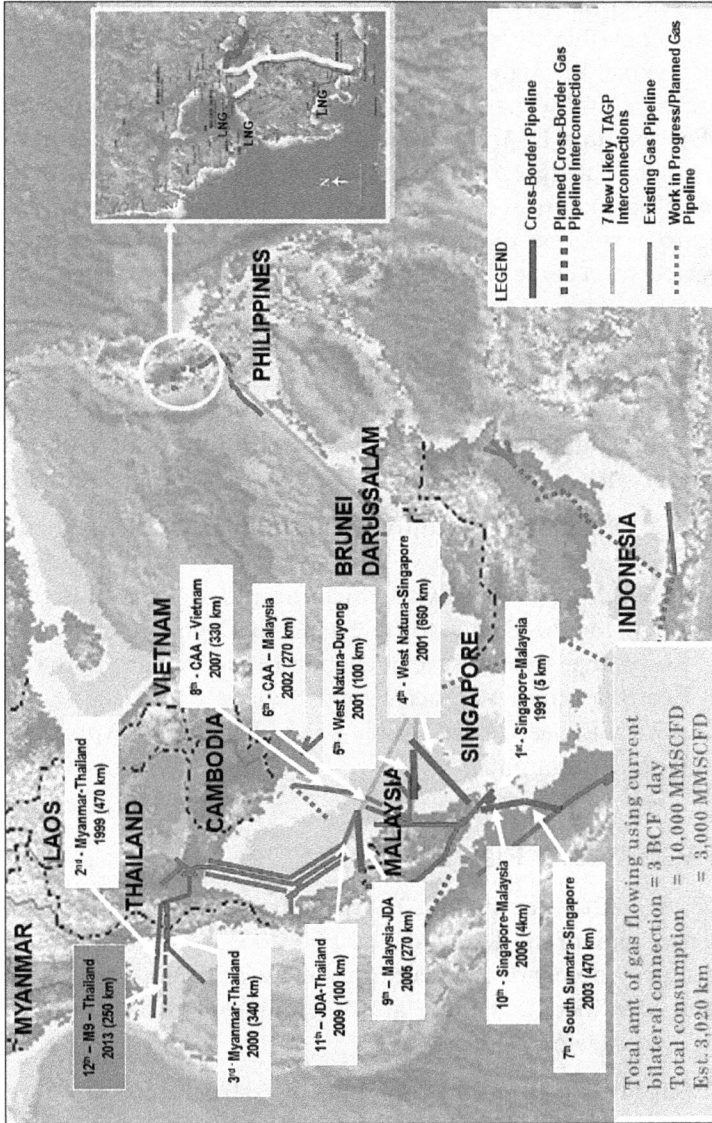

Source: HAPUA Report on the 9th Regional Energy Policy and Planning–Sub Sector Network (REPP-SSN) Meeting, Singapore, 6–7 July 2010.

Since 2000, the gas pipeline infrastructure has grown by 180 per cent from 815 km to 2,300 km of cross-border gas pipelines in 2008. These pipelines formed part of the TAGP, but all are bilateral in nature. To date, it is possible to transport gas molecules from Jakarta to Yangon and vice versa, through 3,020 km of bilateral connections.

But, there are no new significant gas reverse discoveries since year 2000. East Natuna D-Alpha remains the single largest resource but the major pipeline to the ASEAN region has yet to be developed because of pending commercial issues. Efforts are still going to bring the largest hydrocarbon resource to the market and this major pipeline infrastructure is expected to become the main TAGP carrier for the ASEAN region.

APAEC 2010–2015 for TAGP

The key objective of the TAGP, under APAEC 2010–2015, is to facilitate the implementation and realization of the project itself with a view of ensuring greater security of energy via gas supply. The strategies are:

1. ASCOPE member countries to collectively implement an ASEAN MOU on TAGP;
2. PERTAMINA and PSC Partners to undertake detailed feasibility study for the East Natuna Gas Field Development;
3. Respective ASCOPE member countries to implement the approved Roadmap for TAGP accordingly; and
4. ASCOPE Gas Centre (AGC) to implement the Approved 5-year Work Programme.

The TAGP Master Plan 2008

In 2008, ASEAN adopted the TAGP Updated Master Plan 2008 as an updated version of the TAGP Master Plan 2000. Following the conclusion of the supply-demand data verification by ASCOPE member states, it has been identified that there are no significant or major additions to the updated Master Plan due to:

a. Supply constraint — Pipeline infrastructure is a consequence and depends on confirmation of supply;
b. Energy security provided via LNG Regas Terminal — Gas transportation is not only via pipeline but also via LNG tankers.

Preliminary analysis has identified a significant supply gap to be faced in the future with the following observations:

a. There have been no new significant gas reserve discoveries since year 2000. The East Natuna D-Alpha field remains as the single largest gas resource and its commercialization, therefore, becomes even more crucial for the region;

b. There is a widening supply gap as early as 2015 rising to more than 12 BCF/day by 2025;

c. The gas supply shortfall reflects declining gas reserves causing gas supply to plateau and start to decline, while at the same time demand continues to rise strongly;

d. The supply shortfall could be addressed by new discoveries in the region, additional alternative supply from Coal Bed Methane (CBM), or by increased imports of LNG Gas to satisfy consumption; and

e. East Natuna commercialization is key at the ASCOPE level.

Scoping on the hypothetical model of the ASEAN Potential Pipeline Joint Venture Company (JVC) has been finalized and targeted for completion by the end of 2008. Development of a model JVC pipeline, the Gresik-Semarang gas pipeline pilot project, has progressed from a mere MOU to a signed Project Development Agreement (PDA) between two participating member states, namely Indonesia and Thailand. This pilot project is eyed as the prototype for a bigger scale ASEAN Pipeline JVC in the future.

Challenges and Barriers

As ASEAN heads towards the 2015 goal, further optimization of the power grids and gas pipelines would be necessary to minimize any unnecessary cost for the integration of energy infrastructure or what we call the Trans-ASEAN Energy Network.

For the grid, utilities and governments from each ASEAN member state must continuously keep assessing the needs and have the political will to carry out the interconnection projects as recommended by AIMS II. Member countries also need to establish a more cooperative structure to facilitate trading and oversee the physical stability of interconnected systems. System operators need to regularly meet in order to establish a transparent and standardized process to facilitate harmonization for cross-border interconnection and trade. A similar platform needs to be established for regulators and governments to collaborate in addressing regulatory issues, and thereto facilitating the harmonization of all power market structures in ASEAN.

For the pipeline, present bilateral interconnections should be optimized for the benefit of the region. The ability of all markets to access gas resources from almost any location in ASEAN will not be achieved until ASEAN makes a concerted effort on complex issues such as an open access system and the harmonization of gas specifications and transit principles. This will only promote gas trading beyond bilateral connections. Nevertheless, this would still be applicable beyond satisfying domestic consumption.

For the future, TAGP should continue and speed up its current work on the required framework where the entire network could be optimize for gas trading beyond bilateral interconnections. The required framework, government support, and business models need to be ready when the time comes to transport gas in the most economical and efficient manner. This proactive initiative is important for the region to understand the key success factors required for market readiness.

But among all of these issues, as there are no new significant gas reserve discoveries since year 2000, East Natuna D-Alpha remains as the single largest gas resource; ASEAN needs to aggressively explore potential leads and prospects in ensuring that current and future demands will be met.

Acknowledging the importance of regional energy cooperation and the need to build a strong foundation to expedite the implementation of the programme, and to ensure that the programme works efficiently, ASEAN should consider binding this as a Memorandum of Understanding (MoU). This MoU should aim to stipulate broad guiding principles to address critical issues including cross-borders issues. The MoU should include, amongst others, the following:

- Legal instruments — those that can endure the test of time and withstand changes in leadership;
- Regulatory framework — which promotes investments and addresses cross-border issues and barriers, so as to facilitate the implementation of the APAEC including the ASEAN Power Grid and Trans-ASEAN Gas Pipeline; and

- Technical considerations — which harmonize and standardize technical specifications to facilitate grid and pipeline interconnections across borders.

Among all the issues stated above, continuous and strong commitment from ASEAN member countries to cooperate and collectively pursue initiatives towards realizing the Trans-ASEAN Energy Network is the key.

REFERENCES

ACE and IEEJ. *The 3rd ASEAN Energy Outlook.* The ASEAN Centre for Energy and the Institute of Energy Economics, Japan, February 2011.

International Energy Agency (IEA). *IEA World Energy Outlook 2010.* Paris Cedex, France: OECD/IEA, 2010.

ANNEX 1

Status of Fifteen ASEAN Interconnection Grids

No.	Project Description	Utilities Involved	Status
1.	PENINSULAR MALAYSIA–SINGAPORE (Short term)	TNB SPPG	• Commissioned in 1985. • The interconnection is between Plentong 275 kV Substation in Johor, Malaysia and Upper Jurong 230 kV Substation in Singapore • For year 2007, the availability of the interconnection has been at 99.82 per cent.
2.	THAILAND–PENINSULAR MALAYSIA a. Sadao–Bukit Keteri (Short term) b. HVDC Links between Khlong Ngae–Gurun (Medium term) c. 132 kV Transmission Line between Golok Th–Rantau Panjang, Kelantan, PM	EGAT TNB	• The stage I interconnection is now used as a backup interconnection. • The Stage II (HVDC) interconnection project (transfer capability of 300 MW) was completed in September 2001. The HVDC system comprises a 110 km DC transmission line capable of transferring 300 MW between a 275 kV DC converter substation in Gurun, Kedah, Malaysia and a 230 kV DC converter substation in Khlong Ngae, Thailand. • Meetings have been held to study the upgrading of project from 300 MW to 600 MW. However based on the preliminary findings of the AIMS, the need to upgrade to 600 MW is found to be feasible only in 2024. • Newly proposed, the 1st Meeting between TNB and EGAT is under preparation.
3.	SARAWAK–PENINSULAR MALAYSIA (Medium term)	SESCo TNB	• Detailed technical studies are currently being undertaken in view of implementing the HVDC interconnection between Sarawak and Peninsular Malaysia for transferring 1,600/2,000 MW power from Bakun HEP to the TNB Grid system in Peninsular Malaysia.

No.	Project	Parties	Status
4.	PENINSULAR MALAYSIA–SUMATRA (Medium term)	TNB PLN	• The 1st stage of the 800/1,000 MW power transfer is targeted for completion in 2013. • Detailed feasibility study carried out jointly by TNB and PLN in collaboration with Shaw PTI USA (now Siemens PTI USA). Study completed in December 2005. Results presented to management of both TNB and PLN in February 2005. • TNB and PLN have agreed to further study the financial viability of the project. • Technical and financial studies have been done. Awaiting next level decision to steer the project forward. • Joint Workshop between PLN, TNB and Japan Bank for International Cooperation (JBIC) held in Kuala Lumpur in 14 September 2006. There is an intention of JBIC to finance the said project. • The detail engineering study is completed and seeking for financing support.
5.	BATAM–BINTAN–SINGAPORE–JOHOR (Long term)	PLN SPPG TNB	• PLN has conducted a preliminary study on the project and the study result has been extended to both TNB (Malaysia) and Power Grid (Singapore) in the 12th ASEAN Interconnection Meeting for review. • The Batam-Singapore interconnection has been identified by AIMS for completion by 2014 (1st Stage). • Due to the power market reform in Singapore, the development of this interconnection project would depend on the private sector/third party participation. • The detail engineering study is completed and seeking for financing support.

ANNEX 1 *(Cont'd)*

No.	Project Description	Utilities Involved	Status
6.	SARAWAK–WEST KALIMANTAN (Medium term)	SESCo PLN	• Both PLN and SESCo have completed the Basic Design Studies on the proposed interconnection. • Line route survey from the Mambong substation in Sarawak to the interconnection point at the town of Serikin has been completed since the last quarter of 2003. • AIMS recommended the interconnection in 2007 with maximum capacity of 300 MW as an energy exchange scheme. • The project has been studied in detail under the "Trans-Borneo Power Grid Interconnection Study" funded by EAEF. The Study considered an interconnection by the year 2008. Between 250–350 MW of power export by the year 2020 was considered. • A follow-up meeting between SESCO-PLN was held in Jakarta in December 2004 to discuss the actions necessary to get the groundwork going. • A meeting between SESCO and PLN was held in Kuching in August 2005 to discuss the further bilateral actions necessary to get the project going. • As a result of the August 2005 meeting, SESCO developed the terms of reference for a proposed "Control and Operations of the 275 kV Sarawak-West Kalimantan Interconnection" study to be jointly carried out. • The Special Meeting of Energy Working Group of BIMP-EAGA in November 2006 in Bandung, West Java proposed an action plan for the project.

No.	Project	Operator	Status
7.	PHILIPPINES–SABAH (Long term)		• The detail engineering study is completed and seeking for financing support. • The result of AIMS final report indicates that the project is technically feasible but not economically viable at 500 MW transfer capacities. • TRANSCO will propose further study with possible funding under EAEF. • Under reviewing the project timeline
8.	SARAWAK–SABAH–BRUNEI DARUSSALAM a. SARAWAK–SABAH (Short term) b. SABAH–BRUNEI DARUSSALAM c. SARAWAK–BRUNEI DARUSSALAM d. SARAWAK–BRUNEI–SABAH (Long term)	SESCo SESB DES	• Under study by SESB as part of the Bakun–Sabah Interconnection. • AIMS recommended the interconnection of the Sarawak–Sabah – Brunei Darussalam systems in 2019 with maximum capacity of 300 MW. • The project has been studied in detail under the "Trans-Borneo Power Grid Interconnection Implementation Study" funded by EAEF. The Study considered an interconnection by the year 2008. Up to 250 MW of power export by the year 2020 was considered. • The Special Meeting of Energy Working Group of BIMP-EAGA in November 2006 in Bandung, West Java proposed an action plan for the project.

9.	THAILAND–LAO PDR
	a. Nam Theun 2 (920 MW)
	b. Udon Thani–Nabong
	  – Nam Ngum 2 (597 MW)
	  – Nam Ngum 3 (615 MW)
	  – Nam Theun 1 (523 MW)
	  – Nam Ngiep 1 (261 MW)
		EGAT
		EDL
			• The Power Purchase Agreement (PPA) between EGAT and the developer of Nam Theun 2 Project was signed on 8 November 2003. The feasibility study of the transmission project on Thai side was submitted for approval from the Thai Government in February 2004. The interconnection project is expected to be completed in April 2009.
			• COD 1 November 2009
			• COD 1 March 2011

ANNEX 1 *(Cont'd)*

No.	Project Description	Utilities Involved	Status
c.	Mae Moh 3 (Nan)–Hong Sa		• Under negotiation
d.	Mae Moh 3 (Nan)–Nam Ou		• Under negotiation
e.	Roi Et–Savannakhet (Medium term)		• Under negotiation
f.	Ubol Ratchathani-Ban Sok (Medium term)		• Under negotiation • No progress • Pre-feasibility study completed in 2007 with ADB support
10.	LAO PDR–VIETNAM	EDL EVN	• MOU has been signed by Vietnam and Lao PDR to carry out these projects.
a.	Ban Sok-Pleiku (Medium term)		• The Master Plan was approved by the Ministry of Industry of Vietnam.
b.	Nam Theum 2–Ha Tinh (Medium term)		• COD 2014/15
c.	Nam Mo-Ban La (Medium term)		• Pending
d.	Xekaman3–Thach My (Medium term)		• Pending • COD 2009
e.	Luong Prabang–Nho Quan (Long term)		• The connection is under study now and expected to be completed in 2009.
11.	THAILAND–MYANMAR	EGAT	• Feasibility Study completed mid-2007
a.	Hutgyi (7 × 185 MW)		• Under the EIA study
b.	Tasang		• COD 2014

- Under negotiation for connecting lower dam (120 MW) to the Northern system of Thailand
- Under review pending financial support

No.	Project	Entities	Status
12.	VIETNAM–CAMBODIA (Short term) Chau Doc–Phnom Penh	EDL EVN	• Basic Design for Vietnam had been approved by EVN in 2002. • EVN is started construction of 220 kV transmission line in mid-2003. The project of Vietnam side is completed in October 2006. • The project is under construction and scheduled for commission in 2009.
13.	LAO PDR–CAMBODIA (Short term)	EDL EDC	• MOU already signed in 1999. • Preliminary discussion and site visit has been made in 2001 by EDC/EDL. • EDL is constructing the 115 kV double circuit transmission lines to Ban Hat substation which is 26 km from the border area and will be completed in mid-2005. • The PPA was signed in 2007 and COD in 2010.
14.	THAILAND–CAMBODIA (Short term)	EGAT EDC	• Thailand and Cambodia have reached a conclusion on the revision of tariff structure. • Transmission on both sides have been completed and start energized on 22 November 2007.
15.	Sabah–East Kalimantan	PLN SESB	• Newly Proposed

Source: HAPUA Report, Progress APGG 2008–2015.

ANNEX 2

Current and Future Pipeline Interconnections under TAGP by April 2009

No.	Pipeline Interconnections	Actual Date of Completion	Status
1.	Malaysia – Singapore, 5 km via Johore Straits	1991	Completed
2.	Yadana, Myanmar – Ratchaburi, Thailand, 470 km	1999	Completed
3.	Yetagun, Myanmar – Ratchaburi, Thailand, 340 km	2000	Completed
4.	West Natuna, Indonesia – Singapore, 660km	2001	Completed
5.	West Natuna, Indonesia – Duyong, Malaysia, 100 km	2001	Completed
6.	South Sumatra, Indonesia – Singapore, 470 km	2003	Completed
7.	Malaysia – Thailand JDA, 270 km	2005	Completed
8.	Malaysia – Singapore, 4 km	2006	Completed
9.	Malaysia – Vietnam, 325 km through PM3-Ca Mau Pipeline	2007	Completed
10.	East Natuna, Indonesia – JDA – Erawan, Thailand (~1,500 km)	Commencement date will be approximately 7 years from East Natuna gas supply sanction. Approximate volume to make each pipeline viable is 1 BSCF/ day (i.e. 36"–42"diameter of pipeline)	Subject to Supply Commercial viability
11.	East Natuna, Indonesia – Kerteh, Malaysia (~600 km)		
12.	East Natuna, Indonesia – Java, Indonesia (~1,400 km)		
13.	East Natuna, Indonesia – Vietnam (~900 km)		

Further Review

East Natuna – Indonesia – Brunei Darussalam – Sabah, Malaysia – Palawan	In the updated Masterplan, the proposed East Natuna–Indonesia–Brunei Darussalam–Sabah, Malaysia–Palawan, Philippine pipeline was deferred in view of the commercial viability and other economic considerations in establishing the interconnection for the Philippines leg. Moreover, regional assumptions on East Natuna Gas field have changed since the 2000 Original TAGP Masterplan. Much higher demand and limited gas supply plus high unproductive CO_2 content has increased cost of development of this pipeline.

Source: ASEAN Plan of Action for Energy Cooperation 2010–2015.

10

ASEAN ENERGY INTEGRATION: Interconnected Power and Gas Pipeline Grids

Tilak K. Doshi

ASEAN was established in 1967 with the signing of the Bangkok Declaration by the five founding members: Indonesia, Malaysia, Philippines, Singapore, and Thailand. Its stated goal was to promote regional stability, cooperation, trade, and economic growth.[1] During the 1990s, the bloc's membership expanded. Brunei Darussalam joined on 7 January 1984, Vietnam on 28 July 1995, Lao PDR and Myanmar on 23 July 1997, and Cambodia on 30 April 1999, making up what is today the ten member states of ASEAN.[2]

ASEAN Vision 2020, adopted by the heads of member states in 1997, calls for integrating ASEAN economies into a single production base, creating a regional market, fully integrated into the global economy and characterized by equitable economic development of its constituent members.[3] The Declaration of ASEAN Concord II in 2003 (also known as Bali Concord II) envisions a "stable and highly competitive ASEAN region in which there is a free flow of goods, services, investments and a freer flow of capital ...".[4] The Eminent Persons Group report on the ASEAN Charter in December 2006 recommends "particular attention should be given to strengthening economic linkages, (and) ensuring infrastructure and ICT connectivity between ASEAN Member States".[5] In 2006, ASEAN Economic Ministers recommended accelerating the integration process and creating a full-fledged economic community by 2015 rather than 2020 — a recommendation that was adopted by the ASEAN Summit held in January 2007.[6]

For regional economic growth to occur, infrastructure development and logistics are essential for increased intra-regional flows of goods, services, and investments. The "sinews" of regional economic development, quite literally, are the roads, bridges, ports, rail, airways, and energy and telecommunication networks. Cross-border infrastructure (CBI) development is crucial for enhanced regional cooperation and economic integration. There have been a series of policy declarations, summit agreements, and concords in the many ASEAN communiqués that refer to the promotion of CBI development.

Yet, in the midst of a huge and still rapidly growing literature on ASEAN regional economic integration, it is important to note that there is nothing in economic theory that favours "regional" economic integration over paths to economic development that are determined by long-distance international trade and capital investments. These are often shaped by historical relationships that were constituted by colonial rule.[7] Indeed, to most students of economic history it would come as no surprise that ASEAN intra-regional trade has played a minor role in the economic fortunes of Southeast Asian countries.

Energy Integration

Energy was identified as a key area for cooperation early on since ASEAN's founding. In the aftermath of the oil crisis in 1973, the heads of ASEAN member countries formed the ASEAN Council on Petroleum in October 1975, to promote cooperation among its member countries in times of emergency due to oil shortages. Initially, cooperation was viewed as a way of enhancing energy security, although of late climate change and the environment are also viewed as factors in support of a regional approach to the energy sector.

ASEAN Vision 2020 called for an "energy-integrated" Southeast Asia which would "establish interconnecting arrangements in the field of energy and utilities for electricity, natural gas and water within ASEAN through the ASEAN Power Grid and a Trans-ASEAN Gas Pipeline and Water Pipeline, and promote cooperation in energy efficiency and conservation, as well as the development of new and renewable energy resources".[8]

The ASEAN Plan of Action for Energy Cooperation (APAEC) 2010–2015 covers the energy component of the ASEAN Economic Community (AEC) Blueprint 2015 signed by ASEAN leaders in November 2007.[9] The Plan aims to "enhance energy security and sustainability for the ASEAN region including health, safety and environment through accelerated implementation of action plans, including, but not limited to: a) ASEAN Power Grid, b) Trans-ASEAN Gas Pipeline, c) Coal and Clean Coal Technology, d) Renewable Energy, e) Energy Efficiency and Conservation, f) Regional Energy Policy and Planning, and g) Civilian Nuclear Energy".

The Trans-ASEAN Gas Pipeline (TAGP)

The region's most ambitious mega-project, the TAGP aims to connect the gas reserves of the Andaman Sea, Gulf of Thailand, and South China Sea to the urban and industrial demand centres of Southeast Asia. Among its objectives are to ensure the reliability of gas supply to ASEAN members, encouraging the use of an environmentally cleaner fuel, and reducing dependence on oil and coal where economically substitutable.

ASEAN formed the TAGP taskforce in 1999, and ASEAN members signed an MOU on the project in 2002. According to APAEC 2010–2015, the "updated ASCOPE-TAGP Master Plan 2000" involves the construction of 4,500 kilometres of pipelines worth US$7 billion. There are a range of other estimates regarding the size and cost of TAGP, with one source citing $16 billion of investments for 5,100 km of new pipelines.[10] Potential link-ups with East and South Asia could increase investment requirements to over US$65 billion, according to another source.[11]

All large-scale, multilateral infrastructure projects face critical hurdles in the financing, construction, operation, and maintenance of networks. These include the requirements of common technological specifications and standards; stable contractual arrangements to handle supply, transport, and distribution; open access arrangements to common infrastructure; and norms and legal frameworks for arbitration and dispute resolution. The TAGP project is no different, facing key challenges in all these dimensions. The heterogeneity of ASEAN members with respect to income levels, stages of social and economic development, legal systems, and domestic pricing regulations of natural gas all pose significant challenges. Given the scale of the project, it has naturally been a subject of a number of feasibility and planning studies.[12]

Quite apart from the inherent challenges that all large-scale multilateral CBI projects face, the TAGP now faces a more basic question of relevance. From when it was first conceived and discussed,[13] the prospects for the TAGP are now subject to natural gas supply and demand fundamentals in Southeast Asia that have changed profoundly. If the TAGP project seemed overambitious when it was first mooted informally among ASEAN planners and diplomats in the mid-1980s, it now seems that the grand vision of a regionally interconnected grid of natural gas pipelines for ASEAN faces the threat of redundancy by fast paced developments in the natural gas industry over the past decade or so.

Current Status of Cross-border Natural Gas Pipelines in Southeast Asia

Currently, there are eight cross-border natural gas pipelines that are operating, with a total length of over 2,500 km (see Figure 10.1 and Table 10.1). The cross-border pipelines connect Peninsula Malaysia to Singapore (delivering gas since 1992), Myanmar to Thailand from the Yadana (1999) and Yetagun (2000) fields, Indonesia to Singapore with two pipelines, one from West Natuna (2001) and the other from South Sumatra (2003), and Thailand to Malaysia from the Joint Development Area in the Gulf of Thailand (2006).[14] An estimated US$14.2 billion has already been invested in some 3,900 km of bilateral pipelines in 2008.[15]

The successful financing and construction of these cross-border pipelines have occurred on the basis of commercial consortia that involve a range of private and public sector stakeholders in the energy sector, not as part of state-led multilateral negotiations envisioned by ASEAN communiqués of the TAGP project. Finance by multilateral agencies such as the Asia Development Bank (ADB) has played a role in some of the pipeline projects involving the less developed member countries of ASEAN with weak fiscal systems, such as Indonesia.[16] Nonetheless,

FIGURE 10.1
Existing Pipelines in Southeast Asia

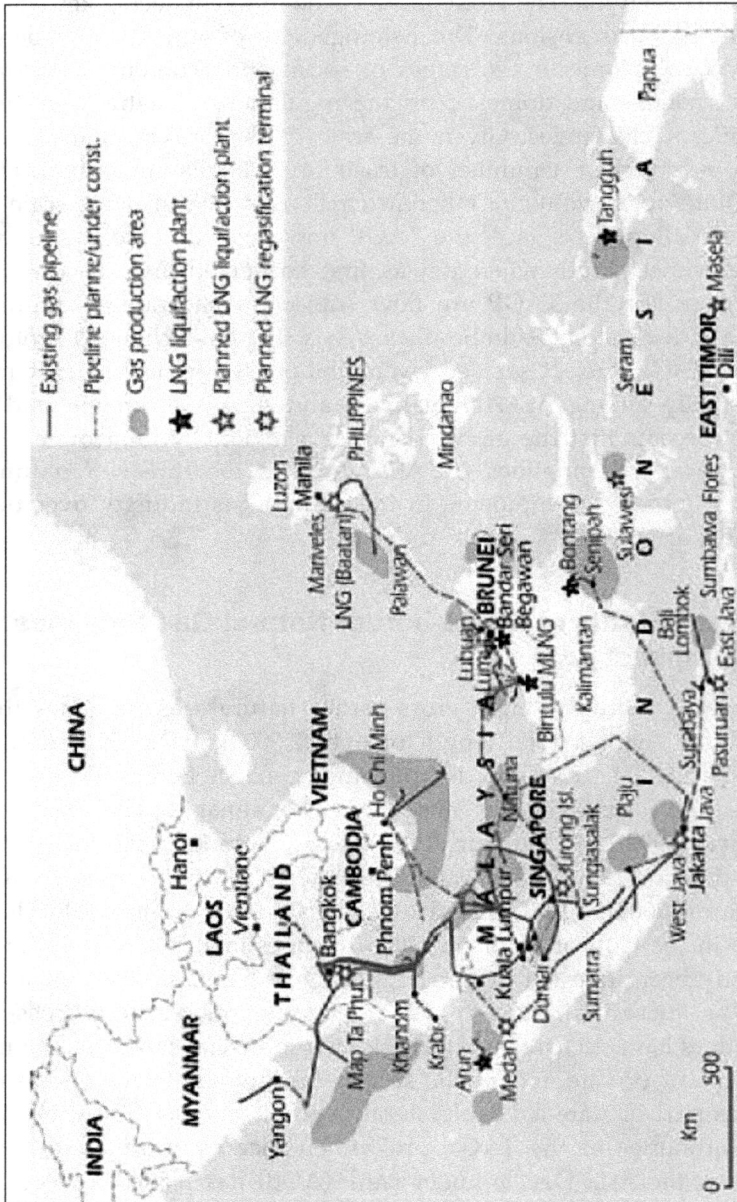

Source: IEA, *Natural Gas Market Review 2009* (Paris: IEA, 2009).

TABLE 10.1

Details of Existing Pipelines in Southeast Asia

Current gas pipelines	Distance (km)	Commissioning date	Capacity (mcf/d)
Peninsular Malaysia–Singapore	5	1991	150
Yadana (Myanmar)–Ratchaburi (Thailand)	470	1999	200
Yetagun (Myanmar)–Ratchaburi (Thailand)	340	2000	260
West Natuna (Indonesia)–Singapore	660	2001	325
West Natuna (Indonesia)–Duyong (Malaysia)	100	2001	250
South Sumatra (Indonesia)–Singapore	470	2003	350
Malaysia–Thailand Joint Development Area (JDA)	270	2005	1,020
Malaysia–Singapore	4	2006	110
Malaysia–Vietnam Joint Development Area (JDA)	325	2007	n/a

Source: International Energy Agency (IEA), *Medium-Term Oil and Gas Markets 2010* (Paris, France: IEA, 2010), p. 268; B.K. Sovacool, "Energy policy and cooperation in Southeast Asia: The history, challenges and implications of the trans-ASEAN gas pipeline (TAGP) network", *Energy Policy* 37 (2009): 2360.

existing investments in cross-border gas pipelines in Southeast Asia are the result of successful negotiations between sovereign owners of natural gas resources in the region and the international oil and gas companies who typically provide private equity and commercial debt instruments, along with the requisite technology and expertise to exploit such resources. Where commercial criteria of risk and reward simultaneously satisfied policy-makers' perceptions of national interest in the exploitation of gas resources, projects reached final investment decisions. And if cross-border transportation of gas helped commercialize otherwise "stranded" gas resources, by allowing gas to reach credible customers with long term sales and purchase agreements, then pipelines got built.

The Natural Gas Industry Outlook in Southeast Asia

Gas played little or no role in the early development of the hydrocarbon industry in Southeast Asia. The oil discoveries in Indonesia, Brunei, and Malaysia led to the rapid development of the oil sector in each of these countries. Natural gas, which was found usually as a by-product of oil production as associated gas, was either flared or used to support enhanced oil production via gas injection. Small quantities were used to support oil field facilities' power requirements.

The natural gas industry in Southeast Asia came into its own only as commercial ventures involving huge investments in large scale liquefaction, shipping, re-gasification, and downstream distribution facilities for Liquefied Natural Gas (LNG) became successfully established. For example, the massive US$940 million (or over US$3.5 billion in the 2005 dollar value) Arun plant in Indonesia with a design capacity for 9 million tons per annum was built early on in the evolution of the modern global LNG industry in 1973–74. Arun LNG had a willing and able buyer (Japan), which was ready to invest in order to diversify its fuel source for power generation. Far from domestic population and industrial centres, Arun gas had an insufficient domestic market, and potential demand centres from elsewhere in the region were not ready to finance capital intensive projects to import LNG. The Arun project makes for an interesting case study of how timing can affect the ultimate outcome of investment alternatives. In the mid-1970s, only Japan in East Asia had the financial capacity and the ability to absorb such a large quantum of gas for its energy requirements, and schemes for domestic or regional utilization by building a local pipeline infrastructure were rightly deemed to be inferior alternatives.[17]

Southeast Asia has been among the fastest growing economic regions in the world over the past three decades. Rapid economic growth in the region has been accompanied by rising demand for energy, and in particular, electricity. Natural gas used in Southeast Asia has experienced rapid growth in the power generation, industrial and household sectors, and the outlook is for continued rapid growth in the medium term; particularly now that carbon emission mitigation has become a factor of consideration in the setting of national energy policies everywhere.

The region boasts three well-established LNG exporting countries — Malaysia, Indonesia, and Brunei, two of which (Malaysia and Indonesia) were the world's second and third largest exporters respectively in 2009.[18] However, without further major discoveries and large new gas field development projects, regional gas supplies are dwindling relative to the rapid growth in domestic demand. Both Malaysia and Indonesia have expressed concern over their ability to meet rapidly growing domestic demand while sustaining their LNG and pipeline export commitments.

In recent years, Indonesia has increasingly oriented its gas policy from an almost exclusively export-focused one to one that includes domestic demand as the country's industrial sector faces an acute shortage of natural gas. According to media reports, the Indonesian government would no longer extend existing LNG export contracts in the future to meet the surge in the domestic demand.[19] While the country will continue to remain an important LNG exporter, it expects to be an importer of LNG as well, by as early as 2013. Its first floating storage and re-gasification terminal will be operational by 2012, and a slate of other small re-gasification terminals are planned to come on-stream at various locations in Java and Sumatra.

Malaysia is also expected to become an importer of LNG as its domestic gas supply is expected to drop to 1.4 Bcf/d by 2025 from a projected 2 Bcf/d in 2015.[20] The first LNG import terminal aimed at helping to ease the gas supply shortage in Peninsular Malaysia is expected to be operational from July 2012.[21]

Malaysian and Indonesian officials have been quoted in the press in recent years saying that pipeline gas exports to Singapore will likely diminish due to pressing domestic needs. In one recent media report, Indonesia was said to be looking at re-negotiating with Singapore, to replace its pipeline gas exports with LNG from East Kalimantan or Papua, so that Sumatran gas can be used domestically in nearby Java.[22]

With the increasingly binding constraints on natural gas supplies in the region, in the context of booming domestic demand, extensive new pipeline development for transporting natural gas in Southeast Asia is unlikely. Indonesia's giant East Natuna field (formerly known as Natuna D. Alpha) in the South China Sea — the region's largest gas field by far with an estimated 46 tcf of recoverable gas, is seen as the lynchpin of the TAGP. Among the pipelines envisaged in the TAGP, East Natuna is expected to supply gas via pipelines to Vietnam, Malaysia, Indonesia (Java), and Thailand. Excluding the "deferred" proposed pipeline to the Philippines, the gas reserves of the East Natuna field are to support about 4,500 km of pipeline supplies to demand centres in four countries.

However, given the very high CO_2 content of East Natuna's gas reserves (up to 70 per cent of total estimated reserves of over 220 tcf), exploiting the reserves will be technically and economically challenging. Official projections for gas production from the field see the first output only after 2020, reflecting the sheer scale and complexity of any project to exploit the East Natuna field.[23] In the current context where there are a number of large LNG projects at various stages of construction and planning in the Middle East and Australasian regions, the eventual development and exploitation of East Natuna remains subject to a high level of uncertainty.

Expected Growth in LNG Trade in Southeast Asia

The most notable development in the region's natural gas sector in the past few years has been the number of announcements of new LNG re-gasification terminals being planned, as many governments begin to see LNG imports as offering the better and faster option in meeting domestic energy requirements (see Table 10.2). Among the several countries in Southeast Asia that have announced plans or have already begun construction of LNG import terminals are Singapore, Thailand, Vietnam, and the Philippines, in addition to the several terminals planned by Malaysia and Indonesia as discussed previously.

It is apparent that the ability to import LNG has become a preferred option among ASEAN's policy planners intent on meeting rapid energy demands required for economic growth; it facilitates access to gas supplies quickly.[24] Floating LNG re-gasification vessels make for even quicker turnaround times to project completion for gas importers. For gas exporters, new technologies that support floating gas liquefaction vessels make the quick exploitation of remote and relatively small gas fields viable.

In sum, the prospects for the TAGP project look dim at least in the medium term to 2020, dependent as it is on the successful development of the vast but difficult to exploit reserves of the East Natuna basin. While there have been several studies commissioned on the viability of the TAGP and an MOU has been signed by the Energy Ministers at ASEAN meetings, it is generally expected that further pipeline development will be piecemeal and incremental, constrained by the fact that all cross-border pipeline projects with heavy capital requirements,

TABLE 10.2
Regional LNG Re-Gasification Terminals

Current terminal	Status	Capacity (mt)	Commissioning date
Thailand (Map Ta Phut)	Under construction	5	2011
Singapore (Jurong Island)	Under construction	3.5/6	2013/14
Indonesia (East Java)	Planned	1.5	2011
Indonesia (North Sumatra)	Planned	1.5	2011
Philippines (Quezon)	Planned	1.0	2011
Indonesia (West Java) (FSRU)	Planned	1.5	2012
Philippines (Bataan)	Planned	1.4	2012
Malaysia (FLNG)	Planned	3.8	2012
Vietnam (Vung Tau) (FSRU)	Planned	1	2012
Malaysia (Port Dickson)	Under Construction	5	2013

Sources: International Energy Agency (IEA), *Medium-Term Oil and Gas Markets 2010* (Paris, France: IEA, 2010), p. 269; "Gas using industries to build LNG receiving terminal", *Jakarta Post*, 17 February 2011; Argus Media, "Petronas to Launch FLNG Regasification Vessel in 2012", available <http://www.argusmedia.com/pages/NewsBody.aspx?frame=yes&id =730939> (accessed 25 November 2010); Upstream Online, "Vietnam hungry for gas", accessed <http://www.upstreamonline.com/live/article237625.ece>.

require a conjunction of regulatory, commercial, and technical conditions for successful private sector participation.[25]

ASEAN Power Grid (APG)

The ASEAN Power Grid (APG) was announced in 1997 by the ASEAN Heads of States/Governments under the "ASEAN Vision 2020" declaration, with its aims to ensure regional energy security and the efficient utilization of electricity resources. It envisages development in several stages; bilateral interconnections will be gradually expanded to a subregional basis and then to a completely integrated Southeast

Asian power grid system. There are currently four ongoing projects, with eleven new projects planned through to 2020 (see Figure 10.2 and Table 10.3).[26]

The ASEAN region is sub-divided into three subregional groups as shown in Figure 10.3. In "Group A", the Greater Mekong Sub-region (GMS), a number of interconnections are now under study for cross-border power exchange financed by the Asian Development Bank (ADB).[27] ADB will provide further funding for the GMS Power Interconnection Project Phase I, which will enable the interconnection of the power systems between Thailand, Lao PDR, Vietnam, and Cambodia and later will also include Myanmar.[28]

FIGURE 10.2
Power Grid Interconnection Projects in ASEAN

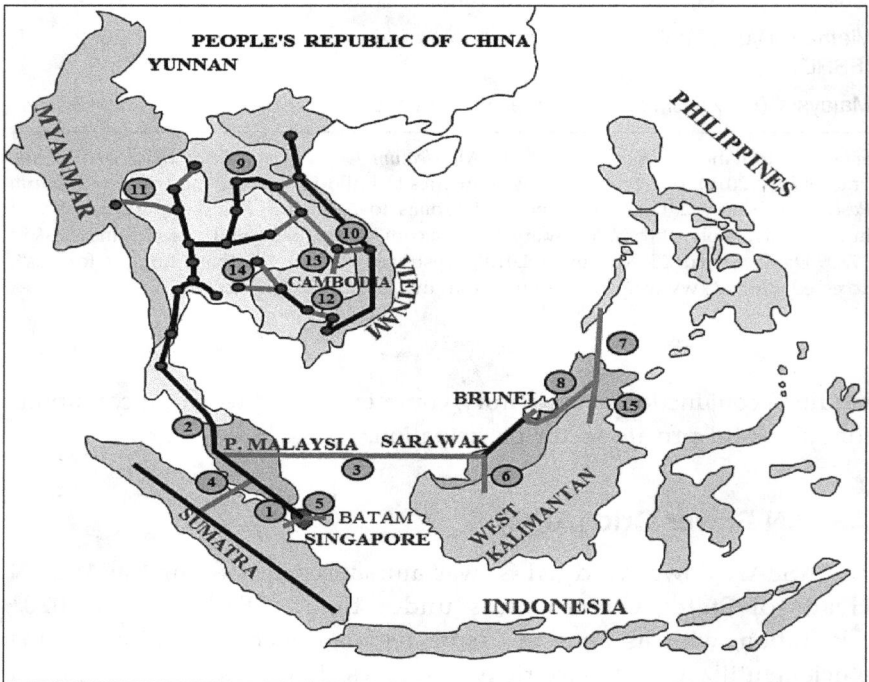

Source: Beni Suryadi, "ASEAN Economic Community 2015: Integration of Energy Infrastructure", *Oil, Gas and Electricity magazine (OGE Asia)*, vol. 5 (August–September 2011).

TABLE 10.3

Status of ASEAN Power Grid Interconnections

	Power grid interconnection	Expected COD
1	P. Malaysia – Singapore	Existing
2	Thailand – P. Malaysia	
	• Sadao – Bukit Keteri	Existing
	• Khlong Ngae – Gurun	Existing
	• Golok – Rantau Panjang	Newly proposed
3	Sarawak – P. Malaysia	2013
4	P. Malaysia – Sumatra	2012
5	Batam – Singapore	2015
6	Sarawak – West Kalimantan	2012
7	Philippines – Sabah	2015
8	Sarawak – Sabah – Brunei	2015
9	Thailand – Lao PDR	
	• Roi Et – Nam Thuen 2	2009
	• Udon – Nabong	2011
	• Mae Moh – Hong Sa	Under negotiation
10	Lao PDR – Vietnam	2010
11	Thailand – Myanmar	2014
12	Vietnam – Cambodia	2009
13	Lao PDR – Cambodia	2010
14	Thailand – Cambodia	Existing
15	Sabah – East Kalimantan	Newly proposed

Source: Beni Suryadi, "ASEAN Economic Community 2015: Integration of Energy Infrastructure", *Oil, Gas and Electricity magazine (OGE Asia)*, vol. 5 (August–September 2011).

In "Group B", which includes Indonesia, Peninsular Malaysia, and Singapore (IMS), the southern power grid of Thailand is integrated with the Malaysian grid. EGAT and TNB, the electric utilities in Thailand and Malaysia respectively, have agreed to review a further increase in the capacity of the interconnection. A study for grid interconnection between Peninsular Malaysia and Sumatra is also being undertaken by TNB, the Malaysian utility.[29]

"Group C" comprises of Brunei, Sabah, Sarawak, West Kalimantan, and the Philippines. The Trans-Borneo Power Grid (TBPG) will constitute one integrated system when the Bakun hydroelectric power station

FIGURE 10.3
ASEAN Subregional Groups

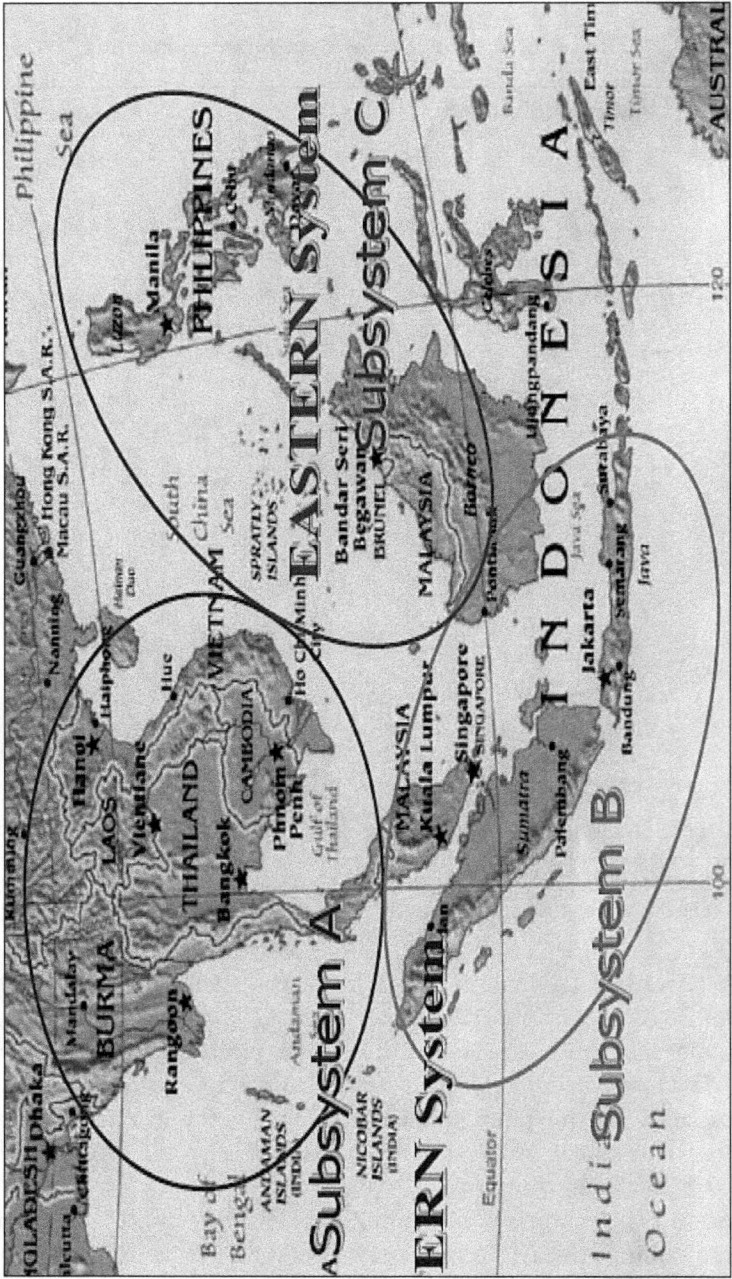

Source: A.P. Roesli, "HAPUA and the ASEAN Power Grid for Optimum Use of Energy Resources", <http://www.asean-sustainable-energy.
net/documents/libraries/001/HAPUASecretary%20akhir%20Bangkok%206-10-06.pdf>.

in Sarawak is commissioned. The TBPG project is a collaborative effort under the ASEAN Centre for Energy (ACE), Brunei–Indonesia–Malaysia–Philippines–East ASEAN Growth Area Business Council and the European Union under the European Union-ASEAN Energy Facility (EAEF).[30] The Philippines would be a stand-alone system, because the interconnection between Borneo and the Philippines is not economically viable within the planning period to 2020.

ASEAN member countries vary considerably with regard to their power sector regulations, market structure and technical characteristics, plant efficiency, transmission and distribution losses, HVAC/DC transmission lines, etc. Reflecting upon the heterogeneity of electric power markets among the ASEAN group, power tariffs for both industry and households differ markedly among different ASEAN member states. Key countries such as Malaysia and Indonesia have subsidized electricity, although both countries have announced their intention of slowly reducing such subsidies in favour of more targeted social welfare programmes.[31]

Brunei, Cambodia, Laos, and Myanmar have traditional vertically-integrated state-owned power utilities, while Indonesia, Malaysia, Thailand and Vietnam have state-owned utilities operating together

TABLE 10.4
Details of ASEAN's Electricity Sector

Country	Installed Capacity (MW)	T&D Losses (%)
Brunei	1,210	5.5
Cambodia	490	10.9
Indonesia	47,033	10.5
Lao	854	8.8
Malaysia	21,820	2.9
Myanmar	2,052	27.5
Philippines	16,845	13.5
Singapore	10,571	5.3
Thailand	35,894	6.8
Vietnam	14,755	10.2

Source: Enerdata, Global Energy and CO_2 Database.

TABLE 10.5
Electricity Prices Paid in ASEAN

Country	Electricity price paid by industry in 2008 (2005 US cents/kWh)	Electricity price paid by households in 2008 (2005 US cents/kWh)
Cambodia	14.41	10.43
Indonesia	4.86	4.59
Lao	4.52	3.27
Malaysia	5.75	5.91
Philippines	9.58	12.66
Singapore	10.91	14.72
Thailand	5.54	6.9

Source: Enerdata, Global Energy and CO_2 Database.

with private independent power producers (IPPs). In ASEAN, only the Philippines and Singapore have "unbundled" power sectors, with privatized power generators and independent grid operators.

There are significant technical and economic benefits to interconnecting power grids as envisaged in the APG. System electricity generation reserve capacity requirements would be reduced the larger the size of the system. Load factors would improve in a larger system due to higher utilization factors. This would allow for diversification of energy supply sources. Integration efficiencies could also encourage electricity market reforms in the region, as the benefits of shared power become apparent. In the Greater Mekong Sub-region (GMS), there is vast potential for exploiting yet untapped hydroelectric power in Laos and Cambodia for export.

However, there are also significant technological, operational, and institutional barriers to interconnecting the different power grid systems in ASEAN. The electric power sectors in different countries have evolved separately, and standards and technologies are different. Policy preferences with respect to reliability and affordability differ across the region. As already mentioned, the market structure in power generation and distribution differ across countries in ASEAN. Some countries still have vertically integrated utilities with a monopoly over generation, transmission, distribution, and retail of electricity, with prices set administratively for social welfare purposes. In gas-exporting countries such as Brunei, Indonesia, and Malaysia, gas is offered to electricity producers at subsidized prices to support electricity tariffs which are below costs of production. International electricity grid interconnections are complex, and power purchase and pricing agreements need to be sorted out prior to the commencement of grid interconnection projects. Liabilities of various parties have to be decided upon across different legal jurisdictions. IPPs and foreign investors cannot compete in an "uneven playing field", unless they are guaranteed off-take at predictable prices.

In countries where market pricing, unbundling, and privatization have not been achieved, the financial burden often falls on already-stretched public sectors in key ASEAN countries such as Malaysia and Indonesia, not to speak of the least developed countries such as Laos, Cambodia, and Vietnam. Market pricing, to reflect real costs of power, can have destabilizing consequences for governments intent on subsidizing electricity for the social welfare of its poorer citizens.

Progress in interconnecting power grids in ASEAN will likely continue on a bilateral basis, except in cases where a regional approach has strong motivation as in the GMS. Countries with a power surplus such as Laos and Cambodia with ample hydro resources could emerge as major electricity exporters within ASEAN, supplying much needed power to rapidly growing large neighbouring countries such as Thailand and Vietnam, as well as China, that constitute a vast market for energy imports.

Progress will likely be slower than as laid out by government planners, since ASEAN member states are still far away from privatizing or "unbundling" electricity sectors and encouraging full-fledged energy trading in open and transparent markets.

Conclusion

Harmonization of rules, regulations, and standards are necessary in ASEAN to achieve gains from trade in natural resources and electricity, and to benefit from market-led investments and trade. To capture economic benefits from market-based pricing in the key natural resource, infrastructure, and energy sectors, several ASEAN countries need to remove gas and power subsidies in favour of programmes that include well-targeted social safety nets. ASEAN governments, like their counterparts elsewhere in the developing world, face critical challenges to ensure popular support from key constituencies for market-oriented reforms in their energy sectors. Market-oriented reforms are needed not only to ensure fiscal health in countries which subsidize gas and power, but also to alleviate shortages of natural gas for rapidly increasing domestic demand. Governments need to maintain stable policy environments for private sector investments which require predictability and transparency.

A McKinsey study commissioned by ASEAN finds the region hindered by "fragmented markets, high transaction costs, and an unpredictable policy environment".[32] According to the study, if ASEAN member states are to remain competitive in the race for foreign direct investment (FDI) and export market share, they will need to step up their integration efforts. The point to note is that while reducing transaction costs in intra-regional trade, investments, and cross-border infrastructure development can assist ASEAN member countries' efforts to promote economic development, that is no substitute to key energy sector reforms that the bloc's constituent members need to undertake domestically.

As markets evolve, reflecting new developments in demand, supply, and technology parameters of the natural gas and power sectors regionally and globally, ASEAN planners will need to re-fashion some of the key "energy integration" initiatives that ASEAN member states have supported. If high profile multilateral cross-border infrastructure projects such as the TAGP are to remain relevant in an era of rapidly evolving markets and technologies, government planners and elected officials will need to be adroit in exerting regional integration efforts that have reasonable chances of success.

NOTES

1. ASEAN Secretariat, "Bangkok Declaration", <http://www.aseansec.org/1212.htm>.
2. "ASEAN Overview", <http://www.asean.org/64.htm> (accessed 27 May 2011).
3. The "ASEAN Vision 2020" declaration can be accessed at <http://www.asean.org/1814.htm> (accessed 27 May 2011).
4. ASEAN Secretariat, "Declaration of ASEAN Concord II", <http://www.aseansec.org/15159.htm>.

5. "Report of the Eminent Persons Group (EPG) on the ASEAN Charter", <http://www.aseansec.org/19247.pdf> (accessed 27 May 2011).
6. Rodolfo Severino, "An ASEAN Economic Community by 2015?", <http://www.iseas.edu.sg/aseanstudiescentre/asco09–10.pdf>.
7. P. Coclanis and T.K. Doshi, "Globalization in Southeast Asia", *Annals of the American Academy of Political and Social Science*, vol. 570, Dimensions of Globalization (July 2000): 49–64.
8. "ASEAN Vision 2020", op. cit.
9. "ASEAN Plan of Action for Energy Cooperation (APAEC) 2010–2015", <http://www.asean.org/22675.pdf>.
10. B. Sovacool, "Energy policy and cooperation in Southeast Asia: The history, challenges and implications of the trans–ASEAN gas pipeline (TAGP) network", *Energy Policy* 37 (2009): 2356–67.
11. P. Ohli, "Trans-Asian gas network could cost $66 billion", *Pipeline and Gas Journal* 221, no. 8 (1994): 1–2.
12. In 1994, for example, ASEAN commissioned a regional "Masterplan Study on Natural Gas Development and Utilization in ASEAN" with technical assistance from the EU. See "ASEAN Plan of Action for Energy Cooperation 1999–2004", <http://www.aseansec.org/11704.htm>.
13. While energy cooperation in ASEAN was first mooted in the aftermath of the oil crisis in 1975 with the formation of ASCOPE, the concept of a network of gas pipelines connecting the region was first discussed in 1986, and formally announced at an ASEAN meeting on Energy Cooperation in 1990. See Sovacool, op. cit., pp. 2357–58.
14. "Natural Gas Infrastructure Development: Southeast Asia", Asia Pacific Research Centre, 2000; various press reports.
15. "ASEAN and ASCOPE lay foundation for growth", *Petromin Pipeliner* (January–March 2011), <http://www.pm-pipeliner.safan.com/mag/ppl0311/r12.pdf>.
16. See, for instance, Asian Development Bank, "Loan 1357–INO: Gas transmission and distribution project", <http://www.adb.org/Documents/Environment/ino/ino_gas_transmission.pdf> (accessed 2008).
17. F. Von der Mehden and S. Lewis, "Liquified natural gas from Indonesia: The Arun project", in *Natural Gas and Geopolitics: From 1970 to 2040*, edited by D. Victor, A. Jaffe and M. Hayes (Cambridge: Cambridge University Press, 2006).
18. BP Statistical Review of World Energy 2010.
19. See, for instance, "Indonesia will no longer renew LNG export contracts", *Xinhua*, 18 February 2010.
20. "Malaysia LNG's new sick man?", *World Gas Intelligence*, 15 December 2010.
21. K.P. Lee, "Petronas CEO: Regas plant to be ready July 2012", *Dow Jones Newswire*, 4 October 2010.

22. "RI may lower gas export to Singapore", *Jakarta Post*, 17 June 2011.
23. In December 2010, Pertamina, the Indonesian national oil company, appointed ExxonMobil, together with Petronas and Total S.A., as partners in the development of the East Natuna gas block. See E. Maulia, "Politicians question ExxonMobil's presence in East Natuna", *Jakarta Post*, 27 January 2011.
24. See, for instance, the forthcoming note on the Southeast Asian gas sector in the IEA's World Energy Outlook 2011.
25. The possibilities for opportunistic behaviour by parties that jointly undertake large, highly specific and irreversible investments to support economic exchange that typically make cross-border infrastructure investments particularly fraught with negotiation failures have been studied by institutional economists. See, for instance, Oliver Williamson, "Credible Commitments: Using Hostages to Support Exchange", *The American Economic Review*, vol. 73, no. 4 (1983): 519–40.
26. The Heads of ASEAN Power Utilities/Authorities (HAPUA) commissioned the ASEAN Interconnections Masterplan Study (AIMS) which was completed in 2003. See A.P. Roesli, "HAPUA and the ASEAN Power Grid for Optimum Use of Energy Resources", <http://www.asean-sustainable-energy.net/documents/libraries/001/HAPUASecretary%20akhir%20Bangkok%206-10-06.pdf>.
27. See Asian Development Bank, "GMS Sector Activities", <http://www.adb.org/gms/sector-activities/archive-energy.asp>.
28. See ADB Project Information Document, <http://www.adb.org/Documents/TARs/REG/tar_oth_36044.pdf>.
29. See ASEAN Interconnections Projects, <http://ace2.aseanenergy.org/energy_sector/electricity/fourteen_projects/fourteen_projects.htm>.
30. See "Trans-Borneo Power Grid Connections", <http://www.bimpbc.org/eabc5.asp>.
31. See, for instance, "Malaysia to revise electricity tariffs", <http://uk.reuters.com/article/2008/02/04/malaysia-economy-fuel-idUKKLR4031820080204>, Reuters, 4 February 2008, and "Indonesia to lift subsidies gradually", <http://www.thejakartaglobe.com/business/indonesia-to-lift-electricity-subsidies-gradually/365652>, *Jakarta Globe*, 24 March 2010.
32. The McKinsey report is cited in "Report of EPG on the ASEAN Charter", <http://www.aseansec.org/19247.pdf>, December 2006.

REFERENCES

ADB Project Information Document. <http://www.adb.org/Documents/TARs/REG/tar_oth_36044.pdf>.
APERC. "Natural Gas Infrastructure Development: Southeast Asia". Asia Pacific Research Centre, 2000.

Argus Media. "Petronas to Launch FLNG Regasification Vessel in 2012". <http://www.argusmedia.com/pages/NewsBody.aspx?frame=yes&id=730939> (accessed 25 November 2010).

"ASEAN and ASCOPE lay foundation for growth". *Petromin Pipeliner* (January–March 2011). <http://www.pm-pipeliner.safan.com/mag/ppl0311/r12.pdf>.

ASEAN Interconnections Projects. <http://ace2.aseanenergy.org/energy_sector/electricity/fourteen_projects/fourteen_projects.htm>.

ASEAN Secretariat. "ASEAN Overview". <http://www.asean.org/64.htm> (accessed 27 May 2011).

———. "ASEAN Plan of Action for Energy Cooperation 1999–2004". <http://www.aseansec.org/11704.htm>.

———. "ASEAN Plan of Action for Energy Cooperation (APAEC) 2010–2015". <http://www.asean.org/22675.pdf>.

———. "ASEAN Vision 2020". <ttp://www.aseansec.org/1814.htm> (accessed 27 May 2011).

———. "Bangkok Declaration". <http://www.aseansec.org/1212.htm>.

———. "Declaration of ASEAN Concord II". <http://www.aseansec.org/15159.htm>.

———. "Report of the Eminent Persons Group (EPG) on the ASEAN Charter". <http://www.aseansec.org/19247.pdf> (accessed 27 May 2011).

Asian Development Bank. "GMS Sector Activities". <http://www.adb.org/gms/sector-activities/archive-energy.asp>.

———. "Loan 1357–INO: Gas transmission and distribution project". <http://www.adb.org/Documents/Environment/ino/ino_gas_transmission.pdf> (accessed 2008).

Coclanis, P. and T.K. Doshi. "Globalization in Southeast Asia". *Annals of the American Academy of Political and Social Science*, vol. 570, Dimensions of Globalization (July 2000): 49–64.

"Gas using industries to build LNG receiving terminal". *Jakarta Post*, 17 February 2011.

"Indonesia to lift subsidies gradually". *Jakarta Globe*, <http://www.thejakartaglobe.com/business/indonesia-to-lift-electricity-subsidies-gradually/365652> (accessed 24 March 2010).

"Indonesia will no longer renew LNG export contracts". *Xinhua*, 18 February 2010.

International Energy Agency (IEA). *Medium-Term Oil and Gas Markets 2010*. Paris, France: IEA, 2010.

Lee, K.P. "Petronas CEO: Regas plant to be ready July 2012". *Dow Jones Newswire*, 4 October 2010.

"Malaysia LNG's new sick man?". *World Gas Intelligence*, 15 December 2010.

"Malaysia to revise electricity tariffs". Reuters, <http://uk.reuters.com/article/2008/02/04/malaysia-economy-fuel-idUKKLR4031820080204> (accessed 4 February 2008).

Maulia, E. "Politicians question ExxonMobil's presence in East Natuna". *Jakarta Post*, 27 January 2011.

Ohli, P. "Trans-Asian gas network could cost $66 billion". *Pipeline and Gas Journal* 221, no. 8 (1994): 1–2.

"Report of EPG on the ASEAN Charter". <http://www.aseansec.org/19247.pdf> (accessed December 2006).

"RI may lower gas export to Singapore". *Jakarta Post*, 17 June 2011.

Roesli, A.P. "HAPUA and the ASEAN Power Grid for Optimum Use of Energy Resources". <http://www.asean-sustainable-energy.net/documents/libraries/001/HAPUASecretary%20akhir%20Bangkok%206-10-06.pdf>.

Severino, R. "An ASEAN Economic Community by 2015?". <http://www.iseas.edu.sg/aseanstudiescentre/asco09-10.pdf>.

Sovacool, B. "Energy policy and cooperation in Southeast Asia: The history, challenges and implications of the trans-ASEAN gas pipeline (TAGP) network". *Energy Policy* 37 (2009): 2356–67.

"Trans-Borneo Power Grid Connections". <http://www.bimpbc.org/eabc5.asp>.

Upstream Online. "Vietnam hungry for gas". <http://www.upstreamonline.com/live/article237625.ece>.

Von der Mehden, F. and S. Lewis. "Liquified natural gas from Indonesia: The Arun project". In *Natural Gas and Geopolitics: From 1970 to 2040*, edited by D. Victor, A. Jaffe, and M. Hayes. Cambridge: Cambridge University Press, 2006.

Williamson, Oliver. "Credible Commitments: Using Hostages to Support Exchange". *The American Economic Review*, vol. 73, no. 4 (1983): 519–40.

III

IMPLEMENTATION
AND POLICY
RECOMMENDATIONS

III

IMPLEMENTATION
AND POLICY
RECOMMENDATIONS

11

MASTER PLAN ON ASEAN CONNECTIVITY "FROM PLAN TO IMPLEMENTATION"

Somsak Pipoppinyo

Introduction: Concept and Development of ASEAN Connectivity

ASEAN leaders first discussed the concept of ASEAN Connectivity at the 15th ASEAN Summit in October 2009. The leaders observed that ASEAN has great potential to physically anchor itself as the transportation, ICT, and tourism hub of this region. Enhanced connectivity between ASEAN member states will encourage competitive growth; facilitate economies of agglomeration and integrated production networks; enhance intra-regional trade; and attract investments.

At the conclusion, the ASEAN leader called for development of an ASEAN Master Plan on Regional Connectivity. The task was assigned to the High Level Task Force on ASEAN Connectivity (HLTF-AC), in consultation and cooperation with relevant international organizations — the Asian Development Bank (ADB), Economic Research Institute for ASEAN and East Asia (ERIA), United Nations Economic and Social Commission for Asia and the Pacific (ESCAP) and the World Bank.

In developing the Master Plan on ASEAN Connectivity (MPAC), the HLTF-AC met five times from March to October 2011. The HLTC-AC looked at the state of regional cooperation in ASEAN, including initiatives at the subregional level, in the three dimensions of physical, institutional and people-to-people connectivity. It has been recognized that ASEAN had put in place numerous programmes and initiatives, and some good progress had been made, for building and enhancing regional connectivity. In doing so, the HLTC-AC is able to do a mapping of what are the ongoing programmes, projects and initiatives that are happening both within and outside ASEAN, draw the complementarities and synergies, identify gaps and develop strategies and actions. The Master Plan thus aims to consolidate and provide a more focused approach to these efforts in order to enhance regional connectivity.

In the elaboration, the ADB, ERIA, ESCAP and World Bank had given valuable inputs and support until the Master Plan on ASEAN Connectivity (MPAC) was completed and adopted at the 17th ASEAN Summit in October 2011. To implement the various initiatives under the MPAC, ASEAN leaders called on external partners, multilateral development banks, regional and global funds, the private sector and other parties to take part in realizing the ASEAN Connectivity.

Benefits of ASEAN Connectivity and Importance of Its Master Plan

Enhancing intra-ASEAN Connectivity will facilitate ASEAN Community Building and reinforce ASEAN's centrality, particularly for its driving role in charting the evolving regional architecture. Moreover, enhanced regional connectivity will assist ASEAN member states to achieve economic growth; attract investments; promote deeper ties among ASEAN people and foster cultural and historical bonds. Besides, enhancing ASEAN Connectivity may also bring about greater effectiveness of the web of ASEAN-centred FTAs, and speed up the development of the ASEAN Regional Comprehensive Economic Partnership (RCEP).

Adoption of the MPAC demonstrates the foresight of leaders to help ASEAN stay focus and on track towards ASEAN Community 2015, and to keep the momentum going beyond 2015. It also acts as a string that links and ties the three pillars of the ASEAN Community together — ASEAN Political-Security Community (APSC), ASEAN Economic Community (AEC) and ASEAN Socio-Cultural Community (ASCC). These connections would be forged through the three dimensions: physical, institutional and people-to-people connectivity. Linking various action plans developed from a sectoral perspective, the Master Plan intends to connect the dots and provide greater impetus and synergies to various plans through multi-sectoral cooperation. It also accords great importance and extends its focus to look at subregional initiatives like the Greater Mekong Sub-region (GMS); Brunei Darussalam, Indonesia, Malaysia, and the Philippines-East ASEAN Growth Area (BIMP-EAGA); and the Indonesia, Malaysia and Thailand-Growth Triangle (IMT-GT).

The Master Plan is both a strategic document for achieving ASEAN Connectivity and a plan of action to implement various measures and actions to enhance the connection of ASEAN through physical, institutional and people-to-people linkages. The strategies and key actions to achieve regional connectivity in ASEAN involve measures to ensure an efficient and competitive transport system such as the completion of key land transport components i.e. the ASEAN Highway Network, the Singapore Kunming Rail Link (SKRL), an ASEAN Single Shipping Market, an ASEAN Single Aviation Market, multimodal transport corridors, ICT infrastructure and services, regional energy infrastructure projects, and developing strategy for inland waterways. The institutional and people-to-people connectivity strategies include transport, trade and customs facilitation, liberalization of connectivity-related services as well as investment, institutional capacity building, promotion of tourism and deeper socio-cultural linkages.

Besides the strategies and key actions, the Master Plan also identifies fifteen priority projects under each dimension, in particular those which implementation will have high and immediate impact towards achieving the goals of ASEAN Connectivity. These projects, some of which are national projects that help establish and operationalize critical subregional links, would provide key building blocks to ASEAN Connectivity.

It is also recognized that enhanced connectivity will bring about both positive and negative impacts. While recognizing the tangible benefits of closer connectivity, the problems caused by transnational crime, illegal immigration, environmental degradation and pollution, and other cross-border challenges should be addressed properly.

In summary, the Master Plan pulls all the key actors and actions together — actors such as ASEAN, the subregional initiatives, international organizations and financing sources, and actions such as the various ongoing programmes, projects and initiatives — all with the aim of enhancing the connectivity of ASEAN.

Implementation Arrangement

To oversee the implementation of the Master Plan, an ASEAN Connectivity Coordinating Committee (ACCC) has been established and expected to work closely with the respective National Coordinators and government agencies as well as relevant ASEAN sectoral bodies. The ACCC is also expected to monitor the implementation status and to engage all relevant stakeholders in the process through communications and outreach activities.

As far as the ASEAN Secretariat is concerned, a dedicated unit has been set up to support the ACCC in coordinating, monitoring and

FIGURE 11.1

Implementation Arrangement for the Master Plan on ASEAN Connectivity

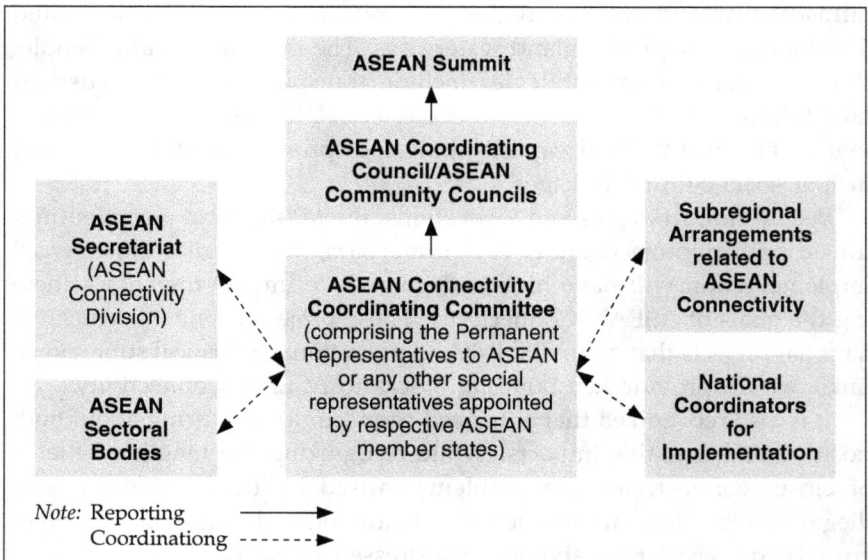

reporting progress of the Master Plan implementation to the ASEAN leaders, through the ASEAN Coordinating Council.

Figure 11.1 illustrates the implementation arrangements for the AMPC. Essentially, the ACCC is expected to work closely with various key external partners, to undertake overall functions related to ASEAN Connectivity and report the progress and issues to the ASEAN Coordinating Council.

Close consultation and coordination among concerned parties in the implementing projects and activities is crucial. In general, relevant ASEAN sectoral committees will be the key implementation bodies on the specific strategies and actions under their respective purview, while the National Coordinators and the relevant government agencies are responsible for overseeing the implementation of specific plans or projects at the national level. Partnership arrangements and regular consultations with the subregional set-ups, private sector, industry associations and the wider community at the regional and national levels will also be actively sought to ensure the participation of all stakeholders in developing and enhancing the ASEAN Connectivity. Given the cross-cutting nature of the ASEAN Connectivity initiative, a dedicated unit within the Office of the Secretary-General of ASEAN is established to support the ACCC in coordinating, monitoring and reporting progress of the Master Plan implementation.

To monitor and evaluate achievements and constraints, a scorecard mechanism will be set up to review the status of the Master Plan implementation and the impact of enhanced ASEAN Connectivity, and especially to ensure that all the list of priority measures and actions undertaken are responsive to the needs and priorities of ASEAN. To ensure cohesiveness and close collaboration among stakeholders or constituents, a communications strategy, aimed at achieving the objectives of ASEAN Connectivity, is envisaged for outreach and advocacy purposes.

Resource Mobilization

Realization of the strategies and actions in the Master Plan will require significant financial resources and human capital. According to an ADB publication, it is estimated that ASEAN countries will require infrastructure investments amounting to US$596 billion during 2006–15, with an average investment of US$60 billion per year. The participation and support of ASEAN Dialogue Partners, multilateral development banks and the private sector in achieving ASEAN Connectivity is thus crucial.

A variety of internal and external financing sources, both over the short and medium-to-long term will be needed. Chapter 4 of MPAC has listed out a number of indicative funding sources, categorized as traditional and new/innovative sources, including private sector involvement and the public-private partnership (PPP).

Traditional funding sources

Among the traditional funding sources include: grants and loans from multilateral development banks (e.g. ADB, World Bank and Islamic Development Bank); bilateral development partners; regional and global funds and facilities (e.g. Regional Cooperation and Integration Fund, and the Public-Private Infrastructure Advisory Facility, which are financed by multiple donors and administered by the ADB); Technical Assistances from ASEAN Dialogue Partners or external partners (see Table 11.1); as well as national government budgets. In the ASEAN's aspirations of greater physical, institutional and people-to-people connectivity, some ASEAN member states could gradually increase financing from issuance of government security as well as tapping part of the region's large aggregate private savings.

New and Innovative Sources

While the multilateral and bilateral development partners, various types of regional and global funds, and national governments, are able to fill part of the total resource needs for priority connectivity infrastructure, the total amount of the resources mobilized from these traditional sources may not be sufficient to implement all initiatives covered under the Master Plan. As such ASEAN will need to explore and tap on new as well as innovative approaches of financial sources, which include, among others, the possible establishment of an ASEAN fund for infrastructure development, public-private partnership (PPP), and development of local and regional financial and capital markets. ASEAN will also need to further strengthen partnership with external partners, including Dialogue Partners, multilateral development banks, international organizations and others for effective and efficient implementation of the Master Plan.

TABLE 11.1

Indicative List of Funding Sources for Technical Assistance

No.	Possible Sources of Available Funding
1.	ASEAN Development Fund
2.	ASEAN Cultural Fund
3.	ASEAN Information Communications Technology (ICT) Fund
4.	ASEAN Energy Endowment Fund
5.	ASEAN-China Cooperation Fund (ACCF)
6.	Japan-ASEAN Integration Fund (JAIF)
7.	ASEAN-ROK Special Cooperation Fund (SCF)
8.	ASEAN-ROK Future Oriented Cooperation Programme Fund (FOCP)
9.	ASEAN Plus Three Cooperation Fund
10.	ASEAN-Australia Development Cooperation Programme Phase II (AADCP II)
11.	ASEAN-India Fund
12.	ASEAN Economic Integration Support Programme (ASEAN-EU)
13.	ASEAN Air Transport Integration Project (ASEAN-EU)
14.	ASEAN Development Vision to Advanced National Cooperation and Economic Integration (ASEAN-US)
15.	Economic Research Institute for ASEAN and East Asia (ERIA)
16.	Asian Development Bank
17.	World Bank
18.	Other Technical Assistance Programmes within ASEAN and with ASEAN External Partners

(a) Establishing the ASEAN Infrastructure Fund (AIF)

One of the new approaches that ASEAN member states and ABD have been working together is the establishment of an ASEAN Infrastructure Fund (AIF). The objective is to mobilize financial resources within ASEAN to support regional infrastructure development. This is a significant gesture as it shows ASEAN's self-reliance and centrality in achieving ASEAN connectivity.

In establishing the AIF, a Task Force on AIF Mechanism composed of representatives from the Ministry of Finance and Central Bank of ASEAN countries was set up, and support of ADB was tapped to help in the design of AIF mechanism. Since 2009, the Taskforce has held a series of meetings together with ADB to deliberate on various issues. Significant progress has been achieved and key issues settled thus far include capital structure, governance, and domicile of AIF.

Under the agreed capital structure, the equity contribution will be funded by ASEAN and ADB at a total amount of US$485.2 million, of which ASEAN will contribute a total of US$335.2 million (69.08 per cent), while ADB will contribute US$150 million (30.92 per cent). In addition, the hybrid capital of US$162 million, as a financial instrument that has both debt and equity characteristics, will be issued after the third and last tranche of the initial core equity contributions. With the confirmation of the pledges, the total capital structure of the AIF is now US$647.2 million. On governance, it has been agreed that the AIF will be established as a corporate entity in a suitable jurisdiction. It will have a board, which will be the decision-making body of the AIF. Each member that contributes to the core equity will be represented in the AIF Board of Directors (BOD). Agreement has also been reached that Malaysia will be the domicile of the AIF, while ADB will manage and administer the AIF on behalf of ASEAN.

Other key issues that have been settled include, among others: the principles for project selection and pricing. ADB has also prepared a list of indicative project pipeline, comprised mostly of transport and energy projects, of which will be further reviewed and consulted with relevant member states.

The Shareholder Agreement on the AIF was signed by ASEAN member states and ADB on 24 September 2011 during the Informal ASEAN Finance Ministers' Meeting (AFMM) in Washington D.C. The member states and ADB are currently on their internal process to complete the first contribution by 30 June 2012.

(b) Role of Private Sector in ASEAN Connectivity

ASEAN has been recognizing the comparative advantages and contributing roles of private sector, as a main player in various ASEAN's works. Private sector inputs and partnership have been promoted to improve coherence, clarity, practicality and synergies of government policies and initiatives across industries and sectors in ASEAN Community Building process, including the realization of the ASEAN Connectivity.

At the operational level, involvement of private sector is important not only as a source of private capital in connectivity projects, but also for the expertise and skill in infrastructure project management and identification of constraints and problems in the implementation of the Master Plan on ASEAN Connectivity.

Chapter 4 of the MPAC identifies the public-private partnership (PPP) as an important approach representing an innovative way for the governments to work with the private sector in providing high quality service delivery and in closing the gaps in fund requirements of the infrastructure sector. To leverage private capital in financing ASEAN's infrastructure development, actions at the country and regional levels would be required to implement PPP projects.

At the country level, the private sector engagement strategy aims to support governments in the region to mobilize and channel private financing into infrastructure development through market-based instruments; while the engagement of private sector at the regional level aims to achieve a well-functioning infrastructure finance market set against changing global financial and macroeconomic realities.

(c) Developing Regional and Domestic Capital Markets

The regional and domestic capital markets are also expected to play an important role in providing available resources to finance certain priority infrastructure projects. Financing of infrastructure requires the availability of long-term capital, on reasonably competitive terms, and preferably in local currency. The establishment of the Credit Guarantee Investment Facility (CGIF), developed under the ASEAN+3 Asian Bonds Market Initiative, has been expected to promote the development of domestic and regional bond markets by encouraging companies' access to bond markets with more liquid local currency and longer term maturity. The CGIF is set up as a US$700 million trust fund, including capital contributions of US$130 million from the ADB. It is expected that the CGIF will provide guarantees on local currency denominated bonds issued by companies in the region. Such guarantees will make it easier for firms to issue local bonds with longer maturities.

Progress has been made in 2011 toward recruitment of key positions, especially the Chief Executive Officer (CEO) and Chief Risk Officer (CRO). Currently, focused works are given to the drafting of business plan and risk management framework for review by the Board of Director in 2012.

Concluding Remarks

The critic will say that ASEAN has too many plans. The advocate will say that ASEAN has vision. This Master Plan on ASEAN Connectivity is among one of ASEAN leaders' strategies to further advance ASEAN Community Building and integration process, as a well-connected ASEAN will bring peoples, goods, services and capital closer together in an efficient and seamless manner.

Through coordination of the newly established ASEAN Connectivity Coordinating Committee (ACCC), relevant ASEAN sectoral bodies will implement the strategies and actions under their respective purview; while the National Coordinators and the relevant government agencies are responsible for overseeing the implementation of specific plans or projects at the national level.

A variety of internal and external financing sources are indicated to make available financial support and technical assistance needs across the ASEAN over the short- to medium- and long term. A communication strategy and regular consultations for partnership arrangements, with the private sector, industry associations and the wider community at all levels, will also be actively sought to ensure the participation of all stakeholders in developing and enhancing the ASEAN Connectivity.

12

CONCLUSION AND POLICY RECOMMENDATIONS

Sanchita Basu Das

In 2010, during Vietnam's chairmanship of ASEAN meetings, the leaders adopted the MPAC. The MPAC aims to provide a framework for regional cooperation on connectivity and a foundation for further connectivity with other regions, such as East Asia and South Asia. The core initiatives of the Master Plan are to improve the economic resilience of the region through improved production and distribution networks and to optimize benefits from the free trade agreements of ASEAN. With the implementation of the MPAC, it is expected to provide economies of scale and generate higher interaction among countries, boost multilateral growth and reduce development gaps. Therefore, enhancing connectivity through the MPAC is seen as a way of promoting ASEAN's economic growth as a whole.

Current State/ Gaps in Connectivity across ASEAN

Transportation

Road and Rail Infrastructure: The two flagship projects — the ASEAN Highway Network (AHN) and the Singapore–Kunming Rail Link (SKRL) — suffer from several missing links and substandard work quality. AHN is targeted for completion in 2015, while the completion of SKRL is likely to be extended to 2020. Once these links are built, it will connect both the mainland ASEAN and ASEAN with China and India.

Maritime Network: Although ASEAN has forty-seven designated ports, there are a number of challenges in providing an efficient shipping network service in the region. According to the UNCTAD Liner Shipping Connectivity Index, except for Singapore and Malaysia, ASEAN countries rank poorly relative to China and Hong Kong. Most of the gateway ports of the ASEAN member states are "fairly full", implying investment needs for capacity expansion.

Air Transport: The connectivity through air is the most developed in the region. The airports of ASEAN capital cities are sufficient in terms of runway lengths to accommodate the existing operation of aircraft. However, some of these airports still face problems in providing airport facilities, particularly warehouses.

Telecommunications

Mobile and Broadband Connectivity: In seven out of ten ASEAN states, mobile connectivity is above 80 per cent and in many cases, one person may own more than one mobile phone. On home broadband, Singapore, Brunei and Malaysia are the leading countries and one-third of the people are connected. However, real connectivity of the ASEAN people is much higher than the figure released by regulators. This is because many people go to Internet cafes or surf the Internet from the office. Hence there is lot of opportunity for local companies to do business in the digital world. Although telecommunications is a very capital intensive industry, there is lot of benefits for an economy as it brings in foreign direct investment (FDI) and generates direct employment.

Currently there are several barriers in adopting broadband techno-logy in ASEAN. It is not easy to build the hard infrastructure in some countries as there is poor electricity infrastructure or copper theft. Getting a license is often cumbersome and expensive. Mobile broadband is still a negative proposition for companies, as wireless networks require significant investment to support high mobile data traffic. ASEAN countries also suffer from the unavailability of good quality, affordable smartphones, which are prerequisites for mobile broadband connectivity.

Information and Communication Technology (ICT)

Internet penetration is at very different stages of development in the ASEAN member states. While Singapore and Malaysia have more than a 50 per cent penetration rate, Laos and Cambodia are below 2 per cent. This disparity shows that a large segment of the ASEAN population is not "connected".

ASEAN is also challenged by the ICT divide between "youth" and "official" ASEAN. The youth of ASEAN are at the forefront of the global social network revolution. Indonesia is among the top five countries in Asia in terms of Facebook users. Against this, "official" ASEAN is still struggling with ICT. In the ASEAN ICT Master Plan 2010–2015, ASEAN ICT initiatives seem to be focused on infrastructure development. However, it should be noted that applications and capacity developments are an integral part of ICT development in the region. A failure to address these three aspects of ICT equally will lead to suboptimal use of ICT for development.

Energy infrastructure

Under the ASEAN Connectivity initiative, there are two major energy infrastructure projects, the ASEAN Power Grid (APG) and the Trans-ASEAN Gas Pipeline (TAGP). APG aims to help member states meet increasing demand for electricity and improve access to energy services. But there are several challenges. ASEAN countries are at different stages in the reform of their respective power markets. While at one end there is the vertically integrated power market with monopoly utility model (Brunei, Cambodia, Laos, Myanmar), at the other, there is the privatized/market friendly model (Singapore, the Philippines). Again, there is a tremendous spread across electricity tariffs with Laos being very cheap (US4.5 cents/kWh) and Cambodia the most expensive (US14.4 cents/kWh). The difference is mainly due to various generation mixes that the countries draw their electricity from as well as installed capacity. Moreover, the countries are very different from each other in terms of legal and financial matters.

TAGP aims to develop a regional gas grid by 2020, by interconnecting existing and planned gas pipelines of member states and enabling gas to be transported across borders. The realization of TAGP is expected to encounter substantial financial and legal complexities, most of which are easier to handle on bilateral basis rather than multilateral. One special challenge for TAGP is that the regional gas supply is dwindling. Countries like Indonesia and Malaysia, who were once significant LNG exporters, are now looking at ways to supply in their own countries. This is because, in recent times, there have not been any new discoveries of large gas fields.

Implementation Arrangement

The overall implementation plan of ASEAN Connectivity will be overseen by the Connectivity Coordinating Committee (CCC). The CCC is expected to work closely with the respective national coordinators for implementation and with relevant ASEAN sectoral bodies. As the implementation of the MPAC will face serious challenges and issues, the ACCC is expected to identify them and make appropriate recommendations to the ASEAN Summit.

ASEAN CCC is also expected to engage ASEAN stakeholders (private sector, subregional groupings, dialogue partners, multilateral development banks) in this process through communication and exchange of information. A dedicated unit will be established at the ASEAN Secretariat to support the CCC in coordinating and monitoring the implementation process. It will also be responsible for connectivity progress reports from time-to-time.

Resource Mobilization

The critical aspect of the master plan is the resource mobilization to implement the key projects under the stipulated timelines. It should be noted that all the projects entail long implementation periods, complex technical issues, sovereign and project risks, and the delicate task of sharing benefits, costs, and risks between two or more countries and the public and private sectors.

The Asian Development Bank (ADB) estimates that ASEAN countries will require infrastructure investment of US$596 billion during 2006–15 (see Table 12.1). According to the ADB, only one-fifth of the requirements has been met so far. Resource mobilization is a concern, as currently 30–40 per cent of the regional funds are expected from public and government contributions, and 10–12 per cent from banks, with almost an entire half of the necessary US$60 billion per annum left to be covered by private investors.

TABLE 12.1

Projected Infrastructure Requirements in ASEAN, 2006–15

(US$ billion)

Sector	New Capacity	Maintenance	Total
Power	170.3	46	216.3
Transport	95.6	61.2	156.8
Water & Sanitation	98.8	60.6	159.4
Telecommunication	30.9	32.7	63.6
Total	395.6	200.5	596.1

Source: ADBI.

To meet this financing requirement, ASEAN is exploring both traditional and new ways of resource mobilization. This includes commitments for funding and loans from international institutions and several dialogue partners, engaging the private sector through approaches like Public-Private Partnership (PPP). The new ways of generating funds include establishment of the ASEAN Infrastructure Fund (AIF), setting up of a regional and domestic capital market like the Credit Guarantee Investment Facility (CGIF), which is a US$700 million of trust fund among ASEAN+3 countries, managed by the ADB.

(a) ASEAN Infrastructure Fund

The AIF is a mechanism in which the ASEAN member states and ADB work together through pooling funds — and promoting the use of ASEAN savings — to foster infrastructure development within the region and make the MPAC a reality. The AIF will have three main development outputs:

    i.   Support the implementation of the MPAC;
   ii.   Provide additional financing for enhanced infrastructure; and
  iii.   Enhance private sector participation in infrastructure development through PPPs.

With voluntary contribution pledges from member states, the AIF consists of US$485.2 million in equity contribution and US$162 million in hybrid capital (see Tables 12.2 and 12.3). The hybrid capital will be launched when the third tranche of the contribution is paid. By 2020, ASEAN is expected to mobilize US$4 billion that will leverage US$13 billion. In the future, the AIF will mobilize resource by buying debt from ASEAN member states' central banks. The AIF will operate as a Limited Liability Company based in Malaysia (before June 2012), and the fund will be administered by the ADB.

TABLE 12.2
ASEAN Infrastructure Fund

Member States	Amount (US$ million)	Member States	Amount (US$ million)
Brunei	10.0	Myanmar	0
Cambodia	0.1	Philippines	15.0
Indonesia	120.0	Singapore	15.0
Lao PDR	0.1	Thailand	15.0
Malaysia	150.0	Vietnam	10.0
Total ASEAN	335.2		
ADB	150.0		
Total Equity	485.2		
Hybrid Capital	162.0		
Grand Total	647.2		

The sectors that could utilize the AIF are energy, transportation and water. The countries that could benefit in its early implementation are Lao PDR, Indonesia, the Philippines, and Vietnam. The AIF board is

TABLE 12.3
Basic Design and Structure of AIF

Equity	Hybrid Capital	Debt	Lending Operations
US$335.2 million from ASEAN member states and US$150.0 million from ADB	Around US$162.0 million in hybrid capital (perpetual bonds)	Debt issued to leverage 1.5 times the equity. Central banks and other institutions, including private sector, may purchase the debt after the AIF has established a clear track record.	Lending to relevant ASEAN member states and based on pipeline projects. Initially only on sovereign and sovereign-guaranteed projects and public portion of PPP projects. Loans to private sponsors can be considered later.

expected to approve about six projects per year. The projects should be economically and financially viable and should have potential to reduce poverty in the region.

(b) Public-Private Partnerships

Another crucial source of funding is the private sector and one way to involve them is through the public-private partnerships (PPPs). PPP describes a government service or private business venture which is funded and operated through a partnership of government and one or more private sector companies. Prior to the 1997–98 financial crisis, ASEAN relied heavily upon the private sector for much of infrastructure investment, especially in energy. In ASEAN, the hydropower sector in Laos provides a recent example of public-private partnership.

PPPs have different forms:

a. Build-Operate-Transfer (BOT): The most widespread private sector financing method is the BOT system. The state grants a 15–35 years concession to a private construction and engineering consortium of firms backed by ample financial resources (the contractors). The private firms build the infrastructure project, operate it for the concession period at the end of which they transfer it to the state without compensation. All the income during the operating period goes to the contractors. If the period of concession is sufficiently long — the contractors have an interest to observe high standards of quality in order to minimize maintenance costs.

b.   Build-Own-Operate (BOO): A private entity constructs and operates a facility for performing public services without transferring ownership of the facility to the public sector. Legal title to the facility remains with the private sector entity.

c.   Privatization: The privatization of utilities has attracted greater attention recently. The privatized companies are expected to operate with greater efficiency and with improved rates of return on capital and many times may provide the service at a lower price.

PPPs can add to public sector investment capacity and provide more efficient management and administrative skills. PPPs require the right policy environment to operate in a country or a region. Projects must also be economically and commercially viable, with risks apportioned between public and private sectors, and returns must be commensurate with risks.

It is however worth noting that there are some issues related to private sector financing of infrastructure projects. The main ones are: (a) avoidance of monopolistic situations, (b) existence of competition, which requires a minimum set of good operators bidding for contracts, (c) avoidance of negative externalities, (d) tariff controls by means of regulation, (e) protection of vulnerable groups by means of budget subsidies, (f) regulation, ensuring independence and credibility on the part of the regulator.

Policy Recommendations

As infrastructure needs are not uniform in the region, harmonious infrastructure development is crucial. Governments have to identify the infrastructure gaps and then plug them accordingly. While the Master Plan has ascertained the stretches of road for regional connectivity, it has missed the smaller details. For example, it did not consider rural connectivity, which is essential to eliminate the rural-urban divide and to distribute the benefits of economic integration to all. Similarly, intra-country integration via gas and power grids can be as important as cross-border grid and pipeline interconnections.

The policies related to legal and regulatory frameworks should be harmonized and synergized among ASEAN member countries. For example, the legal and policy framework on cross-border power trading in ASEAN remains weak. Although Laos' electricity laws address cross-border power trading, they have insufficient and unclear provisions. Conversely, some countries like Malaysia, Thailand, and the Philippines do not have any existing laws or policies on cross-border power trading. Hence, the importance of "legal connectivity", i.e. being on the same page in terms of the existing legal frameworks, common specifications and standards in implementing the various components of the Master Plan, should be highlighted to each member country.

Private sector participation is a key component in the development of ASEAN connectivity as there are limitations to ODA and public resources. While PPP has huge potential, it does not seem to be fully utilized at this point. PPPs bring together the best of the knowledge and expertise of the private sector, and the funds and institutional reach of the public sector. In this vein, it should be beneficial for ASEAN to involve more industrial heads and entrepreneurs during project and financial decision-making processes under ASEAN connectivity. It should also prioritize a small number of regional projects that will deliver quick wins and build momentum, attracting the private investors.

It should also be noted that the investment needs of ASEAN such as physical infrastructure have to be translated into commercially viable projects for private investors to take an interest. In this regard, there has to be a higher quality of information on investment opportunities in the ASEAN countries that are made available to the public. In addition, governments must create an enabling environment that assures investors of predictability, a level playing field, low transaction costs and fair rates of return commensurate with the risks they take.

Finally ASEAN must ensure good governance. The regulatory framework has to be strengthened to make sure that capital is used appropriately for infrastructure development.

Sector-specific recommendations:

ASEAN countries must cooperate on both national and regional levels. While ASEAN has made a good start with cross-border projects, like the AHN, and the SKRL, it has to continue and expand effective cooperation at all levels of government and with multiple stakeholders (central government, local government, the private sector, and civil society). The member countries with the means, expertise and technology should assist the countries who do not have these resources.

As ASEAN is endowed with approximately 51,000 kilometres of navigable inland waterways, waterways transport has enormous potential in reducing freight costs in ASEAN. But the current utilization rate is very low due to the underdeveloped waterways network, poor river ports and facilities, and poor inter-port connectivity. These infrastructure issues need to be addressed, together with improving rules and govern-ance for managing the connected inland waterway transport systems.

ASEAN is not able to turn the demand for the Internet into com-panies that can take benefit from it. Currently, Google takes the lion's share of the search market in ASEAN countries. ASEAN needs to create local champions in the digital industry. In doing so, the public sector can co-invest to encourage private investment in telecom infrastructure. Governments can increase Internet connectivity by pushing more e-services and connecting educational institutions. It must be realized that for rural areas with moderate throughput, mobile broadband is the only affordable solution.

As ASEAN faces the challenge of evolving into a more institutionalized organization, ICT can help ASEAN achieve this goal more effectively. ASEAN can adopt appropriate and cost efficient conferencing software to be used by various ASEAN bodies or at meetings. ASEAN, through the Secretariat, can also develop appropriate e-Participation tools to enhance the engagement with all ASEAN stakeholders.

Regarding energy infrastructure, reducing power and gas subsidies is critical for many ASEAN countries. It is important to capture economic benefits from market-based pricing in key natural resources, infrastructure and energy sectors. Market oriented reforms are neces-sary to ensure fiscal stability in countries which subsidize gas and power, to alleviate shortages of natural gas for domestic demand and to maintain a stable policy environment for private sector investments, which require predictability and transparency. While this is a difficult task as it may hurt constituencies, countries need to move from subsidies to appropriate social safety nets. Flexibility is one of the important criteria for energy security, for example exercising small scale LNG options where viable, exposure to spot and short term LNG contracts form part of a broader supply portfolio.

Summing up

In sum, the ASEAN Connectivity Master Plan is one of the important solutions to the problems obstructing the process of ASEAN Community Building. Road, rail, water and aviation corridors are the most visible face of connectivity due to their importance for the movement of goods and people. It is crucial to promote the utilization of ICT, given the ubiquitous role of the Internet and mobile telephony in business and other economic and social development. The absence of such linkages is likely to threaten the already existing gaps between different countries both within ASEAN and around the world. Lastly, integrated power grids and gas pipelines for ASEAN countries are also important as they aim to improve energy efficiency and develop indigenous energy resources.

Indeed, ASEAN Connectivity is a herculean project, but it is a necessary element in ASEAN Community Building, and in ensuring ASEAN's competitiveness in the world. To stay on track towards ASEAN Community 2015, and to keep momentum going beyond 2015, the MPAC is an important connecting thread that ties the three ASEAN communities together.

It should be noted that ASEAN is a growing infrastructure development market. This is evident from a number of infrastructure projects identified in the MPAC, which are still waiting for investment. Investors should see ASEAN as a more integrated consumer market. The region's "middle-income" (a per capita annual income of US$3,000–12,000) population grew from 140 million (32.7 per cent of total) in the mid-1990s to 250 million (49.5 per cent) in the mid-2000s. By 2015, the market is expected to be more than 300 million. With implementation of the Connectivity Master Plan, the private sector can gain from the improved physical and institutional infrastructure and can take advantage of the remaining disparities in ASEAN (wages, resources, etc) through upgrading supply chains in the region.

INDEX

A

ACE. *See* ASEAN Centre for Energy (ACE)
ADB. *See* Asian Development Bank (ADB)
ADSL broadband services, 88
AEC. *See* ASEAN Economic Community (AEC)
agglomeration forces, 40
    mechanics of, 45
    in new economic geography, 42
Agreement on ASEAN Energy Cooperation, 17
AHN. *See* ASEAN Highway Network (AHN)
AIF. *See* ASEAN Infrastructure Fund (AIF)
AIMS II. *See* ASEAN Interconnection Master Plan Study (AIMS) II
airports, 25–27
air transport, 176
    infrastructure, 14–15
AMPC, implementation arrangements for, 168, 169
APAEC. *See* ASEAN Plan of Action for Energy Cooperation (APAEC)
APG. *See* ASEAN Power Grid (APG)

appropriate technology choices, regulatory levers for, 81–85
APSC. *See* ASEAN Political-Security Community (APSC)
ASAM. *See* ASEAN Single Aviation Market (ASAM)
ASCC. *See* ASEAN Socio-Cultural Community (ASCC)
ASCOPE. *See* ASEAN Council on Petroleum (ASCOPE)
ASEAN
    air and sea ports in, 25–27
    assessment of logistics infrastructure in, 47–49
    Chief Information Officer, 118
    connectivity and community, interaction, 4
    cultures and history of, 113
    economic growth in, 38, 122
    electricity prices paid in, 156
    electricity sector in, 155
    energy consumption in, 122
    energy cooperation in, 17–18, 159n13
    energy integration, 143–44
    E-readiness ranking, 93
    financing requirements in, 23, 179
    gas pipeline infrastructure of, 128

GDP per capita and growth in
2008–2010, 67, 68
ICT. *See* information and
communications technology
(ICT)
initiatives, 20–21
institutional mechanisms of, 123
integrated transport system in, 70
interconnection grids, 126, 134–39
Interconnection Master Plan, 127
Internet penetration rate for, 91–92
Internet users in, 73–76
manufacturing sub-sectors in, 43,
45
McKinsey study, 158
member states of, 142, 143
MoU, 132–33
MPAC in, 112
official, 110–14, 177
online companies, 78
"organizations" of, 113
physical connectivity in, 37–38
planners and diplomats, 145
policy recommendations, 117–18
power generation and
distribution, 156
power grid systems in, 156, 157
power market structures in, 132
production networks and tiers of
economic development in, 38
public sectors in, 157
regional economic integration, 143
regional identity, 116–17
RORO network, 69
subregional groups, 152, 154
TAGP taskforce, 144
telecom development in, 74
transport network in, 69
TTRs in, 12
young, 108–10, 177
ASEAN Broadband Corridor (ABC),
6
ASEAN Centre for Energy (ACE),
155
ASEAN Committee on Culture and
Information (COCI), 113

ASEAN Community Councils, 115
ASEAN Connectivity
aims, 61
and ASEAN community, 4
benefits of, 166–68
Brunei Action and Master Plan
on, 38
concept and development of,
165–66
implementation plan of, 178
Master Plan on, 60, 68
prioritized projects for, 6–8
private sector in, 172–73
realizing of, 60
role of private sector in, 172–73
ASEAN Connectivity, benefits of,
98
connecting for future, 105–6
connecting to collaboration, 102–5
strengthening internal processes,
98–102
ASEAN Connectivity Coordinating
Committee (ACCC), 168
ASEAN Coordinating Council, 115
ASEAN Council on Petroleum
(ASCOPE), 18, 143, 218
ASEAN Council on Petroleum-TAGP
Master Plan 2000, 128
ASEAN Economic Community
(AEC), 3, 59, 66, 70, 117, 167
establishment of, 56–58
2015, 122–23
ASEAN Economic Community
Blueprint 2015, 123, 124, 144
ASEAN Energy Efficiency and
Conservation (EE&C), 20
ASEAN Free Trade Area (AFTA), 10
ASEAN Highway Network (AHN),
5, 68
project, 11, 12, 20–21, 176
ASEAN infrastructure development
challenges for, 30–31
energy, 17–19
ICT, 15–17
importance of, 29–30
transport, 10–15

ASEAN Infrastructure Financing
    Mechanism, 124
ASEAN Infrastructure Fund (AIF),
    8, 179
    design and structure of, 181
    development outputs, 180
    establishment of, 171–72
ASEAN infrastructures
    current state of, 176–78
    energy connectivity policies and
        concerns, 19–20
ASEAN Interconnection Master Plan
    Study (AIMS) II, 127–28
    interconnection projects, 131
ASEAN Master Plan on regional
    connectivity, 165
ASEAN Plan of Action on Energy
    Cooperation (APAEC), 17
ASEAN Plan of Action for Energy
    Cooperation (APAEC) 2010–
    2015, 123, 144
    opportunities and challenges, 124
    for TAGP, 130
ASEAN Political-Security
    Community (APSC), 117, 167
ASEAN Power Grid (APG), 18,
    125–26, 152–57, 177–78
    APAEC 2010–2015 for, 127
    projects, 123, 127
ASEAN Single Aviation Market
    (ASAM), 5
    establishment of, 70
ASEAN Single Shipping Market, 5
ASEAN Single Telecommunications
    Market, 112
ASEAN Socio-Cultural Community
    (ASCC), 167
    implementation of, 117
ASEAN Strategic Transport Plan
    (ASTP), 10
ASEAN Summit, 60, 143, 165
    in Hanoi, 110
    in Singapore, 123
ASEAN Telecommunications
    and Information Technology
    Ministers (TELMIN), 16, 107n7

ASEAN Telecommunications and
    Information Technology Senior
    Officers Meeting (TELSOM), 16
ASEAN Transport Action Plan
    (ATAP), 10, 11
ASEAN Transport Ministers (ATM),
    11
ASEAN Virtual Learning Resource
    Centres (AVLRC), 8
ASEAN Vision 2020, 142–43, 144
    APG, 151
Asia
    FB users in, 108–9
    financial capacity, 148
    mobile phones in, 109–10
Asian Development Bank (ADB), 8,
    22, 165, 166, 169, 179
    role in pipeline projects, 145
Asian Highway and Trans-Asian
    Railway network (AH-TAR),
    22
ATAP. See ASEAN Transport Action
    Plan (ATAP)
Australia, Internet penetration rate
    for, 91

B
Bangkok Declaration, 142
Basin Development Plan, 22
bilateral gas pipeline interconnection
    projects, 19
BOO. See Build-Own-Operate (BOO)
BOT. See Build-Operate-Transfer
    (BOT)
broadband
    access, 72
    adoption, barriers to, 76–81
    ADSL, 88
    connectivity, 87, 176–77
    economic benefits of, 72
    investment in, 72–73
    mobile. See mobile broadband
    penetration. See Internet
        penetration
Brunei Action Plan on ASEAN
    Connectivity, 38

Brunei Darussalam, air and sea ports in, 25
Brunei–Indonesia–Malaysia–Philippines East ASEAN Growth Area (BIMP-EGA), 22
Brunei, oil discoveries in, 148
Build-Operate-Transfer (BOT), 181–82
Build-Own-Operate (BOO), 182

C
CADP, 53
  conceptual framework of, 47
  infrastructure development in tier by, 50, 52, 54
Cambodia, air and sea ports in, 25
Cambodia, Laos, Myanmar, and Vietnam (CLMV) economies, 67
CBI development. See cross-border infrastructure (CBI) development
CCC. See Connectivity Coordinating Committee (CCC)
CERT cooperation. See Computer Emergency Response Team (CERT) cooperation
CGIF. See Credit Guarantee Investment Facility (CGIF)
CLMV economies. See Cambodia, Laos, Myanmar, and Vietnam (CLMV) economies
Computer Emergency Response Team (CERT) cooperation, 111
connecting to collaboration, 102–5
  healthcare, 102–3
  increasing, 103
  reducing cross-border costs, 104–5
  responding to regional crises, 104
connectivity
  ASEAN. See ASEAN Connectivity
  within ASEAN, 3
  broadband, 87, 176–77

domestic, 61
increasing, 81
institutional. See institutional connectivity
mobile, 176–77
people-to-people, 6–8, 33, 166, 167, 170
physical. See physical connectivity
positive impacts of, 61, 62
regional. See regional connectivity
Connectivity Coordinating Committee (CCC), 178
countervailing forces, 40
Credit Guarantee Investment Facility (CGIF), 179
  establishment of, 173
cross-border costs, reducing, 104–5
cross-border infrastructure (CBI) development, 143
  projects, 145
cross-border natural gas pipelines in Southeast Asia, 145–47
cross-border power trading, 183
cross-border trade (CBT), 104, 105
cross-border transport agreement (CBTA), 21

D
data sharing, between governments, 103
decision-makers, 82
Declaration of ASEAN Concord II in 2003, 142
Denmark, E-readiness ranking, 93
device convergence, 95–96
digital media ecosystem, development of, 86
digital subscriber lines (DSL), 84
digital surveillance systems, 101
dispersion forces, 40
  in new economic geography, 42
domestic capital markets, development of, 173
domestic connectivity, 61
DSL. See digital subscriber lines

E

EAEF. *See* European Union-ASEAN
    Energy Facility (EAEF)
e-ASEAN Framework Agreement,
    15, 110
East Asia
    production networks in, 37, 40
    Summit 2010, 38
    U.S.-Mexico Nexus *vs.*, production
        networks, 40, 41
economic activity, accelerator of, 94
economic activity, connectivity
        promoting, 96–98
    connecting for future, 105–6
    creating value in governments,
        99–100
    healthcare, 102–3
    identifying risks and reducing
        graft, 100–1
    internal security, 100
    reducing cross-border costs,
        104–5
    responding to regional crises,
        104
Economic and Social Commission
        for Asia and the Pacific
        (ESCAP), 166
economic community, establishment
    of ASEAN, 56–58
economic development in ASEAN,
    38, 122
economic infrastructure
    development plans, ASEAN, 38
economic integration, ASEAN
    infrastructure hindrance for,
    23–24
Economic Research Institute for
    ASEAN and East Asia (ERIA),
    38, 165–66
Economist Intelligence Unit (EIU),
    92
economy
    CLMV, 67
    interconnected nature of. *See*
        interconnected nature of
        economies

regional connectivity improves in
    local, 61–64
electricity
    grids, interconnected networks
        of, 123
    production, 122, 125
    sector in ASEAN, 155
Electricity Generation Authority of
    Thailand (EGAT), 125
embedded sensors, 105
Eminent Persons Group report, 143
energy
    connectivity policies and concerns,
        19–20
    consumption in ASEAN, 122
    cooperation in ASEAN, 159n13
    infrastructure, 177–78, 184
    integration, ASEAN, 143–44
    renewable, 20
    sectors, market-oriented reforms
        in, 158
    security, flexibility criteria for,
        185
energy infrastructure development
    progress and challenges, 18–19
    strategies, 17–18
energy situation, ASEAN
    challenges and barriers, 131–33
    energy consumption in, 121–22
equalizer, resetting social status quo,
    95
E-readiness ranking, 92
ERIA. *See* Economic Research
    Institute for ASEAN and East
    Asia (ERIA)
ESCAP. *See* Economic and Social
    Commission for Asia and the
    Pacific (ESCAP)
European Union-ASEAN Energy
    Facility (EAEF), 155

F

facebook (FB)
    growth in Malaysia, 109
    growth in Thailand, 109
    users in Asia, 108–9

faster fiber networks, 81
FB. *See* facebook (FB)
FDI. *See* foreign direct investment (FDI)
Federal Communications Commission (FCC), 82, 84
fiber to the node (FTTN), 84
fiber to the premises (FTTP), 84
financing requirements in ASEAN, 23, 179
fixed copper networks, 81
fixed line broadband penetration in Southeast Asia, 76
flexibility criteria for energy security, 185
foreign direct investment (FDI), 60, 64, 158
fragmentation
    mechanics of, 43, 45
    theory, 38–40, 53
    two-dimensional, 40, 42
fragmentation of production, 39, 40

G
gas pipelines
    infrastructure, 129–30
    interconnected networks of, 123
    interconnection projects, 128
Gearing up Internet Literacy and Access for Students (GILAS) project in Philippines, 88
Geographical Simulation Model (GSM), 53, 55, 56
GMS. *See* Greater Mekong Sub-region (GMS)
government services, creating efficiencies in delivery of, 99–100
Greater Mekong Sub-region (GMS), 21, 156
grid interconnection projects, 157
Gross Domestic Product (GDP), 9
GSM. *See* Geographical Simulation Model (GSM)

H
Heads of ASEAN Power Utilities/ Authorities (HAPUA), 18, 19
healthcare, 102–3
High Level Task Force on ASEAN Connectivity (HLTF-AC), 165–66
high-speed broadband (HSBB) network in Malaysia, 85
highway networks, 48
HLTF-AC. *See* High Level Task Force on ASEAN Connectivity (HLTF-AC)
household broadband penetration, 73, 75
HSBB network. *See* high-speed broadband (HSBB) network

I
ICT. *See* information and communications technology (ICT)
Indonesia
    air and sea ports in, 25
    FB users, 108
    LNG, 148–49
    mobile telecommunications company in, 87
    oil discoveries in, 148
    Twitter users, 109
Indonesia–Malaysia–Thailand Growth Triangle (IMT-GT), 22
industrial agglomerations, nominal GRDP per-capita (2005) and, 46
information and communications technology (ICT), 91, 109, 114, 177
    as accelerator of economic activity, 94
    development of, 61
    as driving adoption, 95–96
    as enabler, 93–94
    as equalizer, 95
    as foundation for new service models, 94–95

implementation of, 101
importance of, 110
and inclusive regionalism, 116
infrastructure, 6
liberalization of trade in, 15
Master Plan, 87, 110
MPAC, 111
in people-to-people connectivity,
    113
and policy coordination, 115–16
virtual communities, 96
information and communications
    technology (ICT) infrastructure
    development, 111–12
    progress and challenges, 17
    strategies, 15–16
information technology
    applications, Vietnam's National
        Program on, 87
    ASEAN initiatives in, 21
infrastructure development,
    logistics. *See* logistics
    infrastructure development
Infrastructure Fund Pool, 32
infrastructure funds, management
    of, 30
infrastructure projects, 144–45
    private sector financing of,
        182
infrastructure requirements in
    ASEAN, 179
inland waterways transport, 13–14,
    184
institutional connectivity, 5–6, 166,
    167, 170
    projects under, 7
    strengthening, 7–8
    used in MPAC, 112
integrated transport
    planning, 71
    system in ASEAN, 70
Intel Corporation
    in Malaysia, 87–88
    in Vietnam, 88
interconnected nature of economies,
    98

connecting for future, 105–6
connecting to collaboration,
    102–5
strengthening internal processes,
    98–102
Internet
    connectivity, increasing, 87
    services, demand for, 75
    users in ASEAN, 73–77
Internet penetration, 73, 75, 76, 177
    for ASEAN countries, 91–92
    measure of, 92–93
    rate, 84, 91
intra-ASEAN Connectivity, 166

J
Japan, Internet penetration rate for,
    84, 91

L
land transport, 11
Lao PDR
    airport in, 25
    transit transport routes in, 12
liberalization
    of industry, 79
    of passenger and cargo air
        services, 70
    of trade in ICT, 15
liquefied natural gas (LNG), 19, 148,
    178, 185
    ASEAN's policy planners, 150
    export contracts, 149
    import terminals, 150
    projects, 150
    re-gasification terminals, 151
    trade in Southeast Asia, 150–51
logistics infrastructure development,
    47–49
    strategies for, 49–56
    targets in, 49, 51, 53
Logistics Performance Index (LPI),
    47
low cost carriers (LCCs), 15
LPI. *See* Logistics Performance Index
    (LPI)

M

Malaysia
  air and sea ports in, 26
  FB growth in, 109
  HSBB network in, 85
  infrastructure for LNG
    transportation, 19
  Intel Corporation in, 87–88
  LNG, 148–49
  media users, 109
  oil discoveries in, 148
  online tax returns, 99
Malaysian Government's Vision
  2020 plan, 87–88
maritime network, 176
maritime transport, 14
Master Plan on ASEAN Connectivity
  (MPAC), 3, 23, 29, 38, 60, 68, 110,
  185
  adoption of, 166–67
  ASEAN ICT infrastructure, 112
  core initiatives of, 175
  implementation arrangement for,
    168–69
  institutional connectivity in, 5–6,
    112
  people-to-people connectivity, 6,
    113
  physical connectivity, 5
  PPP initiatives, 32
  priority strategies of, 111
  resource mobilization, 169–71
Mekong River Commission (MRC),
  21–22
Memorandum of Understanding
  (MoU), 132–33
MNEs. *See* multinational enterprises
mobile
  connectivity, 176–77
  phones in Asia, 109–10
  telecommunications company in
    Indonesia, 87
  telephony technology, 88
mobile broadband, 82, 83
  penetration, 89n3
  quality for, 81

in Southeast Asia, 79
mobilization, resource. *See* resource
  mobilization
MoU. *See* Memorandum of
  Understanding (MoU)
MPAC. *See* Master Plan on ASEAN
  Connectivity (MPAC)
MRC. *See* Mekong River
  Commission (MRC)
multinational enterprises (MNEs),
  49
mutual recognition arrangements
  (MRAs), 6
Myanmar
  air and sea ports in, 26
  pipeline linking to Thailand, 19
  transit transport routes in, 12

N

natural disaster, ASEAN, 105
natural gas industry in Southeast
  Asia, 148–50
networks
  faster fiber, 81
  fixed copper, 81
  highway, 48
  maritime, 176
  Next Generation Nationwide
    Broadband, 85
  open-ended, 40
  production. *See* production
    networks
  seamless transport, 30
  "Trans-Asian Highway", 11
  transport. *See* transport networks
new economic geography, 38, 40, 53
  agglomeration and dispersion
    forces in, 42
Next Generation Nationwide
  Broadband Network, 85
non-tariff barriers (NTBs), 5
NTT, 84

O

oil discoveries, 148
online communities, 96

online companies, ASEAN, 78
online presence, 99–100
    businesses develop an, 94
open-ended networks, 40

P
"Peer to Patent" project, 116
penetration
    Internet. *See* Internet penetration
    regional smartphone, 79
people-to-people connectivity, 6–8,
    33, 166, 167, 170
"perfectly integrated economy",
    defined, 56
Philippines
    air and sea ports in, 26
    FB penetration rate, 109
    GILAS project in, 88
    transit transport routes in, 12
    Twitter users, 109
Philippines Nautical Highway
    System, 14
physical connectivity, 5, 29, 60, 166,
    167, 170
    in ASEAN, 37–38
    projects under, 7
policy recommendations, 182–85
Polish National Police, 100
ports in ASEAN, 14
power generation
    coal utilization for, 20
    and distribution, 156
power grid systems in ASEAN, 156
power market structures, ASEAN, 132
PPP. *See* public-private partnerships
    (PPP)
private sector
    in ASEAN Connectivity, 172–73
    initiatives and partnerships, 87–88
    participation, 183
privatization, public-private
    partnerships, 182
production factors, interregional
    flows of, 62
production networks
    in ASEAN, 37, 38

    in East Asia, 37
    mechanics of, 38, 46
    U.S.-Mexico Nexus *vs.* East Asia,
        40, 41
public-private partnerships (PPP), 8,
    31, 170, 173, 181–82
    initiative, 32–33
public sector
    initiatives and partnerships,
        87–88
    investment leadership, 85–87

R
rail infrastructure, 13, 176
regional capital markets,
    development of, 173
Regional Comprehensive Economic
    Partnership (RCEP), 166
regional connectivity, 166, 167
    ASEAN Master Plan on, 165
    challenges in, 64–66
    improves in local economy, 61–64
    natural for, 63
regional economic integration,
    ASEAN, 143
regional identity, ASEAN, 116–17
regional infrastructure development
    programmes, 20–22
regional smartphone penetration,
    79
regulatory models, 82, 84
renewable energy, 20
resource mobilization, 169–70,
    178–79
    new and innovative sources, 170
    traditional funding sources, 170,
        171
road infrastructure, 11–12, 176
Roll-on/Roll-off (RORO) network,
    ASEAN, 69
rural communities, revitalizing,
    101–2

S
Saudi Arabia, citizens interacting
    with government, 99

seamless transport networks,
 30
sea ports, 25–27
sector-specific recommendations,
 184–85
sensors, embedded, 105
Shareholder Agreement on AIF,
 172
short-sea shipping, 69
Singapore
 air and sea ports in, 26
 broadband infrastructure
  development in, 85
 infrastructure for LNG
  transportation, 19
Singapore–Kunming Rail Link
 (SKRL), 5
Singapore–Kunming Rail Link
 (SKRL) project, 11, 176
 ASEAN's initiatives, 21
 missing links in, 13
Southeast Asia
 ASEAN Vision 2020, 144
 cross-border natural gas pipelines
  in, 145–47
 existing pipelines in, 146–47
 fixed line broadband penetration
  in, 76
 Internet users in, 76, 77
 LNG trade in, 150–52
 mobile broadband in, 79
 natural gas industry outlook in,
  148–50
South Korea, Internet penetration
 rate for, 91
subregional groups, ASEAN, 152,
 154
subregional infrastructure
 development programmes,
 20–22
Sweden, E-readiness ranking, 93

T
TagMyLagoon application, 105
TAGP. *See* Trans-ASEAN Gas
 Pipeline (TAGP)

TBPG. *See* Trans-Borneo Power Grid
 (TBPG)
telecom development in ASEAN, 74
telecommunications, 176–77
 ASEAN initiatives in, 21
Telecommunications Act of 1996,
 82
telemedicine, 103
Thailand
 air and sea ports in, 26
 FB growth in, 109
 ICT Masterplan in, 87
 infrastructure for LNG
  transportation, 19
 link pipelines with Myanmar,
  19
Trans-ASEAN Gas Pipeline (TAGP),
 18, 128–30, 144–45, 177, 178
 APAEC 2010–2015 for, 130
 CBI projects, 145
 current and future pipeline
  interconnections, 140–41
 gas trading, 132
 infrastructure, 129
 Master Plan 2008, 130–31
 preliminary analysis, 131
 realization of, 19
 taskforce, 144
"Trans-Asian Highway" network,
 11
Trans-Borneo Power Grid (TBPG),
 153, 155
transit transport routes (TTRs) in
 ASEAN, 12
transportation, 176
transport infrastructure
 development
 air transport, 14–15
 inland waterways transport,
  13–14
 land transport, 11
 maritime transport, 14
 rail infrastructure, 13
 road infrastructure, 11–12
 strategies, 10–11
transport, land, 11

transport networks
    in ASEAN, 69
    seamless, 30
tsunami alert system, 105
TTRs. *See* transit transport routes
    (TTRs)
Twitter, ASEAN, 109
two-dimensional fragmentation, 40,
    42

U
UK Border Agency, 100
United Nations Conference on Trade
    and Development (UNCTAD),
    14
United States
    E-readiness ranking, 93
    Internet penetration rate for, 91
    labour growth in productivity in,
        94
urban mass transit, 61
U.S.-Mexico Nexus *vs.* East Asia
    production networks, 40, 41

V
Vietnam
    air and sea ports in, 26
    Intel Corporation in, 88
    National Program on IT
        applications, 87
village cooperatives, mechanism,
    102
virtual community, 96, 113
Virtual Learning Resource Centres,
    113

W
Wireless@SG project, 85
World, 2007
    exports/imports of
        manufacturing goods to,
        43, 44
World Wide Web, 113

Y
Yeo, George, 117
Yudhoyono, Susilo Bambang, 116

www.ingramcontent.com/pod-product-compliance
Lightning Source LLC
Chambersburg PA
CBHW062025270326
41929CB00014B/2317